Dr. Kimball and Mr. Jefferson

Thomas Jefferson, Architect
Writers of the American South
Colonial Houses
Natchez
House-Dreams
Wright for Wright
The Preservationist's Progress
How Old Is This House?

Dr. Kimball
and
Mr. Jefferson

Rediscovering the Founding Fathers
of American Architecture

Hugh Howard

BLOOMSBURY

This book was made possible in part by a generous grant from the
Graham Foundation for Advanced Studies in the Fine Arts.

Published by Bloomsbury USA, New York
Distributed to the trade by Holtzbrinck Publishers

All papers used by Bloomsbury USA are natural, recyclable products made
from wood grown in well-managed forests. The manufacturing processes conform
to the environmental regulations of the country of origin.

Library of Congress Cataloging-in-Publication Data

Howard, Hugh, 1952–
Dr. Kimball and Mr. Jefferson : a journey into America's architectural past / Hugh
Howard.—1st U.S. ed.
p.   cm.
Includes bibliographical references and index.

ISBN-13: 978-1-58234-455-3
ISBN-10: 1-58234-455-8
1. Architecture and society—United States—History—18th century.   2. Architecture—
Historiography.   3. Historic preservation—United States.   4. Kimball, Fiske,
1888–1955.   5. Jefferson, Thomas, 1743–1826.   I. Title.

NA2543.S6H69   2006
720.973—dc22
2006000155

First U.S. Edition 2006

1 3 5 7 9 10 8 6 4 2

Typeset by Westchester Book Group
Printed in the United States of America by Quebecor World Fairfield

CONTENTS

For Betsy . . .
and, of course,
our two tall daughters,
Sarah and Elizabeth

"Writing about the past, of necessity, is a process of searching for new evidence, restudying original sources, and reassessing the thoughts of other writers on the subject. This may be why the second part of the word history is story."

—ALLAN GREENBERG, *George Washington, Architect,* 1999

AUTHOR'S NOTE

TO TRAVEL BACKWARD: That is the immodest goal of this book.

Thomas Jefferson inspired this attempt at time travel. Some years ago while researching Jefferson's architecture, I encountered Fiske Kimball (1888–1955), the man who had put Jefferson back on the architectural map. As a student, architect, historian, professor, university administrator, and museum director, Kimball became my tour guide in researching this book and, in the coming pages, he will be your *cicerone*, too.

Working in opposite directions—the former advancing from the days of the American Revolution, the latter looking backward from the first quarter of the twentieth century—Jefferson and Kimball are the Johnson and the Boswell of early American architecture. They provide a unique entrée to the world of Federal America, when Englishman Benjamin Henry Latrobe, Bostonian Charles Bulfinch, Samuel McIntire of Salem, a Frenchman named Charles-Louis Clérisseau, Tortola-born William Thornton, and Jefferson himself were in the vanguard of American architectural innovation.

Before Jefferson, there were builders in the Colonies, but no American architects. Thanks in no small measure to him, by the time of his death in 1826 a coterie of professionals had emerged, men who imagined buildings, rendered them onto paper as sophisticated architectural drawings, and then supervised construction not as craftsmen, not carpenter-joiners or masons, but as *Architects*. Because of Dr. Sidney Fiske Kimball, the story of that evolution, which is the matter of this book, can be told.

—HUGH HOWARD,
Hayes Hill, New York

THE PLAYERS

IN THE TWENTIETH CENTURY

Fiske Kimball (1888–1955), graduate student

George Henry Chase (1874–1952), chairman of Harvard's Department of
Fine Arts

Marie Christina Goebel (1889–1955), daughter of a Kimball colleague

Worthington C. Ford (1858–1941), editor of the Massachusetts Historical
Society

R. T. H. Halsey (1865–1942), New York stockbroker and curator

Ferdinand C. Latrobe II (1889–1944), great-grandson of B. H. Latrobe

John D. McIlhenny (1866–1925), president of the Philadelphia Museum of Art

William C. Endicott Jr. (1860–1936), president of the Essex Institute

Franklin Delano Roosevelt (1882–1945), president of the United States

John Russell Pope (1874–1937), New York society architect specializing in the
classical style

Thomas J. McCormick (1925–   ), graduate student

THE EARLY ARCHITECTS AND BUILDERS

William Buckland (1734–1774), English immigrant joiner and carver

Thomas Jefferson (1743–1826), newly appointed minister to France

Charles-Louis Clérisseau (1721–1820), Parisian artist and antiquarian

Major Pierre Charles L'Enfant (1754–1825), French-trained artist and engineer

Charles Bulfinch (1763–1844), a newlywed Boston gentleman

James Hoban (1762–1831), Irish-born winner of the competition for the
President's House

Dr. William Thornton (1759–1828), Edinburgh-educated physician

Étienne Sulpice Hallet (1760–1825), French-trained architect residing in
Philadelphia

George Hadfield (1764–1826), London-born, European-trained architect

Benjamin Henry Latrobe (1764–1820), English-born, European-educated
professional architect and engineer

Samuel McIntire (1756–1811), Salem, Massachusetts, carver, builder, and
designer

Robert Mills (1781–1855), Charleston-born architecture student

THE PATRONS

George Mason (1725–1792), wealthy patriot and Virginia landowner

Mathias Hammond (1748–1786), Maryland planter and patriot

George Washington (1732–1799), former general and president-elect

Samuel Mickle Fox (1763–1808), president of the Bank of Pennsylvania

Joseph Barrell (1739–1804), Boston merchant

Elias Hasket Derby (1739–1799), Salem's wealthiest merchant

James Monroe (1758–1831), newly elected president of the United States

Harrison Gray Otis (1765–1848), Boston merchant, real estate developer,
and politician

FRIENDS AND FAMILY

Charles Willson Peale (1741–1821), Annapolis portraitist

John Trumbull (1756–1843), Connecticut-born portraitist and aspiring history
painter

Maria Hadfield Cosway (1760–1838), Anglo-Italian wife of artist Richard
Cosway

Anna Maria Brodeau Thornton (1775?–1865), wife of Dr. William Thornton

George Ticknor (1791–1871), a well-to-do young Bostonian planning a
Grand Tour

Ellen Randolph (1796–1876), granddaughter of Thomas Jefferson

Thomas Jefferson Randolph (1792–1875), grandson of Thomas Jefferson

Joseph Coolidge Jr. (1798–1879), husband of Ellen Randolph

T. Jefferson Coolidge Jr. (1863–1912), Ellen and Joseph Coolidge's grandson

Jefferson Monroe Levy (1852–1924), owner of Monticello

Dr. Kimball and Mr. Jefferson

KIMBALL'S FIRST DISCOVERY

THE JOB WASN'T MUCH, but he knew he had no grounds for complaint. At the beck and call of Professor George Henry Chase, the twenty-three-year-old graduate student appreciated the work, he really did. But who could blame him for daydreaming about his first visit to Europe the previous summer and fall? The stops on his journey had included London, Paris, Rome, and Vienna. He had walked the Amalfi coast, bicycled through the French countryside, and seen Chartres and Avignon by moonlight.

Yes, Sidney Fiske Kimball had to admit, Harvard had been good to him, bestowing upon him an A.B. in architecture *summa cum laude* in 1909. He had been awarded a Sheldon Fellowship, too (a "loafing fellowship," as it was known about campus, its sole requirement being to travel abroad). Next came an assistantship, but here he was, in the winter of 1912, looking out his window not at the neoclassical beauty of Paris or the classical ruins of Rome. All he could see was a snow-covered Cambridge streetscape. He noted in his diary, "I want . . . specially to write about the French eighteenth century, which I had fallen in love with in Paris." Instead, he was working toward an immediate goal, to earn his M. Arch. degree by completing a design for a grandiose governor's palace for Panama. He was teaching a course in art history, too, but wondered all the while just where it would get him.

One day that winter the eminent Professor Chase appeared at his desk. As the newly appointed head of the Department of Fine Arts, Chase explained to Kimball that he had been approached by Harper & Brothers to edit a series of art books. The publisher wanted individual volumes devoted to painting, sculpture, and other arts. Chase had asked a distinguished colleague to write the book on architecture, but the older man was already engaged in a similar project for another publisher, Macmillan.

Sidney Fiske Kimball, circa 1915. *Philadelphia Museum of Art Archives/Fiske Kimball Papers*

"They turned to me," reported Kimball. Not intimidated for a moment, the brash young man accepted the assignment. "It was a wonderful chance, and I started plowing through the antique stuff."

Fiske Kimball—he would drop the "Sidney" prior to the publication of his first book—could hardly have known then how the project would change his life. Or, for that matter, that his research would affect the way every American understands the nation's architecture.

BY FALL KIMBALL WAS IN LOVE. His advance for the book didn't amount to a living wage, so when his assistantship at Harvard expired, he took a job as an instructor at the University of Illinois. He possessed a booming voice and a manner more assertive than subtle, but in Champaign-Urbana he met a professor's daughter, Marie Christina Goebel, and the two were immediately drawn to one another.

A year younger than Kimball, Miss Goebel was worldly. Her father was German, her mother Dutch. Marie and her parents had survived the 1906 earthquake in San Francisco, and her teenage memories of the harsh life in a tent overlooking the ruins of the city would never leave her. She had studied

Fiske Kimball and Marie Kimball, circa 1913. *Philadelphia Museum of Art Archives/Fiske Kimball Papers*

at Radcliffe but completed her degree at the University of Illinois after her father accepted a post there. Though petite, shy, and cautious, Marie wasn't put off by Kimball's rough edges. Even after Professor Julius Goebel had shown Kimball the door when the vulgarity of the younger man's speech had become too much, his daughter's affection for Kimball grew. This serious young woman knew there was a world beyond Champaign-Urbana and, as Professor Chase had done, she recognized that despite his lack of social graces, her young suitor was a man who could show her that larger world.

Marie and Fiske married in June of 1913. Kimball had won few academic friends in Illinois, and the newlyweds returned to Boston for the summer knowing his appointment would not be renewed, thanks in part to the university's nepotism rule. But Fiske had his book project to occupy him, and he worked with characteristic thoroughness, spending the hot summer days doing research at the Harvard Library.

One morning, after Fiske had left, Marie came across a piece of paper in a pocket of his trousers. As she flattened the crumpled sheet, she read the words "Jefferson as an Architect" in her husband's purposeful hand. They meant nothing to her. Thomas Jefferson at the time was remembered as the nation's third president. But an *architect?* She wondered whether the reference was to someone else with the surname Jefferson, but she couldn't think of whom.

On his return that evening, she asked Fiske about the note. He told her he had come across a recent article by Glenn Brown, a respected architect and the author of a two-volume history of the Capitol in Washington. The essay concerned letters between Jefferson and the first designer of the Capitol, William Thornton, regarding the University of Virginia. Brown had concluded that Thornton was to be credited with designing the first buildings at the University of Virginia, but Kimball wasn't convinced.

"It did not seem to me," Kimball observed, "that quite all had been said."

His instinct ran counter to the prevailing wisdom. Since Jefferson's death in 1826, his architectural accomplishments had grown more obscure by the year. As early as 1834, the plan and overall appearance of Monticello had been attributed to another designer by America's pioneer art historian, William Dunlap, in his two-volume *History of the Rise and Progress of the Arts of Design in the United States.* Each of Jefferson's several biographers seemed to have been blithely unaware that architecture interested him. Typical was the 1911 edition of the *Encyclopaedia Britannica,* which devoted almost 8,000 words to chronicling his life but made only one noncommittal reference to any of his architectural works (". . . Jefferson returned to his home at Monticello . . ."). Nothing in the Jefferson literature suggested that the man ever built or cared about a building in his life.

Still, Marie's curiosity had been piqued. "That looks like a good subject," she said to her husband. "Can I have it?" Engrossed in his own research for *A History of Architecture,* he agreed.

As the child of a professor, Marie took the task seriously. She pursued all of Brown's references, but at first her findings were disappointing. One of Jefferson's two homes, Poplar Forest, had burned in 1845. She learned that Monticello's contents had been dispersed at an auction the year after Jefferson's death, and Monticello itself had become a second home to two generations of a New York family named Levy. On the plus side she came across the claim that Jefferson had designed the Virginia State Capitol; on the minus, his French collaborator, Charles-Louis Clérisseau, seemed to deserve most of the credit. Ambiguous as the results were, Marie found them strangely tantalizing and recounted what she had learned to Fiske, whereupon he decided to shift his energies to investigating Jefferson, too.

Months into the research, a short note arrived from Harper & Brothers. Kimball's editor reported, "I notice that Houghton Mifflin Co. advertise a $12.00 book about Thomas Jefferson as an Architect." It was the worst possible news. When Kimball got hold of a copy of the book, *Thomas Jefferson as an Architect and a Designer of Landscapes*, he found it drew upon twenty-odd drawings and specification sheets in Jefferson's handwriting concerning the University of Virginia. Its author, William Lambeth, M.D., had found the drawings in his role as Superintendent of Buildings and Grounds at the University of Virginia.

The Kimballs felt blind-sided. Although Lambeth's book was far from the wide-ranging survey that Kimball himself had begun contemplating, its publication meant that Thomas Jefferson, architect, was no longer a secret. The splash that Kimball had hoped to make by writing about Jefferson had held out the promise that he might escape teaching; but now, it seemed, the possibility had evaporated. He feared he might well be destined to remain a junior professor—that autumn he had accepted a position at the University of Michigan—a role for which he and Marie knew only too well his boisterous personality was ill-suited and one that would earn him only a meager salary. Even when supplemented by occasional fees from his articles and book reviews, their income remained small. Neither her professor father nor his, a school headmaster, could afford to underwrite Kimball's ambitions.

In frustration Fiske wrote a letter to *The Nation*. The magazine had already reviewed the new Jefferson book, but Kimball pointed out a few of its shortcomings. He also confided to his parents, "It is about all I can do after Lambeth has spoiled my subject."

On December 20, 1913, when he posted the letter to his parents in Massachusetts and the article to *The Nation* from the train station in Chicago, he and Marie were on their way to visit her parents in Illinois. It would be Fiske's first holiday season away from home and, as he contemplated the rugged Michigan winter ahead, it was hardly a consolation that Lambeth's book had produced little more than a small ripple among students of architecture.

THEY NEARLY ABANDONED THE CHASE, but Marie played a hunch. She guessed that Jefferson had made many drawings "some of which might well survive among his manuscripts." She persuaded her husband to make one last attempt to find them, and at her behest he wrote to the two known repositories of Jefferson's papers, the Library of Congress and the Massachusetts Historical Society. "I am particularly interested," wrote Kimball, "in locating anything which throws light on Jefferson's activity as an architect."

While the archivists at the Library of Congress offered no encouragement, an intriguing letter arrived from Boston signed by the head of the Massachusetts Historical Society, Worthington C. Ford. It began ominously. "I would say that there are no architectural drawings among the Jefferson papers owned by the Society," Ford wrote. But there was more. "Mr. T. Jefferson Coolidge, Jr. [had] quite a number of such drawings from a family in Virginia, and they are owned by his heirs."

The MacGuffin of this particular story was at hand.

Determined to prove that this message-in-a-bottle was meant for him, Kimball immediately wrote to the executor of the estate of the recently deceased Coolidge. An understanding was reached for the drawings to be deposited with Ford at the Massachusetts Historical Society in order that Kimball might examine them. Money was tight for the Kimballs so they decided Fiske would come alone even though Marie was very much a partner in the project. As he explained in a letter to his parents, "In this way we will limit the resulting expense to about fifty dollars, which we think is amply justified by the scientific results to be obtained."

He wanted to investigate the cache of Jefferson drawings, but there was a larger issue on his mind, too. He chose the term "scientific results" intentionally, as it signified something important. The drawings, Kimball hoped, would represent the means to a larger scholarly end. The study of architectural history, particularly of American architecture, tended to be a "loose jumble of tradition and probability," as Kimball put it. He distrusted the old stories that dominated architectural writing, believing instead that the architectural historian should take his cue from the study of archaeology. He wanted to compare and contrast primary documents with the existing structures; to his way of thinking, family tales and interpretive connoisseurship were unscientific. Kimball saw himself as a pioneer in a fundamental shift in architectural history away from hearsay to close physical examination. And Jefferson just might be his test case, the way to stake out a scholarly position in a widely visible fashion.

Marie went to Champaign-Urbana to visit her parents at Easter and Kimball took the train east. On the morning of April 6, 1914, he traveled from his parents' home in Dorchester to Boylston Street in Boston's Fenway neighborhood. He arrived promptly at ten o'clock, as arranged in advance with Mr. Ford.

He hadn't known what to expect, but the material laid before him looked as if it had been forgotten in an attic for a very long time. The antique ren-

derings Kimball examined were foxed and their edges bore chew marks where
mice had munched the margins. Having seen a few of Jefferson's drawings in
Lambeth's book, he immediately recognized Jefferson's hand as he organized
the drawings into piles and categories. Kimball's mind was soon racing: He
had been confident on his arrival that morning that he knew more of Jefferson's designs than anyone—more even than Lambeth, thought the confident
young man—but here he confronted much he didn't know, many buildings
he didn't recognize. Kimball found himself sneezing as the attic dust swirled
around him. Though peppered by curses at his allergies, the air had a palpa-
ble sense of epiphany.

The Coolidge collection was a treasure trove. "It was marvelous," he reported. "There were three or four hundred drawings, many highly competent,
some were scrap that were in outline only. . . . They constituted a wilderness
of the most obscure kind. There was scarcely a signature in the lot, rarely any
title, and but few dates though many of the drawings were covered with notes
and calculations in Jefferson's handwriting." In his mind, Kimball had envisioned a neat and self-contained Jeffersonian landscape, but that morning he
found himself surrounded by an undiscovered landmass where he glimpsed
many new and important vistas of Jefferson country.

After a time he was joined by Worthington Ford, a man with a high forehead, thinning hair, and a waxed mustache going gray. He was a scholar of
the first order, having come to the society from the Library of Congress
where he had edited George Washington's papers. Ford was surprised at what
he saw. He had thought the young man's visit would be brief, but Kimball remained hard at work, making notes, poring over the drawings.

Observing the sorted piles Kimball had made, Ford asked a series of
questions about the drawings, what they might represent, and about Kimball's training and interests. The older man was nearly deaf, so Kimball
found himself raising his already loud voice to be heard. Ford was pleased
by what Kimball told him, and he ventured to mention that there had been
talk of assembling the drawings into a book. *Nothing concrete yet, just some
thinking out loud.* Kimball could feel his pulse quicken, but his spirits quickly
plummeted when Ford explained that they had an editor in mind. Kimball
had to content himself with carting home photostats of the drawings he
wanted.

Back in Ann Arbor, Kimball drew upon the drawings to write an article,
"Thomas Jefferson as Architect: Monticello and Shadwell." He now knew for

certain that Lambeth's book left a great deal unsaid. Old friends in Cambridge promised that the article would see print quickly, scheduling it for the June 1914 number of Harvard's *Architectural Quarterly*.

Even before the paper's appearance, an unexpected letter arrived from Boston. Worthington Ford offered the news that the publication of the Jefferson drawings seemed to be moving forward. He reported that Clara Amory Coolidge, widow of T. Jefferson Coolidge Jr., might be willing to underwrite the book as a memorial to her husband. But he wanted to know whether Mr. Kimball would consent to edit the drawings and prepare an accompanying text.

"I would give my eyes just for the chance of doing it," Kimball confessed.

Ford's letter contained another question, too: *What would Mr. Kimball consider a suitable fee?* The Kimballs continued to struggle financially, but they did some figuring and Kimball wrote back, asking in an uncharacteristically humble fashion whether five hundred dollars would be too much.

By return mail, Kimball received a response that he remembered as "a letter of kindness which I shall never forget."

"My dear Mr. Kimball," Worthington Ford wrote, "$1,000 . . . is the sum which has been determined upon, in the hope that it will be entirely acceptable to you."

Fiske and Marie basked in the moment. Then they leapt into motion and Fiske's project for Professor Chase, *A History of Architecture*, was quickly put aside. Kimball arranged to spend some of his windfall visiting Virginia to see Jefferson's buildings in the summer of 1914. There he met Lambeth who, Kimball noted, "was most kind to his young rival." He and Marie collaborated on the research for the book, spending many days at the Massachusetts Historical Society and the Library of Congress.

As Kimball told the story, "She undertook the task of canvassing Jefferson's whole correspondence for letters which might bear on the drawings. The Society had earlier received from Mr. Coolidge['s father] Jefferson's private papers, some fifteen thousand, of which only a few hundred had been published. [Marie] plowed through the manuscript of all, turning up ever so many which had a bearing. . . . She went likewise through the published calendars of Jefferson's official papers in Washington, some twenty-five thousand, with equally rich finds. Meanwhile I worked over the drawings themselves, seeking to distinguish the evolution of the major designs."

They made rapid progress and once the manuscript was completed, production of the book went swiftly. Finished copies arrived from the bindery in time for Christmas 1916. *Thomas Jefferson, Architect* was extravagant, manufactured to the highest standards by the Riverside Press, printed in a limited edition of 350 copies. The elephant folio stood nineteen inches high and fifteen wide, and contained facsimile reproductions of all the Jefferson designs in the Coolidge collection, along with Kimball's text and notes. The book would prove to be the largest and most effective of calling cards, an invaluable credential for the young scholar who, to put it boldly, suddenly became the man who rediscovered Thomas Jefferson, Architect.

In the years to come, Kimball would play a leading role in establishing for the first time that American architectural history merited close examination. If he and Marie had not pursued every lead diligently, the Jefferson drawings might have been relegated for another century to an attic, this time one in Massachusetts. Today schoolchildren learn that Jefferson was the first great native-born architect; because of Kimball's persuasive scholarship, it is now regarded as received wisdom that Jefferson, as Kimball asserted, "may truly be called the father of our national architecture."

Kimball himself would soon be acknowledged as "the Dean of architectural history in America," thanks in part to *Thomas Jefferson, Architect,* which was, remarkably, the first critical biography ever written of an American architect.

No one, it seemed, had cared very much before.

CHAPTER I

AN ARTISAN BECOMES AN ARCHITECT

"The art of architecture in the American colonies at the time of Jefferson's youth was still almost entirely in the hands of the craftsmen of the building trades."

—FISKE KIMBALL,

THOMAS JEFFERSON, ARCHITECT (1916)

I.
August 1755 . . . Aboard ship . . . The North Atlantic

WILLIAM BUCKLAND'S HORIZON LOOMED as large as the Atlantic Ocean. With the full confidence of youth, he had chosen to embark on a journey to the New World just days before his twenty-first birthday. He sought the freedom to become a builder in his own right.

In his short life, he had seen his share of abrupt changes. His mother died when he was four. Barely ten years later, he left the familiar confines of his father's farm a few miles from Oxford, armed with little more than a rudimentary knowledge of arithmetic, writing, and the Bible. His journey took him to the City of London to apprentice with his father's brother, James Buckland, a joiner by trade and a member of the Worshipful Company of Joiners. Though not yet fourteen, William signed a binding legal contract agreeing to forgo "Fornication . . . Matrimony . . . Cards, Dice, Tables . . . Taverns or Playhouses . . . but in all Things as a faithful Apprentice . . . [to] behave himself towards his said Master." The term was to be the usual seven years.

Standing on shipboard with a view of nothing but the heaving waves of

Charles Willson Peale's 1774 portrait of William Buckland, Architect . . . and Gentleman.
Yale University Art Gallery/Mabel Brady Garvan Collection

the North Atlantic, Buckland could look back on his training. He had learned to use chisels, saws, and planes to shape wood. In an era when nails and screws were handmade by a blacksmith one fastener at a time, wooden dovetails and mortise-and-tenon joints were the rule. In his uncle's workshop, he had had his first cousin, Thomas Buckland, for companionship. Though Thomas was four years into his own apprenticeship as a joiner when William arrived, the two of them worked at the craft of making doors, windows, and staircases, as well as the fashionable paneling central to the art of the joiner.

William's circumstances were altered once again less than a year later when he found himself attending his master's funeral. Young Buckland's contract was assigned to John Whiteaves, a member of another guild, and Buckland spent the next six years fulfilling his apprenticeship at the Carpenters' Company. He learned a trade that built upon what he had learned as a joiner. He continued to work with wood but members of the Carpenters' Company, which had been chartered in 1477, were responsible for framing the structure of a building and enclosing it. That meant the carpenter, along with the members of another guild, the masons, built the shell, leaving the joiners to finish it. As one contemporary book, *The London Tradesman* (1747), expressed it, "As a Joiner's Work requires a nicer Hand, and great Taste in Ornament, his Busines requires that he should be acquainted with Geometry and Mensuration." Buckland had demonstrated that he had a "nicer Hand" than most, becoming a carpenter, joiner, and carver of extraordinary felicity.

By traveling to America, he left behind more than his homeland. He had completed his apprenticeship, making him a freeman entitled to be called a journeyman carpenter. Had he remained in Europe's largest metropolis, after more years of service he could have earned the right to wear the livery of the Carpenters' Company as a full-fledged member. But he wanted to be his own master much sooner. A fortuitous meeting with a Virginian named Thomson Mason had offered him his chance.

Mason was completing his law studies at the Inns of Court. His chambers were just around the corner from Buckland's lodgings on Duke Street. The two met, and Thomson made Buckland an offer. On behalf of his older brother, George, he would assume the cost of Buckland's passage and agree to pay him a generous wage once he reached America. Even though this meant traveling to "Virginia Beyond the Seas," the opportunity was made to order. Young Buckland would be provided "all necessary Meat, Drink, Washing, [and] Lodging" while he earned his freedom in a new land, a place where skilled tradesmen were rare. Two months were required to make the journey sailing into westerly headwinds, so Buckland had ample time on that long ocean crossing to examine the new document that defined his life. It was a four-year contract, an indenture of service, that entitled him to £20 per annum.

Fresh from his London training, Buckland would assume the "entire direction of the Carpenter's & Joiner's work [on] a large House." Though he was indentured to Mason, Buckland would no longer be laboring for wages or doing the bidding of other workmen; his task was to complete construction of "a substantial brick mansion, 40 by 70 feet." His new benefactor and employer George Mason wanted a stylish house with a degree of finish consistent with the current architectural fashion that Buckland knew in London, and Mason would look to Buckland to exercise all the skills the young man had learned as a joiner and a carpenter.

Mason wanted a house that reflected his station, and Buckland, exhilarated at the opportunity, planned to make the most of it. When William Buckland disembarked in the colony of Virginia in the fall of 1755, he was a young man with great expectations.

II.
June 1759 . . . Gunston Hall . . . Dogue's Neck, Virginia

ALTHOUGH UNDER CONSTRUCTION, Gunston Hall was a surprisingly quiet place. Not silent exactly, but in an age when everything was made by hand, the loudest sounds a carpenter produced were the repetitive rasp of a hand-saw, the *thwack* of a broadax, and the dull thud of a large mallet. Just across the hall from the room where the builders were at work, George Mason sat undisturbed, tending as usual to his reading, writing, and the management of his business from his Little Parlor.

For some months his growing family had inhabited a portion of the house, and as he stepped into the broad central passage, Mason could hear the sounds of his children upstairs, among them an infant son born in the house in March. From near at hand in the room just across from his study came the voices of his master builder, William Buckland, and his chief carver, William Bernard Sears. They conversed in their London accents as they worked. When he approached the door to what would be the house's grandest space, the Palladian room, Mason may have heard the jolly tones of their laughter, but a sound he heard for certain was the soft *scrunch* of gouges and chisels as the men worked to complete the fine, hand-carved woodwork at Gunston Hall.

Mason would soon reach age thirty-four, but he had long since become a public man. In his twenties he had been appointed a vestryman at his church and a county justice of the peace. He served as a trustee in the burgeoning towns of Alexandria and Dumfries, and had been elected to the Virginia House of Burgesses. He wielded considerable local power, and his future as a political man with far-reaching influence seemed assured.

Though still unfinished, the house he inhabited more than fulfilled his desire for a "substantial brick mansion." Fourteen imposing pilasters lined the passage where he stood, an allusion to the Roman courtyard of the sort that Mason knew only from his readings in classical literature. Yet just as this new house expressed in architectural terms his status and his accomplishments, Mason was coming to understand that his role in politics would be more circumscribed than he once had hoped. His temperament was one factor, since he wasn't a man given to hearty handshakes or political manipulations. He disliked travel, too, and the journey to the colony's capital of Williamsburg required a five-day carriage ride of bone-jarring jouncing.

His fragile health would prove another obstacle, because he inherited the family tendency to the gout, a painful joint complaint. The anguish of the gout sufferer involved acute attacks of intense, stabbing pain in the joint of the big toe, and that morning it may have required an act of will for Mason to climb from his chair, gently maneuvering his elevated foot to the floor in order to make his way to where Buckland was at work. But the master of the house was intent upon making his daily rounds.

He wished not only to inspect progress but to complete another errand as well. Virginia's royal governor had decreed that the new county seat was to be at Dumfries, a ten-mile journey from Mason's plantation on Dogue's Neck. As a town trustee, Mason was vitally concerned with the courthouse, a building central to the public life of the county. A fitting design had to be decided upon and, as Colonel Mason walked stiffly along his house's central passage, he knew very well where design guidance was to be found.

Contrary to his own nature, Mason had come to rely upon Mr. Buckland. When the younger man had arrived four years earlier, Mason met his new carpenter for the first time. He gave him a tour of the construction site, where work had already begun on the new house. Brick walls had risen atop a rectangular footprint, the corners decorated with quoins, cut blocks of sandstone quarried in the nearby Aquia Creek. By the standards of rural Virginia, the building under construction was an important house in the making, but to Buckland, seeing it with the eyes of a man fresh from cosmopolitan London, the vernacular Virginia house was little more than an oversized cottage.

The capable Buckland had quickly impressed the ever-cautious George Mason. Not that Colonel Mason was an easy man to please. He was always on his guard, his hazel eyes critical, a man who took nothing lightly. He could cite the proper ratios of lime to sand for mixing mortar although, as a man with ninety slaves, he never mixed a batch himself. Rather, he managed his holdings with great care. As his son, John, would later recall, "My father kept no steward or clerk about him. He kept his own books and superintended . . . all the operations at or about [the estate]." He was his own meticulous supervisor.

In Mr. Buckland he found a man as intent upon the details as he, and Buckland had won his complete trust. The carpenter was to leave Mason's employ that autumn, after completing his four-year obligation. Mason knew well he would feel obliged to pen on the verso of his indenture a fulsome endorsement, offering the sort of praise he rarely uttered, distrusting as he generally did the instincts of others.

But this was June, Buckland was still his servant, and Mason wanted to draw upon his theoretical side. Mason himself was widely read in history and the law, but he owned no important works on architecture or design, nor had he in his voluminous writings attempted to render an architectural likeness on paper. He looked to Buckland for all that, aware of the man's library of architectural references. Buckland had arrived with several volumes, having been advanced £5 by Thomson Mason before leaving London. His books included *The City and Country Builder's and Workman's Treasury of Designs* (1745) by Batty Langley, William Salmon's *Palladio Londinesis: or, The Art of Building* (1734), and *The British Architect* (1745) by Abraham Swan. These books contained not only building advice but plates with carefully drawn architectural illustrations.

When Mason entered the room, his arrival commanded everyone's attention—all the workers were legally bound to him, either as indentured servants or slaves. He made his way to where Buckland stood at his workbench, and in his plain and forthright manner, he described the matter on his mind.

There was to be a new courthouse at Dumfries, he explained. Though the building needn't be large, tradition dictated that certain basic requirements be met. At the rear there should be a curved and raised platform with a low, paneled partition and perhaps a railing to set off the justices' bench. Immediately in front would sit the petit jury and the clerk, flanked by the sheriff and the court crier. Facing the magistrates there must be seating, Mason explained, for the lawyers, litigants, and witnesses. Behind them members of the public could stand. There were also to be two small retiring rooms for the jury. A building of one storey would suffice, and the shape might be rectangular.

Buckland grasped what was needed. The scale was modest, though the elements were to be carefully arranged to reflect the hierarchy of the court. He began to think through the possibilities and to recall buildings he knew, either from having visited them or examined their plans in his treasured books. Some notions that might relate to the task before him began to take shape in his mind.

Designers don't express themselves in thought balloons, they never have; to communicate their thoughts they draw pictures. Buckland was no exception. With Mason standing at his side, Buckland instinctively turned over a board on the bench before him, gently pushing aside the English-made carver's chisels and gouges. He didn't need them at that moment because the board was about to become his parchment. He began sketching the building's footprint and room arrangement for Mason's consideration.

A drawing took shape. It was roughly two-and-a-half inches square, occupying only a small portion of the wooden surface. From experience Buckland knew it would be the opening gambit and, as expected, Mason responded quickly after examining the rough sketch. As both a justice and an expert in colonial land laws, Mason had visited a variety of courthouses in Virginia. He knew the routine of court procedure, and his further explanations led Buckland to draw another sketch of the layout of the rooms.

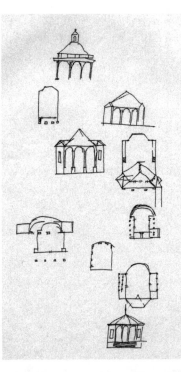

Buckland seized the opportunity to make the functional more exciting by adding architectural drama. In one drawing he placed a cupola atop a steeply sloped roof. In another he turned the jury rooms forty-five degrees, producing an open porch with a series of arches across the front. To the rear of one design he added a projecting bay for the justices' platform. *Carl R. Lounsbury/Colonial Williamsburg Foundation*

After Buckland had sketched several variations of the plan on the board's surface, he took to sketching the face of the building, too. The drawings of the room arrangement and the building's façade made it possible for Mason to visualize the three-dimensional appearance of the structure—it was a means of entry to Buckland's visual imagination. Buckland drew one variation, then another, and another.

Ten sketches emerged for a half-dozen buildings. All were flights of fancy. None mimicked existing Virginia courthouses although, as Mason had specified, each accommodated the necessary functions with distinct spaces for the magistrates, the other participants, and the public. In a matter of moments, Buckland had shifted his focus from the creation of Gunston's intricately shaped interior woodwork (of which Mason was inordinately proud, knowing it to be as fine as any in the land); he had exercised an entirely different set of skills. For the duration of his session with Mason, Buckland had been the designer, reinventing the boxy shapes familiar to his Virginia neighbors, imagining a new geometry. It was a dazzling display of creative energy. And Mason soon limped out of the room, having gotten what he came for, the un-fettered and worldly thinking of his young builder.

As for Buckland, he relished the opportunity to stand shoulder-to-shoulder with Mason, not so much as his indentured servant but as a man whose opin-ions Mason respected. The experience would not be forgotten, and Buckland would prove to have an enduring appetite for being his own designer.

First, though, he had a job to finish. He turned the board over, the pencil sketches untouched on its backside, and resumed carving. Shortly, the board became a part of the window trim, a tabernacle-like frame of carved egg-and-dart and rope moldings, together with applied fretwork and rosettes. After it was fastened in place, the little drawings were hidden and quickly forgotten, awaiting rediscovery two centuries later by restorers of Colonel Mason's house.

III.
Spring 1774 . . . The Artist's Quarters . . . Annapolis, Maryland

SITTING STOCK-STILL WASN'T SOMETHING William Buckland ordinarily did. Not having been born to wealth, he rarely indulged himself in the luxury of idleness. He had worked more than his share of fourteen-hour days during his thirty-nine years, but his life had begun to change.

For his part, Charles Willson Peale was certainly not at rest. A short, en-ergetic young man, he stood before his easel, a bundle of small-motor mo-tion. He peered around the three-foot-tall canvas to view his subject, only to find Buckland looking bemusedly back. Peale glanced at the emerging painted likeness, adding to it in quick strokes.

Watching him work, Buckland could not help but admire Peale's accom-plishments. He had come from less-than-humble beginnings, the son of a forger who had been banished to America. After his father's early death, Charles had been apprenticed at age thirteen to a saddler. He mastered that trade quickly and, led by a restless curiosity, learned silversmithing, the craft of upholstery, and then clock- and watchmaking. All that was before he found his true calling at age twenty-one.

On a journey to Norfolk, Virginia, he had seen a display of landscapes and a portrait by a now-forgotten artist. Peale scoffed, observed that he could certainly do better, and then set about teaching himself to draw. Back home in Annapolis, he traded a saddle to painter John Hesselius for the privilege of watching him execute two oil portraits and then, under the artist's guidance, to complete the second half of a face Hesselius had begun for him. Always a quick study, Peale soon launched himself as an artist. For several years he was on the move, working as an itinerant painter in and around Boston and in Virginia, avoiding his creditors back in Maryland.

If Buckland felt exposed as he sat staring back at Peale, he couldn't help but feel a sense of privilege, too. To be painted by this man meant something. Although seven years Buckland's junior, Peale was on his way to great things; no one in Annapolis would have said otherwise. Eleven of the town's worthies, including the royal governor of Maryland, had recognized Peale's talent. They had underwritten a two-year stay in England for Peale to study with one of the finest American painters of the day, Benjamin West. On Peale's return, he had proved much in demand among the Virginia and Maryland gentry. He had even made the journey to Mount Vernon to paint the reluctant war hero of the French and Indian War, Colonel Washington, whose wife, Martha, had persuaded him to pose for his first portrait. "Inclination having yielded to importunity," Washington wrote to a friend, "I am now contrary to all expectation under the hands of Mr. Peale." Like George Washington, Peale was moving toward greater things.

Buckland knew his own gamble was paying off. His presence in the sitter's chair demonstrated that. He had come to America and spent four years working for George Mason and earning his freedom. In the fourteen years since, aided at first by Mason's recommendation, he had been commissioned to execute woodwork for some of the most influential Virginians of the time, among them scions of the wealthiest Virginia clan of them all, the Carters. He had built a glebe house (parsonage), a prison, and set up his own shop as a joiner and builder. He had taken on apprentice carvers, indentured servants, a convict joiner, and bought slaves. As his business expanded, he took the man who had been his first apprentice, John Randall, as a partner.

The inhabitants of Virginia's Northern Neck helped Buckland establish himself, but in 1771 he had begun to think about moving. On a visit to Annapolis, he found a city large for the region, its streets lined with some five hundred houses. A building boom was under way, as the 1760s and early 1770s saw the construction of not only many modest homes but the appearance of perhaps a dozen fine villas and palazzi. These were major houses, stately homes built on the existing city grid or in the nearby countryside for families with large agricultural holdings further afield on Maryland's Eastern Shore. Buckland recognized that in Maryland's capital his skills would be in demand: If he could establish his reputation here, he had decided, he wouldn't have to seek out customers, they would come to him.

Annapolis was prosperous, a place where the gentry could afford to be conscious of their style and status. The port city was the seat of colonial Maryland's government and its streets and wharves were busy with commerce. All manner of goods, from the mundane to the fancy, arrived from England; most often, returning ships sailed with their holds heavy with tobacco, the major source of the Annapolitans' wealth. Shakespeare was performed at the New Theatre and the Annapolis paper, the *Maryland Gazette*, had a much-read feature, the "Poet's Corner," which featured lines penned by aspiring (but anonymous) local poets. One English visitor reported Annapolis was "the genteelest town in North America" and "its inhabitants . . . the most eminent lawyers, physicians, and families of opulence and note." It was a town with the accoutrements of high culture, among them the fine painter, Mr. Charles Willson Peale.

And an Architect, too, Buckland thought to himself.

An important door had been opened to Buckland in Maryland. His work some years earlier at Mount Airy, a stylish Virginia mansion owned by Colonel John Tayloe, had impressed the owner's daughter, who had more recently become Mrs. Edward Lloyd. When the couple purchased a fine but unfinished house on North East Street in 1771, Edward and Elizabeth Tayloe Lloyd summoned Buckland to Annapolis to survey the work that remained to be done. They promptly hired him to be their "undertaker," that is, to undertake the organization, supervision, and management of the completion of the building. By June of 1772, Buckland had borrowed money from a merchant friend to move his family and his business to Annapolis.

The move had proved a wise one. His transformation of the unfinished shell of the Lloyds' house had gained him professional notoriety in Annapolis society. That was thanks in part to the prominence of Lloyd, a grandee known to his contemporaries as "Edward the Magnificent." He wore his wealth publicly, and his walls were already decorated with portraits of wife Elizabeth, daughter Ann, and himself, commissioned from Mr. Peale. The message he was sending was, *If you want to demonstrate your social status, what better way than by hiring Mr. Peale and Mr. Buckland to do your bidding?*

As the sitting grew tiresome, Buckland had a diversion to contemplate. That evening he and Peale could retire to a meeting of their club. They might join the other members for conversation and gaming until eight o'clock when, "according to Custom . . . the Cards were thrown by, for the much more Important Business of eating & Drinking." Its members were gentlemen of the town, among them Samuel Chase, a patriot who that year would represent Maryland at the first Continental Congress.

Another member of the Independent Club was Mathias Hammond. Born to prosperity, he was a fourth-generation Marylander who had come to Annapolis to read law. He found that he had an instinct for making money, and he enlarged his inherited holdings on the shores of the Chesapeake Bay, where slave labor worked the soil. He worshiped in St. Anne's Parish, and in 1773 had been made a member of the vestry at age twenty-five; in May of that year he was also elected a delegate for Annapolis to the Maryland General Assembly. He was a man on his way with political and social influence to match his wealth. He lacked only a wife and a fine house—but, Mr. Buckland thought to himself with a smile, that would soon change.

Peale welcomed his sitter's distracted half-smile; a relaxed model is easier to paint than a stiff one. The image on the canvas was familiar, both because Buckland's visage was becoming recognizable and since Peale had chosen to record his friend in a familiar pose. He had borrowed the composition from a portrait his own teacher, Benjamin West, had done of him in London as a gift before his return to America.

That portrait was one of Peale's most cherished possessions. In it the artist was poised to draw, his fingers grasping his *porte-crayon;* in the emerging painting of Buckland, the sitter had a tool of his new trade in hand, a draftsman's rule pen. Buckland was flattered that Peale had chosen to mimic his master in portraying him, but the decision represented more than friendship, implying a deeper connection between the men. Buckland and Peale were cut from the same cloth, and it wasn't an aristocratic weave; their fabric was plainer but one of real quality. Each of these men earned his status not as most did by inheriting property but, as Peale explained, because "he can produce by labor of the hands various and wonderful works of art."

The most recent of Buckland's own works on paper were the sketches of a new house for their mutual friend Mr. Hammond. Buckland had been hired by Mathias Hammond not only for his skills as a carver, joiner, carpenter, and master builder; he was truly to be the architect of the fine house, and he had worked on the design over the long, cold winter just ended.

The basic configuration of the place would have been familiar to inhabi-

As illustrated in Charles Willson Peale's sketch, a two-story block would stand front and center at Mathias Hammond's with matching pavilions at either extreme to contain the kitchen and a law office, each linked in turn to the main structure by lower and narrower passageways called hyphens. *Journal of C.W. Peale/American Philosophical Society*

tants of the town, consisting as it did of five aligned parts. Buckland's plan called for an extravagantly carved entrance of the sort only he and his workshop could create. He was confident the grand dining and drawing rooms inside would be the talk of Annapolis society when the house was completed. He and Mr. Hammond had selected with great care a few design elements from the books in Buckland's architectural library, including several from James Gibbs's *A Book of Architecture*. But Buckland already had in mind ways that the bits and pieces were to be improved and made his own. This was not to be a casual compilation of borrowed details; this house would be familiar yet unlike its sources.

Hammond had acquired four in-town lots on which to build the house for himself and his betrothed, rumored to be a Philadelphia beauty. The site was atop a rise, overlooking a garden that sloped gently down to the River Severn and the Annapolis harbor. Devising the final plans for the house hadn't been easy. Buckland's old clients, the Lloyds, lived across the street and out of consideration for their vistas he had had to revise his initial scheme for the Hammond house from three stories to two. But the final design exceeded even his hopes.

Buckland's goal had been a memorable and important house. He had arrived at previous projects—Gunston Hall, Mount Airy, and the Lloyds' house—after the basic shapes had been determined. But Mathias Hammond's house was his from the start. He knew the assignment signified social and professional acceptance in Annapolis, so he had begun styling himself "William Buckland, *Architect.*"

What he could not know as he looked at the back of Peale's easel was the terrible irony that while the Hammond house would indeed establish his reputation, he would not live to see it completed. Buckland would be dead before the year was out and the unfinished portrait would survive him as no more than a disembodied head and hand.

IV.
Early Winter 1783 . . . North East Street . . . Annapolis

IN THE LAST WEEK OF NOVEMBER, Thomas Jefferson journeyed from Philadelphia to Annapolis for a session of the Continental Congress. He still mourned Martha Wayles Jefferson, dead a year earlier from post-delivery complications after the birth of their daughter Lucy Elizabeth. Jefferson had been almost inconsolable in the days after his wife's death, though he found comfort in the company of his oldest daughter, Martha, known affectionately as Patsy. He and the ten-year-old had taken long horseback rides, which she described as "melancholy rambles." His beloved home, Monticello, had ceased to be a happy place for him.

Annapolis wasn't quite Philadelphia, Jefferson allowed. He found Pennsylvania's capital a city of intellectual stimulation; it was also where he would find Patsy, whom he had just settled into school there. But here in Annapolis, there was the satisfaction of being caught up once again in governing and, better yet, in shaping government. Here, too, he could enjoy the company of his protégé James Monroe, with whom he planned to find lodgings.

Rather than riding, as was his wont on his open plantation acres back home in Albemarle County, Virginia, he sometimes chose to negotiate the urban streets of Annapolis on foot, making his way from his temporary rooms to the State House, to the taverns and other meeting places. On one of his constitutionals he first encountered the Hammond House.

Striding down North East Street, he enjoyed the town's finest neighborhood. The nearby streets were lined with colonial mansions, one of which, he knew, had belonged to William Paca, a fellow signer who had been in league with him in Philadelphia when he had delivered his Declaration to the assembled body at the Continental Congress in 1776. But to Jefferson's critical eye, Paca's house looked old-fashioned, with its steep roof and tall chimneys.

Jefferson felt slightly uneasy in this town whose denizens put a great premium on social gaiety and pleasure, where balls and horse races were common pastimes. He was in no mood for such amusements. But the contemplation of architecture was always an escape for him, even though he was a harsh critic of much that he saw. Word had reached him years earlier of the Mathias Hammond house, since little of importance transpired in the small world of American architecture of which Jefferson was unaware. He had been curious about it, but what he had been told left him ill-prepared for the experience of seeing it in person.

He was mesmerized. The front of the Hammond house stretched 131 feet, giving it the scale of a grand country estate despite its in-town setting. The quality of the house surprised him, too. He himself had written of American architecture only two years earlier that "the first principles of the art are unknown, and there exists scarcely a model among us sufficiently chaste to give an idea of them." The shape of the place reminded Jefferson of Monticello, his own, ongoing architectural experiment in Virginia. While that pleased him, any reminder of Monticello was inevitably a source of sadness. The grief he had worked so hard to suppress welled up at the thought of Martha's grave, back on their little mountain in Charlottesville.

If the Hammond house had a desolate air for Jefferson, he was not alone in sensing it. Mathias Hammond had seemed destined to lead a charmed life in Annapolis, but he had tasted failure in love and, having had his marital advances rejected, he abruptly resigned his offices and abandoned Annapolis. Since the early days of the Revolution his newly completed home had stood abandoned. The uninhabited house that enraptured Jefferson resembled a majestic but empty tomb.

The future president reached for the notebook he always carried and set to sketching. He recognized the Maryland five-part plan—Paca's house and another manse in the neighborhood shared the same configuration—but the Hammond house had nuances that he took to immediately. As he sketched the plan, he recorded with care the semi-octagonal façades of the pavilions; they resembled the ends of his own Monticello. Jefferson supposed at once that the builder of this house almost certainly owned a copy of one of his own favorite architectural volumes, Robert Morris's *Select Architecture*, published in England in 1755.

Drawing being the visual equivalent of conversation, Jefferson gained a deeper understanding of the sophisticated design as he recorded the shapes of the Mathias Hammond house. *Massachusetts Historical Society*

He drew the building's front elevation, locating the chimneys, low-pitched roofs, and large windows. But it was the decorative elements at the center of the house that required the closest attention, being the most difficult to draw. The richly carved front door required particular care. Even without reproducing such details as the carved festoons and leafy frieze, Jefferson found the focus of the drawing was unapologetically the doorway. His happy surprise upon first seeing the house gave way to a more studied appreciation that he was in the presence of one of the few architectural masterpieces in America.

V.
1774 and After . . . Lost and Found . . . An Annapolis Story

THE BUILDER OF THE HAMMOND HOUSE AND GUNSTON HALL entered Fiske Kimball's purview in 1914. Kimball had wondered at the mysterious sketch during that inspiring summer he spent with the Coolidge collection. Each evening he and Marie had regaled one another with the findings of the day, and their collaboration in those months had set the tone for their happy marriage.

While most of the Jefferson drawings fitted into categories, a few had not, and the one small, smudged drawing of the multipart house resisted his attempts to tease out its story. Kimball had known it was an early drawing because the sketch was in old-fashioned ink. The kinds of paper used had helped him pigeonhole other drawings, but the laid stock on which this particular drawing had been done resembled none of the others in the Coolidge collection.

He hadn't been content to let it go but kept angling back to look again. *Was there the ghost of a label?* No, he would have noticed that before. *Could they be certain it was the work of Jefferson?* Yes, because Jefferson's drawing style was recognizable in the execution. The geometry of the house seemed to suggest Jefferson, too, thanks to the man's passion for octagonal figures and the building's two, mirror-image octagon shapes. Kimball tried again and again to match it up with a Jefferson building. *Was it an alternative plan for Monticello?* He could find no correlation.

He tried another approach, asking himself, *What if it isn't a building by Jefferson but a study he made of somebody's else's house?* It was not really a very Jeffersonian-looking place, with a brick box at its center of exactly the sort about which the president-to-be had often made disparaging remarks. Still, constructed in bold but uncomplicated brick, it was sophisticated (Jefferson, Kimball knew, would have called it "chaste"). Jefferson had also gone to pains to draw attention to the three openings stacked at the center of the house. The dramatic doorway, the bold central window above, and the round bull's eye window in the attic story. *The combination was . . . could it be . . . familiar?*

He and Marie set to work reviewing all the places where they might previously have encountered the house. They finally found what they were looking for in a grand three-volume compilation titled *The Georgian House* in the library of the Massachusetts Historical Society. The photograph in the 1901 book bore an unmistakable resemblance to Jefferson's sketch. With the knowledge that the house was in Annapolis, Marie found in Jefferson's copious journals references to his months in Maryland's capital. The drawing, they grew certain, was of the Hammond house.

Quite unaware of the existence of William Buckland, Kimball quickly moved on from this unrelated drawing to return to the work on Jefferson's own architecture. Many years would pass before Kimball and others would be able to tell the fuller tale of the little drawing Jefferson had done in 1783 and that he and Marie identified in 1914.

TODAY WILLIAM BUCKLAND STARES DOWN at twenty-first-century visitors. Just a few hundred yards from the River Severn, he seems watchful but welcoming from his perch on the wall of the house museum on Annapolis's Maryland Avenue.

Though painted on canvas, the portrait of Buckland is just a copy, the sort of workmanlike reproduction that comes up as odd lots at country auctions. His hair is dark brown, the eyes gray, and he wears a brown coat and waist-coat. Despite the drab colors, Buckland has an impish, almost winking character about him, with a glimmer in his eye and a half-smile on his face.

Surrounding the bust of the man are symbolic elements the artist incorporated into the image, but the most important is a large sheet of paper filled with architectural renderings. Spread on the dark green tablecloth, the drawings portray the very building in which the portrait is found, a structure now known as the Hammond Harwood House.

The fine home that Buckland built for Mathias Hammond survives, preserved for much of the twentieth century by a foundation that maintains it as a house museum. Its contents include a fine array of eighteenth-century Maryland furniture, as well as several other portraits by Charles Willson Peale. The presence of the immense brick house on the Annapolis streetscape, however, is less remarkable than the survival of Peale's original canvas of Buckland, from which the copy was taken.

Buckland's death in 1774 had been entirely unexpected. Alive in November, he had advertised for workers to help him begin the construction of a new courthouse he had designed for Caroline County, Maryland, a few miles east of Annapolis. Within days of the advertisement's publication, he was dead, circumstances unknown.

If an obituary recorded the event, no one has been able to find it. Some valuable documentary evidence was created after his death, including an inventory of his goods and chattels done in December 1774. While Buckland's abrupt demise in midcareer started the man's reputation on a slide into obscurity, other accidents of history over the years made its restoration possible. The key clue proved to be Peale's unfinished canvas.

The painter had stowed it away after his friend's death. He returned to it only after service in Washington's army during the Revolution. By then Peale had settled in Philadelphia where he executed portraits of many members of the revolutionary generation. Peale occasionally returned to Maryland and on a trip to Annapolis in 1787 he recorded in his diary the delivery of a painting to John Callahan and a payment of £10. John had married Sarah Buckland in 1782 and the subject of the painting was none other than her late father, William Buckland.

Before handing it over, Peale completed the painting he had begun thirteen years earlier. The picture's iconography is rich, starting with the pose.

Royal and aristocratic tradition called for standing figures, with the ruler, lord, or landowner displaying his commanding, noble, and elegant bearing. That had been the rule for public men, especially when the portraits were to be hung in public buildings. But in Buckland's case, the seated pose was informal, with no presumption that the tradesman was the equal of his patrons.

In completing the painting, Peale honored his long-dead friend by adding the drawing of the Hammond house along with a case holding drawing instruments. On a table to one side of the sitter loom two large volumes, no doubt architectural in nature; behind him stands the plinth of a great column and, still farther back, a pedimented portico. The massive edifice at his shoulder was intended to convey something about Buckland: *This* was a man who brought to his work an intimate knowledge of Renaissance grandeur. But Peale had freighted the painting with still another message. *Times had changed*, Peale seemed to be saying. Inherited wealth had long meant power and privilege but in this new world of independence? *Men of intellect and virtue had an inherent right to liberty and status.*

Once delivered, the painting became part of the family patrimony, passed on to John and Sarah Callahan's daughter, Sally. She would marry a man named Richard Harwood, and bear him a son, William, who would eventually inherit not only the portrait, but in a remarkable accident of history, a fine house from another member of the Harwood family. So it was sometime after 1832 that the Mathias Hammond house became the repository for Peale's portrait of his craftsman friend. The architect, in a sense, was reunited with his finest work. Next, both the house and the picture would be inherited by William's youngest daughter, Hester Ann. She would never marry but lived out her life in the house, with the portrait decorating her drawing room, allowing Buckland's shade to regard the architectural masterwork around him.

After Miss Harwood died in 1924, her possessions went to auction. The portrait made its way into the public domain in May 1925, purchased by a New York dealer acting on behalf of Francis P. Garvan, a prominent New York attorney and philanthropist. Although valued at only $25.00 on Hester Ann Harwood's inventory, the buyer reported back to Garvan that "the Architects Portrait is almost certain[ly] by Chas Wilson Peale," so he was "pretty confident" it was a good buy at $375.00. But the reemergence of the man in the picture was not destined to happen quite yet, as Hester Ann had taken to her grave the knowledge of who was portrayed in the painting. Even so, the anonymous subject attracted attention, as more than one observer remarked on the drawing of the Hammond house. The architectural quality of the home was also recognized, and the house was soon sold, purchased by Saint John's College of Annapolis, which established it as a decorative arts museum. Some years later the house would be sold again, this time to the newly founded Hammond-Harwood House Association, Inc., the nonprofit organization that would operate it as a museum.

Kimball proved to be the conduit linking the parties who finally put the story together. In 1929, he received a letter from Daniel R. Randall, a senior partner in a Baltimore law firm. In researching an ancestor, an eighteenth-century master builder named John Randall, Daniel Randall had found that John had apprenticed with a Mr. Buckland and subsequently become his partner. When Buckland died, Randall completed the twenty-one-room Hammond house and also became administrator of his partner's estate. Just as the portrait had been handed down in Buckland's family, a variety of documents had been handed down in Randall's, among them Buckland's indentures.

Daniel Randall wrote to ask Kimball "whether you have among your notes of old Virginia homes run across [Buckland's] name." Randall already knew a good deal about Buckland from the indentures, including the George Mason connection ("On coming to Virginia," Randall reported, Buckland "undertook the building of Gunston Hall"). Kimball wrote back, acknowledging he was "greatly interested" and recommending Randall contact "my great friend R.T.H. Halsey."

Known to his friends as "R. T.," Halsey was a stockbroker-turned-curator, a friend and competitor of Garvan's, whose lectures, writing, and collecting were widely influential. Working as a scout, scholar, and trustee, he helped create the American Wing at the Metropolitan Museum of Art in New York, which had introduced untold visitors to fine American furnishings since its opening in 1924.

Halsey had gone to Annapolis to accept an honorary degree at Saint John's College. There he found a new home, staying on to teach as professor of colonial art. One course he gave, "The Background of American Life," was among the first given in early American culture. He would be the man to restore the name and identity to the anonymous figure in the portrait.

In 1930 Peale's original portrait of Buckland entered the collection at the Yale University Art Gallery in New Haven. Francis Garvan donated it—along with some *five thousand* other antique objects—in his wife's honor as the Mabel Brady Garvan Collection. In comparison to the Annapolis copy, the man in Peale's painting seems positively alive, entombed though he is within a gilt frame on a two-dimensional piece of fabric. The sympathetic understanding between the two strivers, Buckland and Peale, is apparent. They shared bonds of both friendship and ambition in prerevolutionary Annapolis, a place of pomp and pretension where they struggled to better themselves.

On close examination, the painting admits to its own history. Buckland's head, painted thirteen years before the rest of the canvas, stands forth; if it was painted out of friendship, the rest of the work was done by a hand—probably the same hand, but later—bent upon completing the commission in a professional manner but without the same passion.

The painting is evidence of how the cogs of history's time machine engaged to preserve one man's story. The rusty old mechanism began to make sense of disparate data, thanks to the meeting of Daniel Randall and R. T. H. Halsey. There remained missing and misplaced elements, as Halsey in a 1929 essay reported that Buckland hailed from Philadelphia and bore the Christian name Matthew. His full study would remain unpublished when, after being struck by an automobile, Halsey died in 1942. But other researchers, not least Dr. Kimball, managed to complete the reconstruction of a forgotten life.

VI.
The Books in Mr. Buckland's Library

KIMBALL SHARED WITH JEFFERSON a heartfelt belief that the printed word had intrinsic value and importance. Books were to be treasured not for their monetary value but because they offered knowledge, understanding and, very often, connections with the past. When Kimball looked at an antique building, he usually chose to understand it using a book. One was rarely enough and sometimes it took an entire library. Gunston Hall was a case in point.

Kimball was invited as "the best qualified and competent man in the country" to supervise the restoration at Gunston Hall in 1946. He already knew what a fine and important house Gunston Hall was, and he remembered Jefferson's promise to old George Mason, "Whenever I pass your road I shall do myself the honor of turning into it." Jefferson had indeed visited Gunston Hall one last time, just a week before the Colonel died in 1792, but Kimball hadn't been sure at first that he needed to do the same.

Gunston Hall was administered by a board of regents for the National

Society of the Colonial Dames of America. The ladies had been persuasive, and Kimball had given in to their repeated entreaties. Though they had prevailed upon him to take the job, he managed to dictate his terms. The regents had agreed to a contractual clause that his restoration decisions would be final, giving him ultimate authority.

Along the way there had been disagreements about the archaeology, interior decorations, and room configurations. To win at least one crucial argument, Kimball had had to threaten the board with his resignation. When the work at Gunston Hall was completed a few years later, he sat down to memorialize the job in an article for the *Journal of the Society of Architectural Historians*. The writing he had found a "congenial task," not least because it had taken him on a much deeper journey into the past, in particular into the life of William Buckland.

While his work on Buckland was crucial, Kimball alone did not do for the Maryland carver-joiner what he had done for Jefferson. Buckland's emergence as the very model of the eighteenth-century builder-turned-architect would be a collaborative effort, involving the work of Halsey, Randall, and other later historians. The identification of his portrait helped make Buckland's rediscovery possible, along with the Randall documents. Few other eighteenth-century craftsmen have been survived by as much paperwork, not to mention a memorable image, and thus most of them remain little more than shadowy figures.

Kimball in particular put great store in the inventory of Buckland's estate, which had been "legally authorized and sworn [to] 19th December Anno Domini 1774." Like Buckland's portrait, the document was ripe for interpretation. It listed furniture (Buckland owned five bedsteads) and animals (two cows). He also owned five slaves and six indentured servants (a carpenter, painter, carver, manservant, and two bricklayers). The inventory listed tools ("3 Chests Carpenters Tools" and "one Chest Carvers Tools"), clothes, bedclothes, kitchen utensils, and goodly quantities of building material, including boards, nails, and glass. Another entry cites "2 Squares and Bevils and two Drawing Boards," the tools of his adopted trade, that of Architect. Inevitably, though, Kimball's eye fell upon the list of architectural books.

When Buckland died, he owned at least fourteen, a collection that amounted to one of the finest in the Colonies in 1774. Some were the eighteenth-century equivalent of coffee-table books, large folio volumes, elegantly printed and bound, like James Gibbs's *A Book of Architecture* (1728) and the encyclopedic *Complete Body of Architecture* by Isaac Ware (1756), both of which were valued at the then-princely sum of £2. Such books provided a means of admiring fine and important buildings. They were rarely found in the hands of tradesmen but were more likely to be in the libraries of the gentry. Buckland was an exception.

He owned more practical books, too, handbooks to the mathematics of architecture such as *Practical Measuring* by Edward Hoppus (1736). And there were pattern books, most of them pocket-sized, that were effectively builder's manuals. These offered practical knowledge, ranging from pricing data to instructions on the framing of a structure.

Virtually all these books, large and small, contained plates that their authors fully expected would be imitated: That was precisely the point. Buckland often copied elements, meaning that careful comparisons between the books in Buckland's library and the houses he built, in particular Gunston Hall and Mathias Hammond's, enabled Kimball to identify specific printed plates that inspired the builder. "It was chiefly from among [his] books," Kimball wrote, "that came many motifs found in Buckland's works."

Books were essential to Buckland, even more so than to Kimball's generation of architects. Buckland had no degree in architecture. Even if he had had the means, there was no architectural college to attend in his time, even in England. As for America, there wasn't a professional class of designers prior to the 1790s, meaning there were no trained architects to work for the Virginia planters and Philadelphia merchants who could have afforded their services. There were designer-builders, a motley mix of jumped-up masons and joiners who owned a builder's book or two each. Gentlemen amateurs like Jefferson consulted their own libraries for inspiration, but in the eighteenth century fresh architectural plans were almost unheard of. In the context of his time, Mr. Buckland's accomplishments were remarkable: He realized there was a need and, upon moving to Maryland, he set out to fill that need.

Transforming himself into an architect was an audacious goal, and achieving it an immense accomplishment for a penniless farmer's son whose apprenticeship fee had been paid by an Oxford charity. Buckland climbed the socioeconomic ladder, leaping over common laborers, tradesmen, and master builders. He designed houses and even furniture. He desired to be a tastemaker, an American Palladio and Chippendale rolled into one. He wanted to wear the clothes and earn the title of Gentleman. And he succeeded despite his premature death at age forty.

He used his books often, so Kimball and others were able to trace back windows, mantels, and a hundred other details. The books provided the twentieth-century student with an immediate connection: When Kimball held a certain book in his hand, he knew that Buckland had done the same thing. But Buckland had been more than a carrier of old ideas, more than a messenger.

He refined what he saw in his books, adding his own feel for proportion, using the sense of detail that he had developed as a carver and joiner. Sitting at his drafting board, rule pen in hand, he imagined the Mathias Hammond house, a design that Peale recognized as important and added to the composition of his portrait after Buckland's death. As Fiske and Marie Kimball discovered, the Hammond house had caused the next great American architect, Thomas Jefferson, to be struck momentarily dumb before he pulled out his notebook and made his own architectural rendering.

Buckland's buildings continue to command the attention of those who, walking the timeline of American building, experience the same shock of recognition that Jefferson did on what is today Maryland Avenue; Buckland himself straddles an essential moment of transition in American building. The Mathias Hammond house is one that architectural historians recognize as ahead of its time, perfectly proportioned, elegant, and—most important of all—apart from its antecedents. On the basis of the Hammond house alone, Buckland earned the right to be called *Architect*.

CHAPTER 2

AN AMERICAN IN PARIS

"Mr. Jefferson is the first American who has consulted the Fine
Arts to know how he should shelter himself from the weather."
— MARQUIS DE CHASTELLUX (1782)

I.

July 1785 . . . The Minister's Cabinet . . . Paris

THE ANSWER HOVERED in some cavity of his capacious memory. He had considered the problem before, but like the mythical Tantalus who was destined to see the fruit overhead blown out of range each time he reached for it, Thomas Jefferson found himself unable to bring into focus the dimly recollected image.

Two fellow Virginians, William Hays and James Buchanan, had posed the challenge. "We must intreat you to Consult an able Architect on a plan fit for a Capitol, and to assist him with the information of which you are possessed." As Commissioners of Public Buildings they needed architectural plans for a new state Capitol, and they wanted them quickly, preferably by the beginning of August.

Their letter took almost three months to reach Jefferson in Paris, where he had succeeded Benjamin Franklin as minister to the court of King Louis XVI. "Your favor of March 20 came to hand the 14th. of June," he wrote back, adding with regret that "it would be impossible to procure and get to your hands the draughts you desired" on their proposed schedule.

Jefferson found the prospect of the new Virginia Capitol both exciting and daunting. He was passionate about buildings, but in truth he could claim

35

Charles-Louis Clérisseau. *Thomas J. McCormick*

authorship of just one house. As proud as he was of Monticello, the home was far from finished and he was hardly satisfied. In the year since his arrival, his walks around Paris among the the *hôtels* in fashionable neighborhoods left him pondering major changes to Monticello's design. But work on his Virginia house could come later. This new, larger job demanded his immediate attention.

He knew very well that the Commonwealth of Virginia required a new Capitol. Ten years earlier he himself had begun planning one; six years after that, just two days after becoming Virginia's governor, he engineered passage of the Bill for the Removal of the Seat of Government of Virginia. While the state government had duly moved from Williamsburg to Richmond, it hadn't been until after Jefferson's departure for Europe that, tiring of their temporary quarters in a converted tobacco warehouse, the Virginia assembly authorized the directors to commission the construction of "apartments . . . for the use of the legislative, executive, and judiciary . . . under one roof." That had prompted the letter from the commissioners.

As he thought about the matter from afar, Jefferson came to believe the creation of a new Capitol building offered an extraordinary opportunity to educate his countrymen. After receiving the request from Hays and Buchanan, he was inspired to write to his old friend, James Madison, asking rhetorically, "How is a taste for [architecture] to be formed in our countrymen, unless we avail ourselves of every occasion when public buildings are to be erected, of presenting to them models for their study and imitation?" He had derided the public buildings in Williamsburg as "rude, mis-shapen piles" in his *Notes on the State of Virginia,* the book that had come off press only the month before. Now he recognized an opportunity to improve upon existing American architecture.

His immediate problem was that while he knew for certain what he didn't want, he hadn't yet come up with something better. He invested untold hours wandering the Parisian streets considering the matter until, like sunlight streaking through a break in the clouds, a fresh idea illuminated the entire argument. His insight wasn't a new and perfect design; on the contrary, he realized he wasn't looking for a new design at all.

From his desk in his *cabinet,* he wrote again to Hays and Buchanan; he was buying time as he carefully reframed the argument. He wrote that there were two means of fulfilling the charge he had been given. "One was to leave to some architect to draw an external according to his fancy, in which way experience shews that about once in a thousand times a pleasing form is hit upon; the other was to take some model already devised and approved by the general suffrage of the world." By adapting an existing building, he argued, the Virginians would be more likely to produce a satisfactory result.

His Capitol idea was to mime an old building, a notion both simple and radical.

Yet having made the case on paper to his fellow Virginians, he still found himself asking the tantalizing question: *What structure is it that won't come into focus in my mind's eye?*

In France, as in America, Jefferson admitted, he "labored grievously under the malady of Bibliomanie." His first book purchase in Paris had come just one day after his arrival in the French capital. The sight of "Monsieur Chefersone," as the tall American was known to one dealer, quickly became familiar to the printers, publishers, stationers, and bookbinders whose stalls lined the Left Bank streets. In contemplating the new Capitol's design, he turned to his growing array of architectural volumes. He soon identified several buildings from antiquity that he thought worthy of imitation, among them the Erectheum in Athens, the Temple at Baalbec, and the Temple of Mars in Rome. None seemed quite right, so his search continued.

On one of his book-buying ventures, he visited a shop called Chez Crépy in the Latin Quarter. There he found an unfamiliar variety of paper, a woven stock with an embossed grid spaced ten squares to the inch. This "coördinate" or graph paper had been manufactured for silk weavers, but Jefferson purchased a quantity for his own uses. He experimented with the paper and found that it "saves the necessity of using the rule and dividers in all rectangular draughts."

He had only middling talents as a draftsman, so Jefferson understood how useful his new paper would be in limning a likeness of a new Capitol. He also knew that he wanted the source to be "the most perfect model of antiquity now existing." But his sense of certainty ended there: He was, admittedly, no more than a novice designer. Good sense, then, as well as the directors' instructions, led him to seek a collaborator "whose taste had been formed on a study of the antient models of this art."

Undoubtedly his collaborator of choice would have been Andrea Palladio, whose masterwork, *The Four Books of Architecture,* Jefferson later acknowledged was his "Bible" for architectural matters. He knew the book well; fifteen years before, the engraving of Palladio's Villa Cornaro had inspired his design of Monticello's façade. But Palladio was not available for consultation, having died in 1580.

Though he still lacked the "able Architect" that Hays and Buchanan requested, Jefferson would soon find another author—one who happened also to be an antiquarian and architect—who was alive and well and living in Paris.

II.
August 1785 . . . Champs Elysées . . . Paris

THOMAS JEFFERSON COUNTED HIS FOOTSTEPS. He habitually kept track of distances traveled, goods manufactured, and bushels produced, but his new gadget, a "pedometer," mechanically registered his steps ("dble. steps," he noted in his *Memorandum Books,* because the device was attached to one leg, registering every other footfall). Using the machine, he was able to calculate both distance and pace. "I walk then at the rate of 4 3/20 miles an hour," noted the long-legged Jefferson.

For a man intrigued by the craft of building, walking the streets of Paris in 1785 was pure theater. Scaffolding shadowed many buildings, piles of stone obstructed the roadways. Builders' shacks, crowds of workmen, the ringing of chisels, and the thunking of hammers were ubiquitous. A real estate boom produced new mansions as whole sections of Paris were developed.

Jefferson strode purposefully toward the Louvre. No longer a royal residence, the Louvre was not yet an official museum although some Parisians talked of making it into one. The logic was impeccable, given that portions of the building had already become the repository for various collections, among them those of the Royal Academies of Painting, Sculpture, and Architecture. The transition seemed inevitable.

Jefferson visited the immense old palace often, but today a specific errand crowded out other distractions. Some of the building's cavernous halls led to offices, studios, and lodgings, and Jefferson was headed for one atelier in particular. There were enormous, light-and-airy studios and tiny apartments reached only by trudging down long, dark halls and climbing shadowy stairways. It had become an address much sought after by artists. The Louvre also housed one of Paris's artistic and social highlights when the Royal Academy of Painting and Sculpture opened its month-long show each August. The art hung in the Salon Carré, an arena-sized drawing room where hundreds of paintings crowded the walls up to the coffered ceiling some fifty feet above. Jefferson would show an ability to pick winners from this crowded field when he recognized the "best thing" at the Salon of 1787 was David's *Death of Socrates*.

Jacques-Louis David worked in a studio at the Louvre, but this day Jefferson's interest was not in paintings. He strode through the entrance of the Cour du Louvre, his mind too preoccupied to take note of the stalls and easels and the bustle of business in the art market beneath the tall vaulted ceiling.

He was going to visit another man who believed in calculating things. Charles-Louis Clérisseau's specialty was the mensuration and recording of buildings, especially ancient ones. In nineteen years spent in Italy, he painted thousands of drawings, watercolors, and gouaches (in which watercolor pigments were mixed with gum to produce opaque colors). His pictures portrayed in meticulous detail most of the ancient sites in Rome, as well as many in Paestum, Tivoli, Pola, and Spalatro. On his return to France, his much-admired paintings had earned him a place at the Royal Academy, entitling him to a space in the Louvre.

When Jefferson arrived at M. Clérisseau's door, determined to advance the cause of the new Virginia Capitol, he had a proposition to make.

III.
Spring 1915 . . . University of Michigan . . . Ann Arbor

KIMBALL PREFERRED WRITING IN PENCIL. He positioned his pencil between the index and middle fingers of his right hand, grasping it with the thumb and two finger tips. The penmanship that resulted from his unusual grip retained the loopy elegance of the nineteenth century but suggested the brusque urgency of a young man in a hurry.

Even at twenty-six, he had the look of authority. His thick, dark hair was brushed back; a dense mustache combed outward balanced the broad forehead above. And the eyes were dark, always penetrating.

He had launched a small architectural practice, designing a few homes. He wrote reviews, articles, and essays for publication, but there was no getting around the fact that his day job, at least for the time being, was on the teaching track. That posed a small dilemma: He had no Ph.D. and having one would automatically make him an assistant professor and entitle him to a much-needed pay increase.

He thought the solution might be quite literally at hand. He had Jefferson's drawings in his possession, Worthington Ford having entrusted them to his care in Ann Arbor to facilitate work on the Jefferson book, which was not yet complete. Never a man to attack just one project at a time, Kimball had also embarked on a history of the Virginia Capitol, the building that he had come to believe was Jefferson's most influential. He had imagined the subject would be suitable for an article or two, but then it occurred to him to wonder about it as a possible topic for a Ph.D. dissertation. Despite his difficulty in seeing himself as an academic, the words of an old history professor at Harvard had come back to him. According to Charles Homer Haskins, it was easier for a scholar to get a Ph.D. than to explain why he hadn't one.

"It was obvious," Kimball concluded, "that a doctor's thesis could well be extracted from [the drawings] in passing, and I registered in the Graduate School at Michigan as a candidate for a degree of Doctor of Philosophy." His department head was unsympathetic ("What time do I ever have to write?" he inquired impatiently). But a more congenial archaeology professor bound for sabbatical offered Kimball his large fireproof office. Its big tables were ideal.

With the Jefferson drawings spread out around him, Kimball made rapid progress. As a pencil man himself, he noticed an important pattern in Jefferson's drafting—at some point, the Virginian had shifted from working in ink to pencil. The change seemed to coincide with Jefferson's shift to graph paper, the large fourteen-by-eighteen-inch sheets with the grid of red lines. Then Fiske found the watermark, *Richard Auvergne, Paris 1782*. Soon Marie

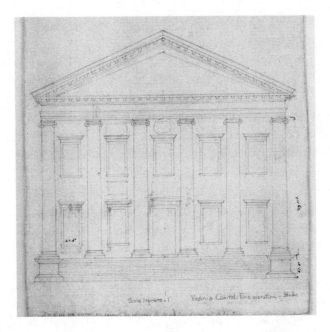

The front elevation as drawn by Jefferson . . . but, perhaps, as emended by Clérisseau (note the elliptical opening at center and the brackets or consoles sketched in on the lower left window). *Massachusetts Historical Society*

came across a letter in which Jefferson told of his discovery in France of drafting pencils. The drawings he produced were more satisfactory than the ink he used previously, he told a Philadelphia friend. "Using a black lead pencil, the lines are very visible, and easily effaced with Indian rubber to be used for any draft."

Kimball wished to tell the story of the Virginia Capitol, and the pieces began to come together. He studied all the drawings that seemed to relate to the project and with Marie's help, compared them to the correspondence to try to date them. They looked for common watermarks, sheet sizes, and paper qualities. He soon established a rough chronology for the drawings that related to the Capitol. They were in Jefferson's hand, but Kimball noted that some bore freehand changes. He hypothesized that the additions might be the work of Jefferson's collaborator, M. Clérisseau.

He would tell the story with typical thoroughness and for the first time. His thesis would fill three issues of the *Journal of the American Institute of Architects* and, on a hot summer day in June of the following year, he became *Doctor* Kimball.

IV.

1570 to 1785 . . . Classicism on the March . . . Rome, Venice, Paris, and London

IN MATTERS OF ARCHITECTURE, Jefferson was an autodidact. There had been no professor of architecture at the College of William and Mary to drill him on its rudiments. He found no "faithful and beloved mentor" to shape his architectural urges as George Wythe had done with his legal and political aspirations.

Thomas Jefferson purchased his first architectural volume a few months into his studies in Williamsburg in 1760, buying the old tome from a cabinetmaker who lived near the gate to the College of William and Mary. More interested in drink than in his dwindling library, the aging craftsman parted with the volume for a handful of shillings. The eager teenager—Jefferson was seventeen—carried the big book back to his rooms and studied it for hours. There were no photographs (another century would elapse before that technology would be developed) but engraved plates of drawings portrayed symmetrical structures with classical columns and bold cornices.

The book Jefferson purchased from the rummy old woodworker probably was Andrea Palladio's *I Quattro Libri dell' Architettura*; over the decades, in fact, the acolyte Jefferson would own at least five different editions of *The Four Books*, and he came to regard its author as his architectural mentor. The pictures he examined were *orthographic* drawings, meaning the buildings were portrayed as if seen from straight on. The human eye doesn't actually see things that way—another kind of drawing, the *perspective*, more closely simulates the sophisticated means by which the brain interprets visual data. In a perspective drawing, the corner of a building is set in the foreground, making some elements appear closer, others farther away. But Palladio, having apprenticed at thirteen as a stonemason, knew that perspective drawings were of very little use to a builder. To avoid the distortion of the perspective drawing, Palladio drew *elevations* (views that reveal the face of a building from the point of view of an observer looking straight-on from a horizontal vantage) and *floor plans* (which show the location of the rooms in a structure, drawn as if from a vantage directly above a building that has had its roof removed). The result was an almost scientific recording of his buildings.

Palladio had been the first to use floor plans and elevations of the same house on the same page in a book, and as the youthful Jefferson taught himself to interpret or "read" Palladio's orthographic drawings, the temples and villas

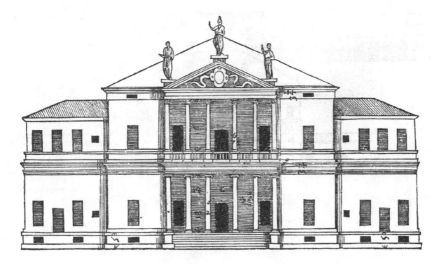

From *The Four Books*, Palladio's design for the Villa Cornaro. It's a design that Jefferson
would echo when he first imagined Monticello circa 1769. *I Quattro Libri dell'Architecttura*

came to life in his imagination. To that time, the farthest he had ever traveled
from his native Charlottesville was the hundred miles to Williamsburg; the
finest buildings in his personal experience loomed as no more than large and
boxy plantation houses of uncertain style. Yet in this book he saw buildings
conceived as objects of beauty, as works of art to be admired.

Jefferson also recognized in Palladio's text the voice of a kindred soul, one
that spoke in terms he could embrace. Palladio wrote of *virtù*, a word that implied both excellence and civic action in his native Italian vernacular. Palladio believed virtuous architecture embodied ideas about how people should
live together. The idealistic young Jefferson couldn't help but agree.

Palladio had been trained not as a designer but as a craftsman when, in his
early twenties, a Venetian nobleman had made him his protégé. The older
man took him on the first of the five visits Palladio would make to Rome.
Palladio had been inspired by what he saw, just as Jefferson was while studying the pages of *The Four Books*. Palladio not only examined but actually
measured ancient Roman temples and other ruins; he was an instinctive ar-
chaeologist, well before the academic discipline of archaeology was created.

What set him apart from the university-educated gentlemen humanists
such as his patron was that he was a working-man's architect. He had been cut-
ting, carving, and laying up stone for many years before he began designing. He
knew how the parts were shaped and assembled, so his book about buildings
was unprecedented in its practicality. He prescribed proportional modules in

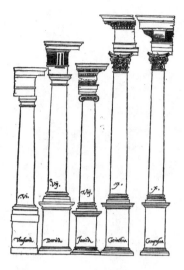

The Orders, as drawn by Palladio's contemporary Sebantiano Serlio: the Tuscan, Doric, Ionic,
Corinthian, and Composite. The Ionic Order has scroll-shaped volutes on its capital; acanthus
leaves decorate the Corinthian capital; and the Composite features both volutes and leaves.
The simpler Tuscan and Doric are differentiated by the curved profiles of their moldings.

minutes and fractions. His buildings offered readers dream fulfillment, too, but
The Four Books was well ahead of its time as a utilitarian how-to book.

The first of *The Four Books* had reappeared over the decades in pirated editions as a freestanding volume on its own. Devoted to "the Orders," it made
comprehensible the rudiments of Classicism (as the English architect
Christopher Wren once aptly expressed it, the Orders are the "Latin" of classical architecture). Classical architectural grammar derives from decorative
features used in ancient Greece and Rome, in particular the various combinations of vertical posts and horizontal beams that form the structure of a
building. Each Order is distinguished by its columns (posts), as well as its
proportions and the distinctive decorations applied to or just beneath the
roofline. Palladio made the ancient systems usable, expressing them in words
and pictures that builders and clients alike could understand.

Something else explains why Jefferson and others made *The Four Books*
the most influential architectural treatise of all time. What Palladio saw in
Rome became a source for his work; he chose to design buildings *all' antica*
("in the antique manner"). His buildings are immediately recognizable as descendants of ancient ones, yet he never copied old buildings, demonstrating
instead a visionary talent for building new. Perhaps most important of all,
he chose to adapt the forms of temples, basilicas, and theaters to domestic

architecture. He was the first great architect to devote the bulk of his practice to designing *houses,* and he did so by basing his designs on antiquity. When he published *The Four Books* at age sixty-two, he chose to include not only his designs of villas and palazzi but also woodcuts of ancient buildings, edifices that Jefferson liked to call "the remains of Roman grandeur."

As Jefferson's library grew, many of the books he acquired demonstrated how Palladio's genius had repeatedly bobbed back to the surface just when it appeared ready to sink from sight. One of those books, *The Designs of Inigo Jones,* presented the work of England's first great "Palladian," as the heirs to Palladio came to be known. A painter and scenic designer, Jones had traveled to Italy in 1614. There he purchased a copy of *The Four Books,* and it became his architectural guidebook. Jones inserted his own sketches, annotations, and commentaries into whatever white space he could find in the book's pages, and fell so deeply into Palladio's thrall that he purchased more than 250 drawings from Palladio's studio (probably from his heirs), many of them executed and signed by the master himself. Jones returned to London and set to work designing new buildings in a manner unknown to his homeland. As a result, he is credited with nothing less than launching Renaissance architecture in England. His immersion in Palladio's designs was such that his drafting techniques so closely resembled Palladio's that centuries would elapse before scholars were able to separate some of Jones's drawings that got shuffled into his collection of Palladio's.

Palladio's drawings continued to inspire people, even after Jones's death in 1652 and his style of Palladian classicism began to fade. Jones's assistant, John Webb, drew upon them for several buildings before his own end came twenty years later. The drawings were then dispersed, though a London architect, an Oxford patron, and others who studied the drawings produced a handful of buildings recognizable as Palladio's children in the next few decades. Then in 1715 the first complete edition of *The Four Books* appeared in English, although its copperplate engravings were, in many instances, reversed and reproduced out of order. The book's appearance led to a new interest in Palladio.

His paper trail carried on through time with a momentum all its own, and November 3, 1719, stands out as an essential date. That day an English peer, Richard Boyle, the third Earl of Burlington, bought his own copy of the 1601 edition of *The Four Books.* Inspired to retrace Inigo Jones's steps, he crisscrossed the Veneto, the mainland region near Venice that had been Palladio's home and where virtually all his work was constructed. He studied the buildings and, as Jones had done, he bought a collection of drawings by Palladio in Venice; then, in 1720 and 1721, he purchased from the estate of a

London architect many of the very sheets Inigo Jones had owned, along with some of Jones's own drawings and his annotated edition of *The Four Books*. Soon Burlington's collection amounted to seventeen bound volumes containing almost all of the surviving drawings by Palladio.

Like Jefferson, Burlington was an amateur smitten with buildings. With his wealth and influence, he became both a patron and a designer in his own right, just as Jefferson would do in the years after his French sojourn. Together with other English writers, publishers, and architects, Burlington helped launch the "Palladian Revival," the architectural style that dominated much of the eighteenth century in England. The *temple front* distinguishes the style, in which an uncomplicated box-shaped building faces the world with a central triangle at its roof-line (the *pediment*), supported by columns. In Burlington's time, the British Empire was emerging as the dominant world power, and rich and influential Britons wanted houses that made a statement. Palladio's temple-front formula fit.

A publishing frenzy in eighteenth-century London produced not only *The Designs of Inigo Jones* but various versions of Palladio's *Four Books* (including a definitive edition underwritten by Burlington). The library of the Palladian Revival featured many other books, volumes found in Jefferson's library as well as William Buckland's, books that dictated the architectural ground rules of the time.

The authors and designers—Palladio, Jones, Burlington, James Gibbs, Robert Morris, and others—shared many things but one in particular: They believed in a usable past. It was as if Palladio, having measured and recorded the buildings of antiquity, rendered their essence into his drawings; it was as if a tube containing his drawings got handed like a baton from runner to runner in a marathon relay race that would last for centuries. Palladio ran the first leg, Inigo Jones came next, and later Lord Burlington took a turn.

Now Jefferson was poised to take his.

V.
September 1785 . . . The Louvre . . . Paris

THE AGING ARTIST COULD HARDLY HAVE ANTICIPATED a visit from the American minister plenipotentiary to France. But the unexpected had come to be usual in a life of high expectations and dashed hopes.

The son of a Parisian *parfumier*, Clérisseau trained as an architect in Paris. At the unlikely age of twenty-eight he won the Prix de Rome, an honor that gave the over-aged student the privilege of studying as a *pensionnaire* at the French Academy in Rome. More surprising still, his three-year fellowship became a two-decade Roman hiatus.

Soon after his arrival he formed a fond friendship with the Professor of Perspective at the Academy, Giovanni Paolo Panini, the man charged with teaching him to paint architectural views. Clérisseau quickly adopted Panini's fondness for ruins, the half-collapsed buildings and monuments, eroded by the centuries, that survived from antiquity. He soon excelled even his master in archaeological accuracy.

The man Jefferson came to visit some thirty years later lived on the fringes of greatness but knew the frustration of never quite tasting it. He had departed the French Academy angry at not having gotten a second extension to his fellowship. The director called him arrogant; in turn, Clérisseau called his French friends at the Academy dissipated and lazy. This would prove to be an unhappy pattern in the years to come, when temperamental displays accompanied his leave-takings when he felt his trusting nature had been abused by others. Upon his departure from the Academy in 1753, however, Clérisseau felt he could afford the luxury of his anger because he had discovered a ready market for his gouaches. His atmospheric paintings of ruins proved the perfect take-home reminder for the well-to-do Grand Tourists who flooded into Rome.

Thousands of Englishmen took the Grand Tour in the eighteenth century, visiting the Netherlands, France, Germany, and especially Italy. They came to complete their educations, to learn about foreign cultures, manners, and languages. Once in Italy, they sought to admire the vestiges of ancient Rome, as well as the paintings, architecture, and sculpture of the Renaissance. But the *Milordi Inglesi* also came for the shopping: Returning to England in 1715 from his year-long Grand Tour, Lord Burlington filled *eight hundred and seventy-eight* trunks and crates. His shopping spree dwarfed the eighty-six crates Jefferson would ship to himself on his return to America in 1789.

The English visitors proved to be eager customers not only for Clérisseau's work but for etchings by another member of his Roman circle, Giovanni Battista Piranesi, who sold his prints at his own shop opposite the Academy. The atmospheric art of Piranesi evoked a sense of drama and decay in illustrating the ruins of Rome. Using dramatic lighting effects, he depicted arches and pyramids and obelisks and columns, producing a sense of the fantastic.

A *cappricìo* of the Temple of Minerva, as imagined and painted by Clérisseau.
Thomas J. McCormick

Clérisseau learned much about the picturesque from his friend, and himself often painted sunlight pouring through collapsed ceilings, creating the illusion of an ancient past that seemed preserved and somehow alive amid crumbling masonry overgrown with vegetation.

Clérisseau had felt very much at home in Rome. Unlike the bustling metropolis that was his native Paris, Rome was a city of artists and students of the past. He made another enduring friend in Rome in Johann Joachim Winckelmann, the founder of modern archaeology, who at the time was undertaking his systematic excavations at Pompeii and Herculaneum. In his major work, *History of Ancient Art* (1764), he looked for historic context rather than to admire randomly what had been found, an approach characteristic of earlier students of antiquity. Winckelmann also played a role in another of Clérisseau's careers, recommending that his students employ Charles-Louis as their painting master. Clérisseau hired himself out as a *cicerone*, too, giving walking-and-talking tutorials around ancient Rome.

After his departure from the Academy, Clérisseau earned an adequate living selling his paintings and his services, but a more comfortable life offered itself when his path crossed that of Robert Adam. Arriving in Italy in 1754, the twenty-six-year-old Scotsman was prepared to spend whatever was necessary of his capital of £5,000 on his Grand Tour. Though he had already practiced architecture with his late father and older brother, he knew that his work needed something to set it apart. His sketchbooks on arrival in Italy contained little more than fashionable but unremarkable Palladian buildings, a mode fast becoming passé. Adam's ambitions led him to aim higher. He didn't know how he would achieve it, but he planned to become the leading architect in Britain.

When they met in Florence in January 1755, Adam recognized Charles-Louis Clérisseau as the catalyst he needed. The younger man envied the ease of Clérisseau's work, remarking that he "drew delightfully in the free manner I wanted." Adam knew immediately that this man had a great deal to teach.

"I found out Clerisseau," Adam wrote home the following month, ". . . in whom tho' there is no guile, Yet there is the utmost knowledge of Architecture of perspective, & of Designing & Colouring I ever Saw, or had any Conception of; He rais'd my Ideas, He created emulation & fire in my Breast. I wish'd above all things to learn his manner, to have him with me at Rome, to Study close with him & to purchase of his works." Adam had found his mentor and Clérisseau his patron.

Upon their return to Rome, Clérisseau took up residence in the Scotsman's palatial apartments above the Spanish Steps. For two months, he played *cicerone*, showing Adam the ancient city he had come to know well. On a journey to Naples in April, Clérisseau the drawing master began to discipline his student, and together they began to draw what they saw. In the coming months, they established a daily routine of working at home in the morning, studying perspective and practicing draftsmanship; then, after the midday meal, Adam reported, we "ride out to see palaces and draw on the spot." The program was rigorous and Clérisseau, as his own teacher Panini had done, forbade work on architectural design ("Clerisseau preached to me to forbear inventing . . . till I have made more progress in seeing things and my head more filled with propper ornaments"). Adam copied his master's drawings, too, a routine part of an artist's training in the eighteenth century. From Clérisseau he learned what he described to his brother James as those "knacks so necessary for us architects." Through Clérisseau he met Piranesi, too, reporting home that his new friend "is becoming immensely intimate with me . . . and says I have more genius for the true noble Architecture than any Englishman ever was in Italy."

Adam proved an apt pupil and by the following spring, Clérisseau loosened the reins. Adam himself hatched a plan to publish a book that would launch his career in London, as he put it, with a "great puff." After a time, he settled on Spalatro as his subject, a collection of Roman ruins on the Adriatic coast not far from Venice. Clérisseau's status then changed again—Adam took to calling him his "Antiquarian," but in reality Clérisseau became head draftsman, preparing many of the finished drawings and supervising their engraving onto copper plates in Venice. Proof sheets were sent for approval to Adam, who had resumed his architectural practice in England.

Adam got from Clérisseau and his Grand Tour exactly what he wanted. He returned home with a collection of ancient building fragments along with so many renderings of his and Clérisseau's that he had had to commission a special trunk "of the most enormous magnitude, made a-purpose to contain all my drawings, sketches and studies." His book, *Ruins of the Palace of the Emperor Diocletian at Spalatro in Dalmatia*, would be a landmark when it appeared in 1764, both as a work of archaeology and as means of creating an appetite for Adam's new architecture. The young Scotsman began integrating antique decorative elements into his designs, applying swags, friezes, arabesques, and other ancient details to ceilings, vaults, niches, and arcades. A new style emerged from the drawings he had done under Clérisseau's tutelage, as literal recordings of the past gave way to newly imagined spaces decorated with authentic elements. The Adam style would prove broadly popular in the late eighteenth century as the principal successor to the Palladian Revival's durable mode of building.

For his efforts, Charles-Louis Clérisseau got little beyond a stipend to live on and unfulfilled promises. Although much of the work on *Spalatro* had been Clérisseau's, Adam buried his name in the list of foreign subscribers, acknowledging him only as "Mr. Clérisseau, a French artist" who accompanied him on the expedition. Relations between the two men, having been almost that of father and son, had grown distant as Adam gained confidence and Clérisseau's role devolved from *professore* to draftsman. For a time Adam actually paid Clérisseau *not* to come to England for fear his evident expertise would distract from Adam's own growing reputation. When he finally did get to work in Adam's offices in London, Clérisseau's employment abruptly ended when Adam went temporarily bankrupt. Clérisseau returned to France, once again with little to show for his labors.

When Jefferson met him years later, Clérisseau's pride had sustained still another wound. Catherine the Great of Russia commissioned him in 1773 to design a house in an antique style, but she had rejected his plan, dismissing it as too big and ill-suited to her harsh northern climate. Clérisseau, never a man to forget a slight, snubbed her son Prince Paul when the Russian visited Paris. Again Clérisseau had had to content himself with mere money, selling Catherine an immense cache of his drawings. Despite the welcome revenue, the sale of the portfolios proved painful for the artist, who described the 1,170 drawings he sold as "my blood, the purest of my blood."

Clérisseau could hardly have known that yet another collaboration was in the offing that, in the fullness of time, would be essential to his architectural legacy.

VI.
September 1785 . . . Clérisseau's Atelier . . . The Louvre

CLÉRISSEAU? EVERYONE CALLED HIM THE RIGHT MAN FOR THE JOB. Not only had he trained as an architect—his skills as a draftsman were unsurpassed—but no one in Paris knew as much as he about ancient Roman buildings. Jefferson's stated goal was a building "to improve the taste of my countrymen," and it appeared that as the recognized authority on classical ornamentation, M. Clérisseau could easily satisfy the Virginian's concern that the proportions, the Orders, and other detailing on the new Capitol be entirely correct.

Still, Jefferson was nervous. Clérisseau's contretemps with Catherine the Great posed a nagging concern. The gossipy tale had reached his ears, telling of how Clérisseau, apparently overcome by delusions of grandeur at having a client of such wealth and power, produced a design for an enormous villa when the commission had been for a mere garden house. Who could say he wouldn't get carried away again? Jefferson, facing a deadline and a limited budget, knew he could ill afford to waste time and money.

To avoid traveling up a such a cul-de-sac, he devised a strategy. First, he would develop the preliminary design himself. He had begun the job years before and, in any case, he was eager to put to use the coördinate paper he had found on the Rue Saint Jacques. He studied the floor plan the Virginia directors had sketched, mindful that their drawing "altho it contains many particulars . . . is not intended to confine the architect except as to the number and area of the rooms." Inigo Jones would have called the drawing a "scizo," meaning a sketch intended to convey less a design than the germ of its idea. Jefferson reached back into his own memory of the old Capitol in Williamsburg, one of the few Virginia buildings he liked tolerably well ("on the whole," he allowed, "it is the most pleasing piece of architecture we have"). Recognizing that Clérisseau could not "know what number and sizes of apartments would suit the different corps of our government," he adapted the old Capitol's floor plan.

The result was three essential sheets that included plans of the first and second floors, as well as an elevation of the building's side. With these drawings at hand, Jefferson believed, Clérisseau could be kept on course, but to be doubly sure he also prepared a set of instructions written in French and bearing the title *"Notes explicatives des plans du Capitole pour l'état de la Virginie,"* which specified the several ancient temples that Jefferson regarded as the new Capitol's antecedents. He cited the numbers of the plates that illustrated each temple in books Clérisseau would know. Jefferson enumerated the Orders he wanted, too, leaving little to chance in the papers he prepared for his future collaborator.

These he brought to Clérisseau that day.

The man who greeted Jefferson wasn't handsome. He had a protuberant nose, and his features had thickened over the years. But advancing age had mellowed his temperament, and a new stability in his life had replaced the old seesaw pattern of initial eagerness to please giving way to angry partings. Construction was well under way for the Governor's Palace he had designed in Metz, the capital of the French province of Lorraine. In his personal life, too, there were the satisfactions that he and his wife, Thérèse, had enjoyed as they watched their daughter grow into a handsome young woman who captured the attentions of an up-and-coming young architect, Jacques-Guillaume Legrand.

Although denied proper credit by Robert Adam for his contributions to the Spalatro book, Clérisseau had set aside his resentments, resolving to undertake his own publishing venture. He had embarked upon a thorough study of the Roman ruins in his native land. Over a period of almost ten years, he laboriously prepared the drawings and text for *Antiquités de la France: Première Partie, Monumens des Nismes,* published in 1778. In assembling the book he brought a new rigor to the recording of ancient buildings, taking the dictates of his friend Winckelmann to heart. "One has no right to omit or neglect anything," Winckelmann had written before his death in 1768, "even if it seems unimportant to the ordinary person, because it may be important to the enlightened." *Monumens des Nismes* immediately became the standard work on the subject.

When welcomed to Clérisseau's studio late in the summer of 1785, Jefferson towered over the hunched, sixty-three-year-old Frenchman. He hadn't known quite what to expect, but the man's manner was ingratiating. They discovered a common passion for ancient monuments; Clérisseau recognized the presence of a kindred spirit.

He quickly warmed to the young American whose attempts to speak French were endearing if not altogether fluent. As they talked of the possible candidates on which to model the new Capitol for Virginia, the conversation inevitably turned to the one Clérisseau knew best of all. He brought forth a copy of his grandly proportioned book, *Antiquités de la France*. Too big to be held comfortably in hand, it was spread before his guest on a tabletop. Jefferson was always one to admire fine bookmaking, but this volume presented a truly intoxicating blend of artistry, craftsmanship, and architecture.

Antiquités de la France was the first of a planned series of volumes, and its subject was the Roman town of Nîmes in the south of France. Perhaps Jefferson sensed something familiar in the immense creamy white pages of the folio—had he perused this book on one of his many forays to the Left Bank searching for books? The printer had been the same Philippe-Denys Pierres who had just produced his own book, *Notes on the State of Virginia*. Had he encountered the book there?

Yet the book itself seemed unimportant once Jefferson realized what it contained. Clérisseau directed his guest's attention not to his meticulous renderings of the amphitheater or the other ruins in Nîmes, but to one building in particular. It was a Roman temple, constructed a few years into the Christian era, on which Clérisseau and Jefferson could quickly agree: There was no more perfect monument than the Maison Carrée, not even in Rome.

Jefferson realized that, yes, indeed, he knew the building from his many perusals of Palladio's *Four Books*. It hadn't made it onto his short list of potential models for the Capitol, but seeing it in the pages of M. Clérisseau's *Antiquités de la France*, the Maison Carrée took the place of the other buildings. Thanks to his new friend, Jefferson found himself looking at the model he wanted, the very image that he had been unable to bring into focus in his imagination.

VII.
August 1786 . . . Halle aux Bleds . . . Paris

JEFFERSON CAME TO LOOK AT THE CEILING. Built on a footprint 120 feet in diameter, the walls of Paris's grain market formed a cylinder capped by a flattened dome. That morning, the great interior courtyard of the Halle aux Bleds buzzed with the business of farmers and millers buying and selling grains.

Although it served a utilitarian purpose, the surprisingly elegant building had become a requisite stop on the connoisseurs' tour of Paris; that was why Jefferson's companions had come along on this unusually warm August day. But Jefferson himself had a different motivation. He was mulling over a plan for a public market back in Richmond. He had heard much about the dome of the Halle aux Bleds, added to an earlier building by Clérisseau's son-in-law, J. G. Legrand, just prior to the building's acceptance by the city of Paris in 1782. While Jefferson had seen more majestic domes since arriving in the Old World, the one a hundred feet over his head was remarkable in its own way. The others had been built of stone, the result of masonry traditions that reached back centuries, but this dome employed very different techniques: The structure was of wood, with short lengths of lumber cut into arcs then overlapped and laminated together to form the ribs of the dome.

Jefferson declared the saucer-shaped curve above him a "noble dome" despite its humble materials. The twenty-five windows inserted between the wooden ribs flooded the expansive interior with light. The vast rotunda pleased his companions, but Jefferson continued to regard the building in a way those around him did not. Always attuned to the practical and the mechanical, his mind registered that here was an adaptable and affordable design. The idea of masons in Virginia raising a stone dome like the cathedrals of Europe was almost unimaginable; but a wood-frame dome like this one? That would surely be within the skills of Virginia carpenters using native materials. Jefferson filed the idea away; in the years to come, at a market or elsewhere, he would find a place for which just such a design would be the perfect solution.

Jefferson turned his attention to his companions.

One he had come to know well, a fellow American named John Trumbull. They had met that spring in England, on Jefferson's journey to meet with his old friend John Adams, who was serving as minister to the Court of St. James. Though the son of a Connecticut governor and an aide-de-camp to General Washington during the Revolution, Trumbull had chosen to employ his political connections in the service of art. As he confided to his brother, "the great object of my wishes . . . is to take up the History of Our Country, and paint the principal Events particularly of the late War." Despite being blind in one eye, Trumbull had found a place in the London studio of Charles Willson Peale's old teacher, expatriate Benjamin West, joining another countryman already ensconced there, a Rhode Islander named Gilbert Stuart.

Trumbull's passion for the arts had impressed Jefferson. At one of their London meetings, Jefferson extended an invitation, Trumbull reported, "to come to Paris, to see and study the fine works there, and to make his house my home, during my stay." Taking Jefferson at his word, Trumbull had arrived for a visit a few days earlier.

The two Americans were not alone that morning. Trumbull had invited along two new friends he wanted Jefferson to meet. He himself had only just been introduced to the Cosways, Richard and Maria, at the painter Jacques-Louis David's studio in the Louvre. An Englishman, Richard Cosway was in Paris to paint miniature portraits of the children of the influential Duc d'Orléans, and had brought his young wife with him for a holiday.

A contemporary described Richard Cosway as "very like a monkey in the face," but no one ever offered such unkind remarks concerning Mrs. Cosway. When Jefferson's gaze fell upon her, he experienced sensations and feelings he had for years denied himself. This woman had the delicate beauty of the wife he mourned—slim and graceful, she was gentle of manner yet accomplished, too, an artist in her own right. Born in Italy to English parents, she spoke a polyglot of European tongues, and her conversation revealed a refined taste for the arts. Jefferson found her deep blue eyes, cascade of wavy blonde hair, and artistic sensibilities irresistible.

He came to the Halle aux Bleds to raise his eyes at the domed ceiling; having done so, he found himself falling into an infatuation with Mrs. Cosway. A plan was quickly made for the new friends to extend their time together, requiring Jefferson, a man usually punctilious about his duties, to postpone another engagement. The minister dispatched a "lying messenger" to the elderly Duchesse de la Rochefoucault d'Anville, excusing himself on the grounds that newly arrived dispatches required his immediate attention.

The foursome dined on the outskirts of Paris at the Parc de Saint Cloud, a royal landscape park. They visited the palace there and examined the pictures in its gallery before returning to Paris for a fireworks display. The day drew to a close with musical entertainments at the home of harpist and composer Jean-Baptiste Krumpholtz. Mrs. Cosway's gifts, Jefferson learned, included a lovely singing voice and considerable facility at the forte piano. It was well into the night before they went their separate ways.

The two Americans returned to the Hôtel de Langeac, the three-story house Jefferson had leased the previous fall. Located on the outskirts of the city, the house had "a clever garden to it," Jefferson had written John Adams; it more nearly resembled his rural Virginia mountaintop than had his earlier residence closer to Paris's busy center. The Hôtel, though facing the Champs-Elysées, had been constructed by a French nobleman for his mistress on land that previously had been the royal nursery. In other ways, too, the accommodations compared favorably with his beloved Monticello. For one, construction had been completed at the Hôtel de Langeac; for another, it was a very stylish accommodation, with its three separate suites, several salons, stables, and full staff of servants.

A generous dose of comfort and joy was overdue in Jefferson's life. Ordinarily a man of robust good health, he had arrived in Paris only to spend his first six months in late 1784 and early 1785 dogged by a cold he couldn't shake. In January of 1786, the still-mourning widower received the devastating news from his friend the Marquis de Lafayette that his daughter Lucy back in Virginia had succumbed to whooping cough. On his journey to England a few months later he found himself snubbed by King George, who pointedly turned his back on Jefferson and Adams, adding insult to heartache.

As the summer of 1786 waned, Jefferson had begun to find a new equilibrium. He was falling in love with France, with its food and wine, its salon society, its painting and sculpture, and he felt its people and its government reciprocated his affections. "This country . . . is the only one on which we can rely for support, under every event," he wrote to Madison. "Its inhabitants love us more, I think, than they do any other nation on earth." Despite the excesses of the monarchy, the private life in France seemed to Jefferson a logical extension of the revolution just won at home, since religion and the state held less sway in the drawing room than science, reason, and personal responsibility. Jefferson's own Hôtel—for which he, in his usual fashion, had drafted detailed plans for a renovation—proved commodious, and familiar, too, with a kitchen garden that provided "Indian corn for the use of my own table, to eat green in our manner." Under such auspicious circumstances, then, perhaps it is not surprising that Maria Cosway seemed like a vision come to life.

In the presence of this woman Jefferson felt his feelings and senses opening, and embarked on a flurry of daylong expeditions. While the painters Trumbull and Cosway pursued other obligations, Jefferson and Maria Cosway alone often visited statues and paintings and attended musical events. But the itinerary grew weighted to architecture, to the new as well as the ruined buildings of old.

Their intense flirtation took them to sights in and around Paris. Almost daily Jefferson arrived at her doorstep on the Rue Coqhéron and they ventured out in his phaeton, as he himself noted, to "hie away to the Bois de Boulogne, St. Cloud, Marly, St. Germain, etc." The presence on his arm of his "vastly pleasant" companion colored everything he saw. "The day we went to St. Germain," he reported, "how beautiful was every object!"

Fortresses, casinos, and châteaux stood atop the itinerary most every day. One of Jefferson's most detailed recollections of their times together concerns not the justly renowned gardens and cascades at the Château de Marly: It was the Machine de Marly that excited Jefferson the most. The celebrated Machine was hardly a romantic destination. Its great wooden wheels raised river water from one pumping station to another before delivering it to an aqueduct and a series of reservoirs that, in turn, fed the many water features in the gardens. The hydraulic wonder so enthralled Jefferson that, though he had visited before, he took Maria to admire the useful invention, too.

Their journey on September 16 would remain in their memories the rest of their lives. That day they traveled a dozen miles west of Paris to the village of Chambourcy. There they spied the grotto that marked the entrance to an immense landscape garden called Le Désert de Retz. Its owner, a self-made man named Racine de Monville, had begun dotting his acres with follies, fantasy buildings often with little or no purpose. Jefferson and Maria encountered several of these "eye-catchers," as their English friends liked to call them. One was an icehouse in the shape of a pyramid. They saw temples, an open-air theater, and an *orangerie*. Each was artfully constructed to appear as a ruin.

When they came upon *La Colonne*, it was if they stumbled into an interrupted dream. The "Column House" appeared to be the remains of an immense Tuscan column that had collapsed at midshaft. Jefferson was immediately taken by it—"How grand the idea excited by the remains of such a column!"

They soon found the exterior was but half of the elaborate display of architectural wit. Inside the Column House their guide showed them a spiral stair, topped by a glass skylight, connecting the four levels of living quarters. The elliptical and round rooms on each floor conformed to the building's circular footprint; windows peered out from recesses in the fluted column. The interior decorations bore the signs of the archaeological researches conducted by Clérisseau and the other Neoclassicists, with motifs and details drawn from antiquity.

That September day proved the climax of the month-long escape Jefferson shared with Mrs. Cosway. Within hours, it came to a crashing conclusion when he fell and broke his right wrist. He consulted two surgeons but neither could satisfactorily relieve his pain. He secluded himself for some days, sleepless and

The fifty-foot-tall folly resembles a Clérisseau *vedute ideate* (imaginary composition),
with the column's base built into grade while greenery emerged from the jagged remains
at the top.

uncomfortable. The spell was broken, and two weeks later Maria and Richard
Cosway returned to England.

Like a chastened child, Jefferson allowed the relationship to end. In the
days after Maria Cosway's departure, he composed one of the most emotional
letters of his life (it is his only surviving love letter), in which his head and
his heart engage in a dialogue. In a crabbed, painstaking script written with
his left hand, the dense paragraphs constituted catharsis for him. The long
letter recalled some of their Parisian day trips, the visits to the Machine at
Marly, the Halle aux Bleds, and Le Désert de Retz. He described the natural
wonders of America at Niagara Falls and the Blue Ridge Mountains, as well
as "our own dear Monticello." But the letter proved to be a last outpouring,
followed by an irregular and diminishing correspondence.

VIII.
1950 . . . Fairmount Park . . . Philadelphia

THEIRS WAS A PRODUCTIVE PARTNERSHIP. The tiny woman grown stout
over the years gave the great bear of a man at her side the confidence to accomplish what he did. The Kimballs were a team: Loud and fond of off-color

jokes, he could be the life of the party, while she, well-mannered and soft-spoken, was the perfect dinner companion. He would laugh the hardest at the theater or snore loudest at the opera, but Marie was always at hand, as Kimball himself acknowledged, to "pick up many good points of information and reaction on the side." They were childless—some mix of biology and busy lives had allowed parenthood to pass them by—but they expressed no regrets.

Marie and Fiske made a formidable pair. She was forever copying out references and pursuing research leads for him. Marie made a substantial contribution to his work, but even while helping her husband, she managed to pursue her own writing. Her principal subject was subsidiary to Fiske's, but her commitment was unflagging.

Fiske almost immediately broadened his scope after his 1915 Ph.D. dissertation, *Thomas Jefferson and the First Monument of the Classical Revival in America*, and his book, *Thomas Jefferson, Architect* (1916). He moved on to investigate other architects and artists, but Marie Kimball remained engaged by Jefferson. At first she did what in her time was regarded as the womanly thing and did it well (her book, *Thomas Jefferson's Cook Book*, remains in print many decades later). But she was a professor's daughter and regarded scholarship as the paramount pursuit in life. Despite many social opportunities to join them, she was never interested in women's clubs, gardening groups, or charitable boards.

She began writing articles about Jeffersonian matters. They appeared regularly throughout the 1920s and 1930s in prestigious, male-dominated publications like *The North American Review, Antiques,* and *The Virginia Quarterly Review.* In 1943, the first of her multi-volume Jefferson biography, *The Road to Glory: 1743–1776*, was published, followed in 1947 by *Jefferson, War and Peace: 1776 to 1784.* She had become so consumed by the third president that Kimball took to referring wryly to her favorite subject as "brother Jefferson." And she was quick to acknowledge her debt to her husband: "[The author] wishes particularly to thank Fiske Kimball. He has patiently discussed all phases of the book with her. He has given her the benefit of his wisdom, and he has made her fight, bleed, and die for her opinions." They were a couple who hardened their formulations by testing them on one another.

The first two books had been well executed and reviewed, but she brought a unique sensibility to the third volume of her life of Jefferson, *The Scene of Europe: 1784–1789* (1950). Having traveled abroad often with her husband, Marie understood the milieu Jefferson encountered in Europe; as the child of European parents, she knew intimately the feeling of being an outsider, of the foreignness that accompanies one's arrival in a strange land where the natives speak a foreign tongue.

In a sense, she had begun working toward the book that would become *The Scene of Europe* in the years before World War I. When Fiske moved on to other artists and designers, Marie remained in Jefferson's company. She made her share of discoveries, too. In the 1920s she found the cache of *billets-doux* that Maria Cosway had written to Jefferson, a sheaf of papers effectively lost in the archives at the Massachusetts Historical Society. She soon knew more about his love life than anyone else. Twenty years later she found new materials about the Clérisseau collaboration at the Huntington Library in California when she accompanied Fiske west on a trip.

Their friends joked that Marie was in love with Jefferson, but she dismissed that. His politics were too liberal, too changeable for her. She was hardly blinded by her passion for her subject, and retold the events of Jefferson's days in Paris without resorting to the literary equivalent of violins or jelled lenses. She observed coolly that "this informal association with artists [gave him] the opportunity of looking at works of art through the eyes of professionals." She described his days with Maria Cosway and, at times, her husband, Richard, and John Trumbull, as "artistic pilgrimages."

She found in Trumbull an important ally in her telling of Jefferson's Paris years; the Connecticut painter had contributed in his own time to shaping the Jefferson mythology.

On his arrival in France in 1784, Jefferson had been a shadowy figure. To the Europeans, George Washington bore a recognizable resemblance to royalty, while the much-loved Benjamin Franklin embodied the Enlightenment as a man of science, philosophy, and wit. So often had Parisian artists asked Franklin to sit for artists that his likeness, on Jefferson's arrival in France, seemed to be everywhere.

Jefferson himself knew no such notoriety. At the time neither he nor the document he penned back in 1776 were much recognized beyond the small circle of politicians who served in the Continental Congress. Had Jefferson's ship foundered on its way to France, no likeness of the man would have survived, since up to that time he had not sat for a portrait.

Marie Kimball told the story of the first one, undertaken during the same trip to London during which Jefferson and Trumbull met. Mather Brown, yet another young American abroad, agreed to a fee of £10, but the canvas he produced displeased Trumbull ("Your [likeness] I do not think so well of," he reported to Jefferson). But Jefferson and Trumbull soon cooked up another notion for a painting that would involve a better image of the statuesque Virginian. It would also serve his place in history.

Between their artistic pilgrimages with the Cosways in the late summer of 1786, Trumbull and Jefferson got talking about Trumbull's aspirations. Jefferson became keenly interested in Trumbull's "national work," a proposed series of paintings recording revolutionary battles, among them Trenton, Saratoga, and Yorktown. Trumbull had brought with him two finished canvases, one each commemorating the battles at Quebec and Bunker Hill. He planned to leave shortly to find an engraver in Germany or the Low Countries to publish them as affordable prints for sale in America.

As they talked in Jefferson's library, a new notion emerged. *Why limit the subject matter to battles?* The history of the conflict remained fresh in their minds, and some of its events were political rather than military. Soon a great idea was brought forth: *Why not record the events surrounding the Declaration of Independence?*

The conceit pleased them both. Having played a principal role, Jefferson volunteered his assistance and advice regarding the composition. The two men talked at length about how, as Trumbull put it, "to convey an Idea of the Room in which congress sat." Jefferson, always happy to sketch out his thoughts, found a small sheet of paper and drew a floor plan of the assembly room where the Continental Congress gathered. Soon Trumbull sketched a much more sophisticated rendering of the room on the same sheet, drawing likenesses of Jefferson, Adams, Franklin, Roger Sherman of Connecticut, and Robert Livingston of New York as they presented the Declaration to John Hancock, president of the Congress. In Trumbull's sketch, Hancock sits in an oval-backed Louis XIV armchair copied from one in the salon at the Hôtel de Langeac where Trumbull and Jefferson planned the painting.

Back in London that November, Trumbull worked in earnest on *The Declaration of Independence*. First he painted in the background, allotting spaces for the figures and faces to be added later. Before John Adams left that summer to return to America, Trumbull painted him from life directly onto the canvas. The following winter Trumbull returned to Paris and painted in Jefferson.

Marie Kimball admired the likeness. "It seems the most sensitive of all the Jefferson portraits," she observed in *The Scene of Europe*. "In the eyes and in the aspect of the face, the artist has caught the visionary that was Jefferson at this period of his life. He wears a dark coat, a red waistcoat with gold buttons, and white stock. The powder, characteristic of the time, had been brushed from his hair, revealing its natural reddish hue. The cheeks are highly colored, as family tradition tells us they were. Jefferson towers straight and strong above the other signers."

The painting, with all forty-eight figures, would require more than thirty years to complete. It would help place Jefferson in the American memory as a central figure in the founding of his country.

IX.
March 20, 1787 . . . Maison Carrée . . . Nîmes

JEFFERSON TOOK THE JOURNEY ON DOCTOR'S ORDERS. The broken wrist produced by his untimely tumble the previous autumn had been tended by several physicians who made no fewer than twenty house calls at the Hôtel de Langeac. After several months, Jefferson's arm showed few signs of repairing and he resumed planning a journey to the south of France that he had long contemplated. He decided to take the trip, "one object of which," he wrote to James Monroe, "is to try the mineral waters there, for the restoration of my hand."

On February 28, he departed alone; Maria Cosway, with whom he had often discussed the journey, was gone, if not forgotten. He justified his solitary travel, explaining "[I] think one travels more usefully when alone, because he reflects more." He headed for Aix-en-Provence to take the waters, but planned many stops along the route to visit seaports, canals, and vineyards about which he would take detailed notes regarding trade and viticulture. Although he felt his efforts would benefit his country, he decided not to submit his expenses for repayment. This trip, he knew, represented his chance to be a Grand Tourist, his opportunity to see in person the sites he knew from books and, in particular, the plates in M. Clerisseau's *Antiquités de la France*.

After one-night stops at Fontainebleau, Dijon, and numerous villages, he arrived in Nîmes on March 19. The ancient city, founded by the Romans in the first century B.C., was home to the first coliseum Jefferson had seen. It was a town rich in the monuments of antiquity and Jefferson found himself aroused by what he saw. His five days there would be the longest stay of his three-month journey; a week later, he would spend less time at his original destination, Aix, pursuing his cure.

Charles-Louis Clérisseau's friend Winckelmann had once advised him, "Write as much as possible in the presence of the actual object and return to it if you have second thoughts." It was as if the old German spoke his sentiments in Jefferson's ear when, on his second day in Nîmes, the American composed a letter to a distinguished lady of his acquaintance in Paris, Madame de Tessé. They had been introduced by her nephew, the Marquis de Lafayette, and became fast friends. Though her facial features were marred by smallpox, Madame de Tessé was wise, witty, and liberal. She surrounded herself with a circle of family and friends at both her Paris and country homes. Jefferson had dined with her at least once a week, often strolling in her gardens, discussing their common passion for botany.

The Virginian sat down in the town square at Nîmes and wrote. He professed a passion for what he saw in a way that, at least in writing, he had never been able to describe with any consuming human affection. "Here I am, Madam, gazing whole hours at the Maison quarrée, like a lover at his mistress." He lightheartedly remarked that weavers nearby "consider me as a hypochondriac Englishman," but he made no apologies.

"From Lyons to Nismes I have been nourished with the remains of Roman grandeur. . . . From a correspondent at Nismes, you will not expect news. Were I to attempt to give you news, I should tell you stories one thousand years old. . . . I am immersed in antiquities from morning to night. For me, the city of Rome is actually existing in all the splendor of its empire."

The enthusiasm of those days continued to enthrall him even after his departure. The following week he wrote to his secretary, William Short, "The remains of antiquity . . . are more in number, and less injured by time than I expected, and have been to me a great treat. Those at Nismes, both in dignity and preservation, stand first." He would soon be advising other travelers to visit there.

He went on to Arles and admired more Roman ruins. He briefly detoured into northern Italy, remarking of his two weeks there that "my time allowed me to go no further than Turin, Milan and Genoa: consequently I scarcely got into classical ground." But soon he was back in Paris, newly confident that now that he had seen it for himself, he could affirm wholeheartedly that, as he had told the Virginia directors, the Maison Carrée looked very much "the most perfect and precious remain of antiquity in existence."

He had all but abandoned work on Monticello following Martha's death. In Paris he felt the stirring once again of his architectural desires and while in the French capital he redoubled his commitment to the arts, mentoring young men like John Trumbull. His Paris years would inhabit his imagination for the rest of his life; his architectural collaboration with Clérisseau taught him important lessons.

Before his sojourn in Paris, American builders rarely if ever worked from detailed plans. Instead, masons and carpenters, typically having agreed on the basis of a single sheet, just went ahead and built. But Jefferson's Paris years proved a fulcrum in American architectural practices as he helped initiate a major transformation—the plans he sent home for the Virginia Capitol in a tin box may well have been the first complete set of working plans ever prepared for an American building.

Clérisseau had been duly paid. The fee was 288 francs for the drawings, a sum for which Jefferson, seeking reimbursement, would rebill the Commonwealth of Virginia on his return to America. On the day he paid the Frenchman's fee, Jefferson also recorded in his Account Book, "pd. Clerissault for a book 72f." The book he bought—a copy of Clérisseau's *Antiquités de la France*—would return with him to Monticello. It was no mere souvenir but a building block in a library that would prove to be the foundation of Jefferson's subsequent architectural exercises. Surely Clérisseau's book deserved a place of honor since, thanks to him—along with Andrea Palladio, the anonymous Roman architect of the Maison Carrée, and, of course, Thomas Jefferson—Virginia had a new Capitol. It was a building that Kimball, a man not given to understatement, termed "a frontispiece to all Virginia."

CHAPTER 3

CREATING THE FEDERAL CITY

"When ever it is proposed to prepare plans for the Capitol, I should prefer the adoption of some one of the models of antiquity, which have had the approbation of thousands of years; and for the President's House, I should prefer the celebrated fronts of modern buildings, which have already received the approbation of all good judges."

—THOMAS JEFFERSON,
WRITING TO MAJOR L'ENFANT, APRIL 10, 1791

I.
April 30, 1789 . . . Broad Street . . . New York, New York

THE BOOM OF GUNS ACCOMPANIED THE DAWN. No battle ensued since the thirteen cannons fired from the Battery signaled not war but a celebration. America's first president would be inaugurated at midday, and Congress had ordered all possible pomp and ceremony.

America's indispensable man, George Washington, waited impatiently. His weeklong journey from Mount Vernon had included stops in Baltimore and Wilmington to greet cheering crowds of ten thousand people and more. A reception twice that size greeted him in Philadelphia where, persuaded to mount a white charger, Washington received a crown of laurel upon passing beneath a celebratory arch of triumph designed by Charles Willson Peale, his once-and-future portraitist. A crew of thirteen sailors in white dress uniforms

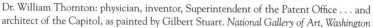

Dr. William Thornton: physician, inventor, Superintendent of the Patent Office . . . and architect of the Capitol, as painted by Gilbert Stuart. *National Gallery of Art, Washington*

had ferried the president-elect from New Jersey's Hudson shore to Manhattan on a barge accompanied by a flotilla of decorated ships.

Even after his arrival in New York, General Washington had little time to discharge his duties. Never a man absorbed by social niceties, he complained, "I was unable to attend to any business whatsoever; for gentlemen, consulting their own convenience rather than mine, were calling from the time I rose from breakfast, often before, until I sat down to dinner." To his relief, the much-anticipated Thursday had at last arrived. His inaugural address completed, he breakfasted and attended to his toilet.

Clothes mattered to General Washington, and he debated which suit to wear. For forty years he had been ordering fabric, gold shoulder braid, silk sash, and lace from London merchants, but on this occasion he worried about looking too magisterial. Certainly the day's events resembled a coronation and he might have opted for the sartorial splendor of his suit of imported black velvet, but he wished to avoid appearing kingly. Months earlier Washington had asked his old colleague-in-arms, Major General Henry Knox, for a quantity of Connecticut broadcloth and this morning he chose the suit made of Hartford-spun fabric, with its silver buttons decorated with eagles. He belted on his dress sword in its steel scabbard and was ready.

The day dawned cloudy and gray, but by nine o'clock sunshine accompanied the peal of church bells. Before moving to lower Manhattan, the American government had operated in eight different cities in fifteen years, among them Philadelphia, Princeton, Annapolis, Baltimore, and Trenton. New York's citizens took pride in its new role as capital, and the biggest crowd yet of Washington's inaugural journey filled a streetscape of brick and wood-framed structures. The jumble of low buildings and tall on Broad Street, some with stepped Dutch parapets, others with fancy Georgian façades, lined the east and west sides of the street, funneling the crowd's attention northward. There, where Broad terminated at the crossing of Wall Street, stood the nation's Capitol, the first under the Constitution ratified just the previous year.

Constructed as City Hall, it had been among the earliest buildings north of what had been the city's protective boundary in the seventeenth century (thus its name, "Wall Street"). Built in 1703 to house the administration of Lord Cornbury, the royal governor, City Hall in its first incarnation looked as if it had been transplanted from Christopher's Wren's London, with tall chimneys, red brick walls, and a Baroque cupola. But in the preceding seven months, a radical remodeling had been effected.

Pierre Charles L'Enfant planned and supervised the renovation. The French soldier had attained the rank of major in the corps of engineers in the Continental Army and, as war gave way to peace, he demonstrated himself to be a designer with a talent for ornament, using a bald eagle and thirteen-pointed star in the insignia of the newly founded veterans' organization, the Society of the Cincinnati. He later found work designing houses in New York, and his skills as a builder, combined with his gift for patriotic symbolism, made L'Enfant the logical choice to remodel City Hall into the nation's architectural centerpiece.

He tripled the building's footprint. A grand, three-story vestibule rose at its core, paved with American marble and lit by an immense skylight. L'Enfant designated generous chambers for the Senate and the House of Representatives, decorating them with carved trophies featuring the letters "U.S." encircled by a laurel wreath. There were offices, committee rooms, and other apartments, as well as a second-floor lobby to serve as a saloon or picture room, soon to be hung with John Trumbull's portraits of American leaders, among them one of George Washington himself. But the richly ornamented façade of Federal Hall, as the reinvented building was renamed, would be the focus of everyone's attention this day.

Many people from other states had traveled to New York to join the on-lookers on Broad Street, including a Massachusetts couple on the final leg of their wedding journey. "We begin to wish to be home," the dutiful son wrote to his parents a few days before the inauguration, "and shall hasten there with diligence as soon as we have seen General Washington. The sight of this great man is all that is wanting to make our pleasures complete." But it was the appearance of Federal Hall that proved to have most lasting impression on the young Bostonian.

More than anyone else awaiting the ceremony that morning, Charles Bulfinch knew what he was looking at. Few of his fellow Americans had traveled abroad; even George Washington had only once left his "Infant Woody Country," as he called it, traveling as a nineteen-year-old to Barbados. But Bulfinch had sailed to Europe for a Grand Tour after completing his studies at Harvard. He had seen much of England, with stops in France and Italy. His fellow Bostonian, John Adams, proved hospitable in London, but in Paris he found his taste for architectural matters nurtured by a man with a great passion for both the old and the new styles.

"At Paris," remembered Bulfinch, "I tarried some time to view its buildings & other objects of curiosity, to which I was introduced by . . . Mr. Jefferson, then minister there." On that trip three years earlier, he had studied the sites of Paris closely, where his sometime companions included Trumbull and the Cosways. In New York, upon casting his gaze on the new Federal Hall, Bulfinch had the wit and experience to recognize elements that were based upon emerging archaeological knowledge of ancient Rome and Greece. He saw, too, L'Enfant's carefully wrought symbols of the newly independent America, including an eagle on its pediment. Well on its way to becoming the nation's symbol, the great bird seemed to be bursting through the clouds, surrounded by thirteen stars, one for each of the states in the new constitutional union. Bulfinch knew that Federal Hall was perhaps the finest building in the new nation.

A few blocks away, his hair powdered, clubbed, and ribboned, Washington emerged from his quarters. Alone, he climbed into his grand coach, attended by three coachmen and pulled by four fine horses. After inching through the gathering crowd, the coach halted two hundred yards from Federal Hall and Washington clambered down. He continued on foot, accompanied by sena-tors, secretaries, and federal department heads. They trooped up Broad Street, the crowd parting to let them pass.

The official congregation disappeared into Federal Hall, only to reemerge on the second-floor balcony. The worthies included Vice President John

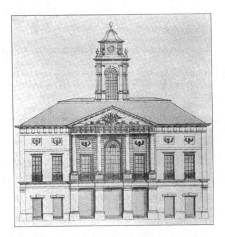

The building before Bulfinch inspired in him the desire to record what he saw, and he set to sketching a likeness of Federal Hall. He drew the sturdy Tuscan piers at the basement level and the Doric columns above that defined the broad porch and supported the pediment.
Massachusetts Magazine

Adams, New York Governor George Clinton, Secretary of Foreign Affairs John Jay, various members of Congress, and other dignitaries. Washington bowed to the crowd before him. His gesture was met with a cascade of cheers from the thousands standing in the surrounding streets. Out of every window more people hung, and still others looked down from nearby rooftops. He bowed again, his hands on his heart, and the cheers redoubled before he stepped wordlessly back and sat down in the armchair designated for him. He awaited quiet.

Once the crowd grew silent, Washington rose and stepped to the railing with its elaborate design, its focus a central medallion composed of thirteen arrows, another motif of Major L'Enfant's. A simple ceremony commenced, with Robert R. Livingston, Chancellor of New York, administering the oath of office while Washington rested his hand on a large and elegant Bible. Livingston soon announced to the dignitaries around him, "It is done." Turning to the crowd, few of whom had heard his unamplified words, he called, "Long live George Washington, President of the United States!"

Church bells rang out, cannon fired, and the flag rose atop Federal Hall. After a time the cheering crowd watched the balcony empty, as Washington retired within to deliver his inaugural address to Congress.

Celebrations, high and low, large and small, carried on for many hours. The French minister in attendance would report to his government, "Never has [a] sovereign reigned more completely in the hearts of his subjects than did Washington in those of his fellow citizens. . . . He has the soul, look and figure of a hero united in him." Charles Bulfinch returned to Boston within the week. In the next issue of the *Massachusetts Magazine*, an engraving based upon his finished drawing appeared, together with an unsigned but detailed description of L'Enfant's building.

As for the new president, he felt free to go to work at last. He had goals to reach as he helped launch the young country. Among them was a plan to initiate the process of establishing an entirely new capital city. Bringing that particular notion to fruition would require the services of many, among them Pierre L'Enfant, Charles Bulfinch, Thomas Jefferson, and eventually even Fiske Kimball. Over time, each contributed to the architecture that would express Washington's vision of the country he was shaping.

II.
June 28, 1791 . . . Jenkins Hill . . . The Banks of the Potomac

GEORGE WASHINGTON STILL FELT MOST AT HOME ON HORSEBACK. The leather reins rested easily in his large hands. His body had softened over the years as his weight increased by some thirty pounds, but he rode deep in the saddle, his muscular legs maintaining that familiar mastery of the animal beneath him. As a soldier, he had been a legend on horseback, the kind of rider who inspired sculptors to fashion great equestrian statues.

Descending from the river village of Georgetown on this Tuesday morning, he couldn't help but think like a surveyor. It had been his first profession, after his widowed mother had rejected the idea that young George might make his fortune at sea. Part of his legacy from his father had been a set of surveyor's tools stored in a barn, and he dusted them off, executed a few practice surveys in his schoolboy copybooks, and embarked on a surveying mission to Virginia's western frontier. By age seventeen, he received his first official appointment as Surveyor for Culpeper County and, with the knowledge he gained and the money he earned, he began acquiring land, the foundation of his eventual wealth. That had been half a lifetime earlier.

The previous day Washington had departed from Mount Vernon before sunrise. He had reached Georgetown for a nine o'clock meeting concerning land grants and conveyances, but today he could afford to empty his mind of such matters as deeds. He had left his three commissioners behind him in Georgetown to sort out the paperwork. He trusted these men, having appointed them himself to administer the new Federal District. Their task was to prepare for the signing ceremony where the nineteen owners in the new Federal City would put their land in trust to him as president. But as Washington would note that evening in his diary, this morning would be spent "with Majr. L'Enfant and Mr. Ellicot to take a more perfect view of the ground, in order to decide finally on the spots on which to place the public buildings."

Washington was a man almost fastidious about keeping his emotions to himself, but as he rode south and east into the center of what was to be the new city, a sense of great satisfaction accompanied him. The previous July, the Act for Establishing the Temporary and Permanent Seat of the Government of the United States had become law. The Residence Act, as it was known, called for the establishment of a new capital near the geographic center of the young country; and here was the chosen location, straddling the river he had known since boyhood, the site barely a dozen miles north of Mount Vernon.

Pierre Charles L'Enfant was to be its designer. Never bashful about offering his services, he had written in September 1789, shortly after the ratification of the Constitution, which called for the establishment of "the seat of government." He had addressed Washington directly: "Your Excellency will not be surprised that my Ambition and the desire I have of becoming a useful citizen should lead me to wish a share in the undertaking." Perhaps the recipient had smiled at this, knowing Major L'Enfant was possessed of both boldness and great confidence. The letter went on at length, but the message was straightforward enough: "I view the appointment of Engineer to the United States," concluded L'Enfant, "as the one which could possibly be most gratifying to my wishes."

Washington had been able to think of no better candidate. L'Enfant had first come to his attention when, at age twenty-three, he had arrived from France as a volunteer to the American cause. L'Enfant made himself indispensable to Baron Friedrich von Steuben, the Army's Inspector General, training raw recruits at Valley Forge and, during that winter of 1778, the commander-in-chief and the French lieutenant had met. Known for his pencil portraits of fellow officers, "Monsr. Lanfang," as Washington rendered his name, arrived at the general's tent to take a likeness of Washington for the Marquis de Lafayette. Washington grew testy during the prolonged sitting that winter day, but the artist and his talent remained in his mind.

By the end of the war, L'Enfant had been promoted twice, to captain, then to major in the Corps of Engineers. His later work for the veterans' organization, the Society of Cincinnati, and at Federal Hall had further elevated him in Washington's eyes. He had given Martha Washington, at her personal request, a guided tour of Federal Hall. The Washingtons had come to value his company, as L'Enfant had been their guest at Mount Vernon only a few days before, dining at their table.

His purpose then had been to deliver a "progress map" of the Federal City, the very map that was to be their guide this day as they reviewed the sights together. As the two men stood tall in their saddles, they made an imposing pairing. The president had the bearing of a natural aristocrat, a large man whose physical presence seemed to imply leadership and strength. At his side, L'Enfant's finely proportioned features and courtly manner gave him the air of a trusted courtier, one whose presumed intimacy with the great man beside him gave him special access.

Major Pierre Charles L'Enfant needed Washington's approval of several important recommendations he had made and, by sunset, he hoped the Federal City would have a basic configuration. They would visit the proposed sites of the "congressional building" and the "presidential palace," as L'Enfant called them, the two buildings around which the life of the city would emerge. Yet even as L'Enfant contemplated the execution of his plan, Washington remained aware that L'Enfant's character did allow for misgivings.

Was he an artist in engineer's clothing? Or an engineer with an artistic gift? The task before them—designing an entire city—posed a challenge almost as complex as that of inventing a new form of government. The Federal City held immense symbolic importance, and Washington knew better than anyone the importance of symbols. He himself had come out of retirement to assume the presidency because he recognized that his mere presence brought iconic weight to the new constitutional adventure that he knew must succeed. In the same way, he wanted the Federal City to anchor the new country, to become a place that not only would be the nation's governmental center, but would look the part. For that, he needed L'Enfant's visionary talents.

Yet the major had already shown signs of suffering from inflexibility, perfectionism, and, odd for a military man, a willful disregard for the chain of command, wanting to deal only with Washington himself. He did come by his artistic temperament honestly, since L'Enfant had studied at the Royal Academy of Painting and Sculpture at Versailles, set amid the royal park with its tree-lined avenues projecting like rays from the royal palace. But as their horses climbed toward the summit of Jenkins Hill, the men were surrounded by a landscape that could not have been more different from the manicured symmetry of the immense French garden at Versailles. The Federal District consisted of rugged terrain, with wooded thickets, meandering watercourses like Goose and Rock Creeks, swamplands, and few signs of habitation.

Washington hoped that the third principal in their party that morning would prove to be a counterbalance to L'Enfant. He was Major Andrew Ellicott, another veteran of the war, and his official task was to stake out the bounds of the city and to produce "a survey and Map of the Federal Territory." Ellicott, having previously completed the Mason-Dixon line and made the first topographical study of Niagara Falls, had a reputation for superior accuracy. He used a transit of his own manufacture, one that he boldly claimed "may safely be considered as absolutely perfect." Together L'Enfant and Ellicott were to prepare a plan of the city for publication, and Washington hoped that the utter precision of Ellicott's surveying might complement the expansiveness of Major L'Enfant.

The men dismounted to consult the rough map. The landscape that spread before them, according to a contemporary, was "a morass and forest, the abode of reptiles, wild beasts, and savages." It was a wilderness untamed and, though he later shared the thought with his wife rather than Washington, Ellicott for one had doubts about the future of the site, suggesting it was better suited to the stall of an ox. Yet that was not what Washington and L'Enfant beheld.

From their hilltop position they imagined the landscape's future. To their eyes, the summit of Jenkins Hill was "a pedestal waiting for a monument," as L'Enfant described it. Although a dense forest stood behind them, L'Enfant envisioned the "Congress House" rising in its place to embrace the view. He read the prospects of the landscape to Washington, explaining how the low-lying strip of land that extended west to the river from the base of the slope would become a "grand and majestic avenue." While Ellicott saw a thousand acres of woods and underbrush with a few scattered farmsteads, L'Enfant's broad gestures over the rolling landscape transformed it for Washington, giving shape to the dream the two men shared.

They climbed back onto their horses, and the tour continued. The party descended the hill, then forded Tiber Creek, the major stream that ran westward toward the river. After retracing their steps on the Georgetown road, they veered off and, two miles west of Jenkins Hill, ascended to higher ground once again, this time to the proposed site of L'Enfant's "President's Palace." Behind them stood an apple orchard and beyond that a cottage with a graveyard at its front door. But they gazed in the opposite direction, regarding the memorable river view that reached "10 or 12 miles down the Potowmack." In the middle distance, where the presidential gardens would meet the main avenue of the city, L'Enfant explained, was "the proper [place] to erect a grand Equestrian figure." Perhaps equally important, according to L'Enfant's plan, the Capitol— which was to be the symbolic and political center of the new nation—would be visible from the surrounding landscape, the terminus of all the major radial avenues.

Washington could not help but be impressed. To use the hilly acres as they found them posed a great challenge. The nation's resources were limited and opposition remained in Congress to the Potomac site. If the delays were too great or the costs too high, loud objections would soon be voiced and, inevitably, malcontents would advocate relocating the capital. But L'Enfant's plan took fine advantage of the up-and-down topography, setting the major buildings on high ground, producing what he called "grand and far-distant points of view." His plan for using existing roads for two of the major diagonal streets would reduce development costs.

The tour completed, the party returned to Georgetown. Washington would remain in the village for two more nights to execute the deeds, putting in place the business plan, which apportioned roughly half the plots to the nation to be sold to underwrite construction costs, with the balance retained by the sellers to sell for their profit. Upon showing the plan to the commissioners and the proprietors, Washington made his satisfaction explicit, noting his "pleasure that a general approbation of the measure seemed to pervade the whole."

On Thursday Washington would resume his journey back to the temporary capital of Philadelphia, pleased that in the remarkably short span of three months, Major L'Enfant had conceived a master plan that was to be engraved and printed for distribution to Congress and potential investors. With the deeds signed and the sites for the public buildings established, the streets could be laid out. The felling of trees, the staking out of building sites and streets, the digging of foundations, and the firing of brick kilns could commence in the weeks that followed.

The cliché tells us that Rome wasn't built in a day and, to be certain, neither was the new capital city on the Potomac. Nevertheless June 28, 1791, may be seen as the day America's Federal City began its rise.

III.
March 1792 . . . The President's House . . . Market Street, Philadelphia

EVEN HIS PATRON FOUND Major L'Enfant's behavior inexplicable. As Washington sat in his private office, a small converted bathing room on the second floor of the rented house, he felt bewilderment at the man's "perverseness." The optimism for the future of the Federal City that carried the president northward the previous summer had utterly disappeared.

In the interim, the Frenchman had refused to hand over the city plan to the commissioners in time for an October land auction, sabotaging a key event in the carefully assembled financial plan. A month later, upon determining that the footprint of a new house overlapped the proposed site of New Jersey Avenue, L'Enfant had ordered the structure demolished—knowing full well it belonged to the city's largest landowner, who also happened to be the nephew of one of the commissioners. Outraged letters had quickly made their way from Georgetown to the president's desk, presenting him with a difficult dilemma.

Washington had placated the commissioners then because he continued to believe that L'Enfant's skills outweighed his liabilities; to lose the man's services, as he told his secretary of state, Thomas Jefferson, "would be a serious misfortune." In his letter to Commissioner David Stuart, Washington chose to explain L'Enfant's actions as a consequence of the man's artistic temperament. "Men who possess talents which fit them for peculiar purposes [are] almost invariably . . . possessed of some disqualification by which they plague all those with whom they are concerned." He wrote to L'Enfant separately, issuing him another of the several stern warnings he was forced to dispatch in those months.

Yet L'Enfant had proved unable to change his ways. As February came to an end, L'Enfant's continued defiance of the commissioners led Washington to send an emissary to his quarters, only to have the major send him packing, shouting after the man that he "had already heard enough of this matter." Personally insulted by this behavior, Washington felt that L'Enfant left him no choice. He ordered the dismissal of his trusted former adjutant. In a letter dispatched at "4 o'clock, Feb. 26th, 1792," Secretary of State Jefferson informed the inflexible and impetuous L'Enfant that "your services must be at an end."

That left Washington without the one man he believed capable of handling the immense task of creating the Federal City. With L'Enfant gone, Washington felt his own desire to manage the process waning. He had turned sixty just days before, and the burdens of his office were beginning to weigh on him; he even harbored thoughts about the wisdom of running for a second term as president. Washington understood the connection between correct paperwork and property, so he could content himself that the map for the city was complete. But there was no building progress: The President's House remained a muddy hole on the top of a hill with the first loads of foundation stone, delivered by boatmen from the Aquia Quarry, barely visible below at the mouth of the Goose Creek.

The building of both the President's House and the Capitol required immediate attention and that was work that exceeded Washington's expertise. Yes, over a period of decades he had overseen the remodeling of his own home, but he freely admitted "to [having] no knowledge in Architecture." He professed himself ready to obey "the rules laid down by the professors of the art," and he had chosen to believe he had such a one in L'Enfant to mastermind the whole process. But now that would not come to pass.

On the other hand he knew that Jefferson, the secretary of state with whom he often met in this very room, stood at the ready, keen to make a contribution.

As Washington had begun to feel his own age he saw that the forty-eight-year-old Jefferson was approaching the peak of his powers. He stood tall, his trim figure unstooped. He donned no powdered wig, but wore his mane of red hair brushed back, revealing few signs of gray. Although their acquaintance dated to their service in the Virginia House of Burgesses twenty years before, they had only rarely resided in the same city, with Washington off fighting the war and Jefferson serving in France after the Treaty of Paris. But Jefferson had demonstrated great discipline in his two years serving the president, as a loyal counselor.

Washington had also observed Jefferson's boldness as he did everything he could to influence the evolution of the Federal City. He had been known to remark, "I am an enthusiast on the subject of the arts. But it is an enthusiasm of which I am not ashamed, as its object is to improve the taste of my countrymen." He wanted to present his fellow citizens, as well as visitors to America, "with specimen[s] of our taste in our infancy, promising much for our maturer age." Washington understood perfectly: They shared the desire to build noble monuments that spoke well of the democratic experiment to be conducted within their walls.

Acting as the intermediary between Washington and L'Enfant in the preceding months, Jefferson had offered ideas and proposals to Washington. He had peppered L'Enfant with letters, offering unsolicited guidance; as L'Enfant's superior, he demanded regular progress reports. He had entrusted L'Enfant with Clérisseau's plans for the Virginia Capitol, and volunteered his collection of printed images of fine buildings to inspire the domestic architecture in the new Federal City. He had even offered his vision of what the major buildings ought to be. "Whenever it is proposed to prepare plans for the Capitol," Jefferson had told L'Enfant, "I should prefer the adoption of some one of the models of antiquity, which have had the approbation of thousands of years; and for the President's House, I should prefer the celebrated fronts of modern buildings." But the haughty major paid little heed to instructions issued by anyone but Washington. He once went so far as to assure Jefferson that the design of Federal City was his to execute—"without any restriction soever."

Only now he was gone. Whatever architectural sketches he had prepared he took with him, along with the tin case containing Clérisseau's plans of the Virginia Capitol. The only evidence of L'Enfant's design for the President's House consisted of a few tiny foundation lines on the plat map of the entire city. With no architect standing by to take L'Enfant's place, both Jefferson and Washington knew they needed to find one quickly.

A proposal from Jefferson required Washington's attention—and, the president thought, it might just provide the solution for moving forward. Jefferson's thinking had begun with the query: *Why not conduct a Competition?* It was an approach he had suggested earlier but the idea's time had now come. Jefferson reported that such competitions were common in Europe. A prize might be offered, he explained, perhaps a sum of money or a medal of equivalent value. They could specify a few basic requirements for the buildings, set a date for entries, and announce the competition. Then the president, along with Jefferson and the commissioners, could review the submissions and choose the best one.

The vacuum left by L'Enfant's departure made the logic of a competition seem somehow inevitable. Washington now examined two advertisements, both drafted by Jefferson, one each for the Capitol and President's House competitions. The premium to be paid the designer of "the most approved plan" for each building would be $500, though the winning designer of the Capitol would also be awarded a lot in the new city. Washington read the sheets with care, making minor corrections on the pages.

It would be done, he decided. He approved the drafts for release to Jefferson. The order of things required the secretary of state to forward the announcements to the commissioners in the Federal City. Then, in the weeks to come, the competitions would become public knowledge as the advertisements for entries appeared in major newspapers. The drafts before him established a deadline for submissions of July 15, 1792.

Washington understood that years would elapse before the buildings could be completed. He could only wish that the process might go as quickly as the naming of it had when the commissioners had decreed the Federal City would be known as "Washington" and the Federal Territory as the "District of Columbia." He was discomfited by the city's name, finding himself unable to refer to the place as "Washington." And he could not help but wonder whether he would live to see the rise of the two principal buildings in the city that now bore his name.

IV.
1916–1917 . . . The Sachs Fellowship . . . On the Road

THE DRAWING PRESENTED A PARADOX. Its paper differed from all the rest, and the fineness of the line suggested that its maker had thorough training as a draftsman. The brushwork, too, distinguished the floor plan from Jefferson's drawings, which tended to reveal a "streaky and uncertain character." Kimball was confident that this large sheet in the Coolidge collection was the work of a man more familiar with drafting tools and techniques than the self-trained Jefferson.

Yet, if Jefferson had not drawn it, then why had he penned a note on the sheet's lower right-hand corner? Kimball recognized the handwriting instantly. The annotation read, in part, "the scale is 1.37*i*. to the foot." Even the words seemed cryptic—not one inch to the foot, or even 1.25 inches to the foot—why "1.37*i*."? A drawing *not* by Jefferson . . . but *annotated* by him . . . one that bore a peculiar arithmetic? "Very curious figures," Kimball concluded, "unlikely to have been originally employed."

In short, he had stumbled across another untold story. The drawing wasn't by Jefferson though the evidence of his association was unmistakable. Then *Who . . . when . . . where . . . ?* Kimball determined to go about discovering the secret of the puzzling drawing. Detective work, it seemed, was proving one of his particular talents.

Once more, Jefferson and the Coolidge collection in Boston set him in motion. His work on *Thomas Jefferson, Architect* inspired Kimball to think big. He nurtured an ambition to study other American architects and write their histories, too. Kimball had solved the Jefferson-as-architect riddle— *Was he or wasn't he? Most assuredly, he was*—by laboriously comparing the buildings in Virginia to the drawings in Boston, then interpreting both in light of Jefferson's correspondence. The process had truly thrilled him, and Kimball found himself admitting to his academic mentor at Harvard, Professor Chase, that "it is research above all things, rather than [architectural] practice, teaching, or interpretation that I am interested in." His adrenaline rose when, like a mathematician solving an age-old conundrum, he found a solution that no one else could. He was an awkward man who felt suddenly streamlined when his instinct and intellect fired in unison to answer a question, particularly one that few had even thought to ask.

The polished drawing at hand posed just such a question, and Kimball had a plan for pursuing its answer along with a number of other lines of inquiry. Confident that repositories in other cities held similar riches to those at the Massachusetts Historical Society, he wanted to take an extended journey to what he called "the older states" to visit buildings and archives. But his desires had to be balanced with his needs, namely the practical matter of how to underwrite the research as well as his and Marie's day-to-day expenses.

Kimball's Harvard contacts and a bit of excellent timing provided the opportunity. He learned of a newly endowed fellowship at Harvard, one underwritten by Samuel Sachs, a founder of the investment firm Goldman Sachs. Kimball made a bold but simple case to the judges. "I turned up clues to much other manuscript material on the history of early American architecture," Kimball noted. He wanted to study not just one or two but *all* the early architects so he "submitted an application on the basis of travel and study of this in America." George Chase wrote him a recommendation.

He was awarded the first Sachs Research Fellowship for the academic year 1916–1917, with its stipend of $2,000 in an era when the average annual income hovered around $1,200 a year. Fiske and Marie felt confident they could make the money last since the couple lived frugally and would be able to stay with friends in some cities. Her brother was in Washington, working at the

State Department on Latin American diplomatic papers on a Columbia University fellowship. Fiske's godfather lived in Nashville. And the cachet of the Jefferson book was sure to open doors, introducing him to a network of people who felt as he did about older American buildings. The fellowship would buy him the time to do the research he wanted and, with his confidence running high, Kimball notified his department head, Sidney Lorch, that he would be taking a year's leave of absence from Michigan. Though irritated, Dean Lorch had little choice but to grant the rising star's sabbatical year.

The tour would take Kimball to Atlanta, Athens, and Savannah, Georgia; to Charleston and Columbia, South Carolina; and to St. Louis, Louisville, and Nashville, where he hoped to find sponsors and tour guides. Chapel Hill, Washington, Baltimore, Annapolis, Philadelphia, Trenton, New York, Hartford, Providence, Boston, and Salem would be on his itinerary as well. He wanted to get his first taste of buildings by the second generation of American architects, men like Robert Mills and William Strickland, whose work had been little studied. He wanted to follow the trail left by the great but surprisingly obscure Benjamin Henry Latrobe, the English-trained engineer and designer whom Kimball believed to have been the first professionally trained architect to work in America. Kimball harbored a hunch that there was a major story there, but he didn't know enough to be sure.

Early in his sabbatical year, Kimball visited the Maryland Historical Society in Baltimore. Among the society's holdings was a pair of scrapbooks deposited by one of Benjamin Henry Latrobe's sons. One contained Latrobe's drawings for the cathedral he designed for the Baltimore Diocese, which Kimball quickly realized held great promise for an article or even two. But soon Kimball set the cathedral drawings to one side. He sensed the other scrapbook held something even more important.

Bearing the label, "Rejected designs for Capitol and President's House, Washington," it contained a miscellany of drawings, though virtually none had been executed by Latrobe. Immediately the portfolio took on the quality of a time capsule, transporting him back to the 1792 design competition for the President's House.

Announced by the Washington Commissioners on March 14, 1792, the competition called for "Drawings . . . of the ground plats, [and] elevations of each front and sections through the building in such directions as may be necessary to explain the internal structure." At least seven entrants responded by the July 15 due date, and the judging began the following day. For the occasion the president had traveled to the Federal City. Jefferson hadn't

James Hoban's original presentation drawing for the President's House, identified by Kimball
in the collections at the Maryland Historical Society. *Maryland Historical Society,
Baltimore, Maryland*

come—*That's rather strange,* thought Kimball—but even without Jefferson
present, Washington and the commissioners had little trouble settling upon
the winner. On July 17 they declared "the best plan of a President's house"
was James Hoban's. The certificate issued on the occasion specified that
Hoban "chuses a Gold medal of 10 Guineas value—the Ballance in Money."
Hoban further agreed "to make the drawings and superintend the execution
of the Palace," in return for three hundred guineas a year.

Five of the contestants were represented in the Maryland collection, one of
whom, despite the label "Rejected designs," was James Hoban. As the winner
of the contest, Hoban's basic life facts were generally known to Kimball. Born
in County Kilkenny south of Dublin in about 1762, Hoban had come to America in his early twenties, spent at least two years working in the building business in Philadelphia, and then five more in Charleston before relocating to the
Federal City in 1792. Kimball studied Hoban's drawings for the President's
House, but the more he looked, the more skeptical he grew about the prevailing theory that Hoban had based his design on the great eighteenth-century
mansion in Dublin, Leinster House. Kimball saw as many differences as simi-
larities. He had a hunch that Hoban had based the building on a plate in James
Gibbs's *A Book of Architecture*, and he noted, too, that Hoban had borrowed
the eagle set prominently in the pediment from L'Enfant's Federal Hall.

Kimball moved to the other entries, the long-ignored submissions by four of
the losers, among them Jacob Small, James Diamond, and Andrew Mayfield

Carshore. Kimball pored over each of their drafts. If the outcome of the competition had long been an oft-told tale—Hoban won, got the premium, and his design was constructed as the building that became known as the White House—then a richer back story revealed itself as Kimball studied the portfolio.

Four sheets bore the mark of Jacob Small, who proposed four different designs. Though of varying size, the buildings closely resembled one another. His drafts suggested that Small, a builder of good repute from Baltimore, lacked the skill to handle the large proportions and detailing of the mansion. Kimball dismissed him as a builder without sufficient formal training to elevate him above the status of carpenter-builder. The work of Andrew Mayfield Carshore, a gifted educator and linguist, was still less inspired, employing the outmoded appearance of three-story colonial houses the likes of which Carshore had seen in New England port towns. As far as Kimball knew, no evidence survived to suggest that he had ever attempted to design another building, before or after his entry in the competition. Kimball shared the opinion of the judges in 1792 who found Carshore's design unrefined. Though James Diamond's drawings were better, his President's House promised to be the kind of overstated royal residence that President Washington wanted to avoid.

After looking at the work of Small, Carshore, and Diamond, Kimball understood why Washington, worried about the quality of the early submissions, had complained to one of his commissioners less than a week before the deadline, "if none more elegant than these should appear . . . the exhibition of architecture will be a very dull one indeed."

Kimball could easily have just flipped through the fifth set of drawings, those submitted by the quasi-anonymous "A.Z." Some years earlier, an architecture student who had examined them attributed the five sheets to a Maryland builder named Abram Faws, presuming the letter that resembled a Z was actually a slightly misshapen F. Given their lack of originality, the drawings gave Kimball no inclination to disagree that they were probably the work of a builder working from a book. At a glance he recognized the design as an inflated version of Palladio's memorable Villa Rotonda, a retirement home Palladio had built for a papal prelate. Kimball also knew from his studies that, like Foucault's pendulum, the Villa Rotonda maintained a motion through time, seeming to swing back into view at regular intervals. The building had aroused Goethe ("Perhaps architecture has never attained such a pitch of splendor"), and Kimball could cite several important incarnations in eighteenth-century England, one of them Chiswick, the home of Palladio's

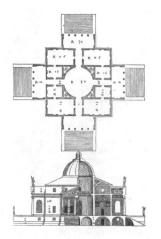

Palladio's Villa Rotonda, in the woodcut from *The Four Books*

great eighteenth-century champion, Lord Burlington. The explanation for the enduring popularity of the design was obvious: With its four matching porticos, one on each side of the square footprint, and the majestic dome that capped the tall cylindrical rotunda inside, this was a building that had come to seem the apotheosis of geometric beauty. For its admirers, Palladio's masterwork made the case that great architecture can truly transcend mere building.

Perhaps for that reason, Kimball didn't flash past the A.Z. drawings. He found himself looking more closely, and the more he looked, the more familiar they seemed. Gradually the cycle of realization washed over Kimball: the surprise, the confusion, the simple satisfaction, then the excited anticipation. Jefferson often reached for his Palladio to help him as he developed an architectural scheme; he had turned to the plates of the Villa Rotonda when making an unexecuted design of a Virginia's governor's mansion, as well as for various domestic projects of his own. The more closely Kimball looked at the sketches, the more confident he became. The notation "sky lights" on the dome caused another synapse in Kimball's brain to fire: This was Jefferson applying the saucer from his old Parisian haunt, the Halle aux Bleds, to a printed plate in Palladio's *Four Books*. By the time he rose from the table, Kimball felt entirely confident this was not the work of Faws or of anybody with the initials A.Z.

The certainty of his attribution was based on more than instinct. He could clearly recall draft versions of these drawings, rough sketches he knew in the Coolidge collection. Plus the Baltimore drawings bore dimensioning

The original elevation Jefferson submitted to the President's House Competition.
Unlike the preliminary drawings Kimball saw in Boston, this presentation drawing
was not done in pencil on the coördinate paper but in pen and ink.
Maryland Historical Society, Baltimore, Maryland

and other jottings unmistakably in Jefferson's hand. In short, Kimball knew
he had identified a pseudonymous submission by the secretary of state, a man
who had been worried, as the president had been, at the quality of the early
submissions. Not wanting personalities to cloud the discussions, Jefferson had
submitted his Palladian plan, coyly signing it just A.Z. "These drawings,"
Kimball would soon write in an article for the *Century Magazine*, "prove to
duplicate Jefferson's studies line for line and distance for distance, and leave
not the smallest shadow of doubt that we have in them a most novel and important item of Jeffersoniana."

Marie's research into Jefferson's correspondence revealed that he had remained silent on the subject of the President's House competition. With his
enthusiasm for architecture and the Federal City, as well as his tendency to
remark upon just about everything else in his life, Jefferson's omission seemed
odd until the drawing supplied the explanation. Little wonder that Jefferson
had absented himself the day of the judging: With a submission of his own
under consideration, he quite naturally stayed away as a matter of con-
science. A serious man with no taste for dissembling or irony, Jefferson could

never have stood by and maintained the pretense of detachment. And after the medal was awarded to Hoban? Jefferson's design had finished out of the running and the true identity of its draftsman no longer mattered.

In the years afterward, the so-called A.Z. entry had gotten shoved to the side, an irrelevancy. It remained in the possession of the District of Columbia Commissioners until, with the incorporation of the city of Washington in 1802, the District Commission ceased to exist. Then President Jefferson created the office of Surveyor of the Public Buildings, and the man he appointed Surveyor, Benjamin Henry Latrobe, became keeper of the nation's architectural documents, which included the working drawings he needed to supervise construction at the Capitol and the President's House. Shuffled among them were the decade-old competition drawings, which by default became a part of Latrobe's archives, and traveled with him over the next two decades to Baltimore, Pittsburgh, New Orleans, and, after his death, back to Baltimore.

Over time, his heirs donated portions of Latrobe's voluminous papers to the nation and various public archives, with the "Rejected designs" scrapbook going to the Maryland Historical Society in 1865. In remarks at the time, John H.B. Latrobe recalled that the drawings "were regarded as rubbish . . . and I well remember, as a child, the amusement they afforded to those to whom they were, then, occasionally exhibited." In the Baltimore archive they remained for a half century until the newly minted Doctor Kimball came along.

Kimball was thinking of writing on the competitions, and had in mind engaging a talented graduate student of his at Michigan, Wells Bennett, to be his coauthor. His notes burst with so many article ideas, he could never complete all of them himself. As he and Bennett would write in the months to come, "There exists no complete or adequate work dealing with the competition for the Federal buildings, or even one devoted primarily to it." Until theirs, that is.

Kimball had a particular motive for wanting to recount those days in detail. The Sachs Fellowship, as the *Christian Science Monitor* reported in October while Kimball was in Baltimore, had been created to "encourage careful study of fine arts by taking up the problems in the history of art in general." In his Jefferson studies, Kimball had begun to sketch a larger theory to which he now wanted to add substance. At the Maryland Historical Society, he found some of the evidence he needed.

Every student of American history already understood that a new form of government had assumed a workable shape under the thoughtful ministrations of George Washington in his first term. Kimball harbored a corollary notion that a simultaneous but largely unrecognized transformation had taken place in the world of American building. The president and his secretary of state masterminded the creation of a new city; the Constitution mandated it. But the manner in which they accomplished the job resulted in a wholesale rethinking of what buildings meant in America.

Kimball needed building blocks to take the next step in his telling of the tale of American architecture. His Jefferson studies had led him to a thesis he wanted to prove. He believed the two competitions represented the moment at which the balance of American architecture shifted; his rediscovery of Jefferson's competition entry, despite the fact it became an also-ran on July 17, 1792, helped to buttress his theory. On one side of the historical seesaw sat the builders and amateurs, the workers who knew how to construct a building and the gentlemen clients whose books led them to think they knew something of design. On the other were the architects, an entirely new species in the American wilderness. "The competition," Kimball soon wrote, "[became] the decisive struggle between the builders and amateurs on the one hand, who, together, had so far dominated architecture in America, and the professional architect on the other hand—hitherto lacking—who henceforth assumed the leading role."

Jefferson and Carshore were the gentlemen amateurs; Diamond and Small were the builders. But James Hoban represented another classification altogether. Hoban had studied drafting in Ireland's capital where he won a prize for his drawing skills. Before coming to Washington, he had run "an EVENING SCHOOL for the instruction of young men in Architecture" in Charleston. In Hoban, Kimball found something important: He was a trained professional from abroad who imagined a building on paper first, in all its rich details. He understood scale, proportion, balance, and pattern. He didn't think first with his hands as builders did; his eye needed initial gratification. And by putting his vision on paper first, the architect accomplished nothing less than establishing control over a building project.

While in Baltimore, Kimball made a smaller discovery, too, one that served to amplify his larger theory. He solved the little mystery of the floor plan he found in Boston, the sophisticated drawing with the odd note in Jefferson's handwriting specifying a 1.37-inch scale. He was certain it was the work of James Hoban. And Jefferson's annotation? When the commissioners had increased the size of the building, Kimball hypothesized, the scale had been adjusted by the man in possession of the plan, namely the secretary of state. Later, when he resided as President Jefferson in the very building represented, he once again possessed Hoban's floor plan. Unlike the other drawings that made their way to the Surveyor, it remained with the Jefferson drawings that eventually made their way to Massachusetts.

To Kimball, the crooked road the drawing had traveled meant less than what it symbolized: Namely, the presence on the federal payroll of a "professional architect." The hiring of James Hoban represented another subtle shift in the new country from the craft of building to the art of architecture.

V.
1792 . . . Trumbull's Lodgings . . . Philadelphia

A MAN WITH A GIFT FOR HAPPENSTANCE, John Trumbull thought he might be able to help. Although Hoban had been selected as architect of the President's House, the competition for the Capitol remained unresolved; Trumbull, his ear always attuned to the talk of the town, knew that any further delay could jeopardize the plan for the Federal City itself. Not a few of the powerful people he knew wished the federal government to remain in Philadelphia.

Quite by chance, Trumbull had visited the future site of the new capital in May 1791. He traveled widely in those years, conducting research for his projected Revolutionary War paintings and, he confided in Jefferson, to sketch likenesses of "those who have been the great actors in those illustrious scenes." On returning from a trip to Virginia, Trumbull stopped in Georgetown where, he recorded, "I found Major L'Enfant drawing his plan of the city of Washington." Knowing Trumbull to be a man well liked in the president's circle, L'Enfant turned their unexpected meeting into a personal tour of the Potomac site. Though Trumbull described what he saw as no more than a "thick wood," he felt privileged to preview the city in its earliest days. He took great pleasure in being close to the seat of power, as intrigued by political events as he was knowledgeable about the arts.

Three months later, Trumbull knew, no Capitol prize had been awarded on the day James Hoban had been given the commission for the President's House. The advertisement had been clear enough: The commissioners wanted a "plan for a Capitol . . . of Brick, and to contain the following apartments, to wit: a Conference room, a room for the Representatives . . . a Lobby or Antichamber to the latter, a Senate room of 1200 square feet area, an Antichamber or Lobby to the last, [and] 12 rooms of 600 square feet area each, for committee rooms & clerk's offices." By the deadline, no fewer than fourteen designs arrived for consideration, some from the same drawing boards as entries to the President's House competition, among them those of Andrew Carshore, Jacob Small, and James Diamond. Well-known builders entered, too, including Samuel Dobie, the man charged with constructing the Virginia Capitol, and Salem, Massachusetts's famed builder Samuel McIntire. But as the commissioners explained, none of the designs had met "with entire approbation."

In 1792, Trumbull had taken a portrait of George Washington, painting the president in his mansion in Philadelphia. An earlier portrayal of the newly inaugurated president, commissioned by the city of New York, already hung in Federal Hall, but this time Trumbull chose to paint a retrospective view. He worked at an immense, life-size canvas of the general on the eve of the battle of Trenton. The finished work pleased both the sitter and Trumbull very much, as the painter felt emboldened to call it "the best certainly of those which I painted, and the best, in my estimation, which exists, in his heroic military character." The work on the painting once more affirmed his relationship with the president.

Over the years, Trumbull had grown accustomed to acting as an intermediary between Washington and the Marquis de Lafayette on his foreign journeys. Thus he would think the request natural enough when a Philadelphia acquaintance, the "English gentleman, Dr. Thornton," asked him to perform the same service. "[He] had made a drawing and plan for the Capital or house of government," said Trumbull. "The doctor requested me to show these drawings to the President, and commend them to his attention, which I did."

The delivery of William Thornton's design was many months after the initial deadline, but, thanks in part to Trumbull, it arrived at the right place at the right moment.

VI.
November 1792 . . . No. 159 Chestnut Street . . . Philadelphia

THE WASHINGTON COMMISSIONERS had earlier received an anonymous letter, its signatory identifying himself only as "FELLOW-CITIZEN." Dated July 12, 1792, the missive arrived from Tortola in the British West Indies.

"By a note lately sent me from Philadelphia," the correspondent began,

"I find you have offered a premium for the best plan of a Capitol for the United States. . . . I have been constantly engaged since in endeavoring to accomplish what you propose. I have made my drawings with the greatest accuracy, and the most minute attention to your directions keeping strictly to the rules of architecture, and would have sent them by the present opportunity, but mean to depart hence in a few days for America, and preferred taking them myself . . . having great hopes that I may not yet be too late."

Almost seven weeks were required for the letter to reach Georgetown but Dr. Thornton need not have worried about missing the deadline since, as the commissioners announced, "the final Decission is put off." The president might not have known exactly what he wanted for his Capitol, but he was certain that he hadn't seen it yet. The best the disappointed judges had been able to do was decide that a successful design *might* be salvaged from one entry, the work of a recently immigrated Frenchman.

Étienne Sulpice Hallet, the only professional architect to enter the Capitol competition, had proposed a rectangular building enclosed on all four sides by columns. Although the president observed that Hallet's drawings might produce "a noble and desirable structure," he also expressed a preference for the notion of another entrant to cap the building with a dome. At Washington's instructions, the commissioners wrote to Mr. Stephen Hallet, his first name anglicized, offering a brief critique and making a request. "On the whole we wish you to visit the Spot as soon as you can, and have a free and full Communion of Ideas with us [as] your Design may perhaps be improved into approbation." Though unsatisfied with his first attempt, the judges hoped to guide him into a design that would please the president.

In the meantime, Thornton's stay in Tortola had been extended when he was "seized with a very violent fever, accompanied with disagreeable symptoms."

Though born on the island in 1759, Thornton barely knew the place. At age five he had been sent to Lancashire, England, to live with Quaker relations. Given a classical education, he then apprenticed at eighteen to an apothecary and physician. Four years later, he enrolled at the University of Edinburgh, where he was awarded a medical degree in 1784 after further studies in Paris and London.

Having attended perhaps the best medical school of the day and won the respect of his professors, Thornton might well have become a practitioner of note in London. But the young man possessed both a wide-eyed desire to experience more of the world and the freedom to do it, thanks to his income from Pleasant Valley, his inherited Caribbean plantation. He toured the Scottish Highlands, journeyed to the Swiss Alps, attended salons in Paris, and established a place for himself among a circle of artistic friends in London. Not having returned since early boyhood, he visited Tortola in 1785, but stayed only briefly, traveling on to the United States. He arrived in Philadelphia for a visit in October 1786, but almost at once found himself caught up in the excitement of the new American republic.

He took a northern tour to Newport and Boston, returning to Philadelphia in time to hear daily reports of the Constitutional Convention from another boarder at his lodgings. James Madison's recounting of the proceedings then in session one block away completed Thornton's conversion. "Men of talents and virtue are here wanted," he explained to a friend. Choosing to take part in the quintessential Enlightenment experiment, Thornton became an American citizen in January 1788.

By the autumn of 1792, as he recuperated from his "tedious sickness," his life in America had already offered him an opportunity to explore his considerable range of talents. "Mine's a greedy eye," Thornton wrote to an English painter friend, "and loves to feast in the luxuries of seeing." His visual gluttony was matched by an inquisitive streak, and he had made himself expert in botany, mechanics, and painting, as well as medicine and pharmacology. Yet his first flush of public success he owed to architecture, a discipline in which he had only an occasional, fleeting interest—and no training whatsoever.

His flirtation with the building arts had begun in 1789. Though engaged in the practice of medicine, he wanted something to distinguish himself in his adopted country. He saw his chance when the Library Company of Philadelphia announced a competition for a new building. "When I traveled I never thought of architecture," Thornton explained, "but I got some books and worked a few days, then gave a plan." Borrowing from the Palladian plates in English architectural books he found in the Library Company itself, Thornton won the competition. The completed library at the corner of Fifth and Chestnut Streets was soon "admired by all strangers who come to the city." For Doctor Thornton, it was as easy as that.

The Washington Commissioners heard again from the long-silent Thornton in November 1792. Having regained his health, he had sailed from Tortola aboard the brig Molly, arriving in Philadelphia on November 1, along with his wife, Anna Maria, whose mother, a Frenchwoman named Ann Brodeau, ran the best young ladies' boarding school in Philadelphia. Thornton had learned to his pleasure that the contest for a Capitol design remained unresolved, and promptly wrote to the commissioners in Georgetown, assuring them that, since "I am not yet too late . . . I will either forward my plans . . . or will wait upon you at the city of Washington." By then he knew, too, that the competition rules did not require anonymity, so he affixed his full signature to the letter.

Thornton had known the recently deceased Benjamin Franklin; among his friends he counted physician Benjamin Rush, Madison, Trumbull, and many leading figures in Philadelphia society. He was quickly gaining a reputation as "a scholar and gentleman—full of talent and eccentricity . . . his company the complete antidote to dullness." His contacts, he found, added up to easy entrée to the wealthy and powerful in Philadelphia.

Such access meant he got to see some of the rejected Capitol submissions. The same friend who apprised him of the contest's status, Judge George Turner, had himself submitted the design with the dome that President Washington had admired. Turner's plans had been rejected, but not before Turner visited Jenkins Hill where he learned a good deal about the judges' thinking. He confided in Thornton about President Washington's preferences, explaining that both a dome and a presidential apartment, requirements that at first had not been specified, had become essential. Thornton's initial drafts had been for a building that resembled many of the English country houses of the day, but he realized he must begin anew. Once again, his drawings would fail to arrive on the promised schedule.

That autumn the competition favorite, Stephen Hallet, traveled to Philadelphia to consult with the president and the secretary of state. The two of them, Hallet sensed, would be making the final decision, but despite repeated redesigns, the "fancy piece" exterior and "internal arrangements" of his design still had not yet coalesced to the satisfaction of the commissioners, who seemed to exercise some sway. Secretary of State Jefferson, with whom Hallet corresponded in French, encouraged him; Jefferson's respect for Hallet as a man of professional training was evident, as he believed Hallet's talents would be invaluable in constructing by far the greatest architectural challenge ever undertaken in the United States.

With a new series of drawings in hand, Hallet made the pilgrimage to the then-capital city to make his case directly to Washington and Jefferson. His plans depicted a monumental building with a high central dome and wings, a building tailored to Jefferson's and Washington's expressed tastes. Hallet was disappointed when his meetings in Philadelphia did not earn him the prize; still, he departed with instructions for the preparation of further drawings, certainly a good omen.

While Hallet seemed to be inching closer to winning, his presence in Philadelphia also worked to Thornton's advantage. Somehow—not even Fiske Kimball would prove able to explain the exact circumstances—Thornton got a glimpse of Hallet's drawings. They contained the key to the prize and, although Thornton spent but little time with them, a record survives of his examination. In Kimball's words, the little sketch is merely "a hasty note from memory," but he connected the dots, recognizing the resemblance between Thornton's speedy study and Hallet's careful drafts.

Drawing came easily to Thornton. As a child, he once showed an uncle two £5 notes. "Which is best engraved?" he inquired. The uncle chose the very one young William himself had just finished rendering in pen and ink. His native skills had been polished at Edinburgh, in a time when anatomy studies required a facility for drawing. He took pleasure in his easy way with watercolors, too, having painted Alpine and Scots landscapes on his travels. His botany studies made him a practiced recorder of the natural world.

Thornton had immediately absorbed the general composition of Hallet's design, with its matching wings and a central dome supported by the colossal columns at center. Then he set to work devising his own solution. He knew Hallet's assemblage held the basic elements but, equally, that he needed to vary them to make the Capitol his own. On the verso of the same sheet on which he sketched Hallet's design was one of the plans for the Capitol scheme he had abandoned; Thornton grafted the two plans together, mounting a rough approximation of Hallet's tall building with its dome onto his own raised basement. He borrowed a balustrade from Turner.

The sketch determined the direction for Thornton's new design, and he set to work in earnest. In preparing the required elevations, plot plans, and sections, he added a range of details, selecting them from architectural books. He produced a finished elevation of the east front and a plan for the main floor of the Capitol, and these he entrusted to Trumbull in January. Trumbull, in turn, delivered them to the president.

The response from Washington and Jefferson came quickly: They were most impressed. On February 1, 1793, Jefferson wrote to the commissioners in Georgetown, "Doctor Thornton's plan of a capitol has been produced, and has so captivated the eyes and judgement of all as to leave no doubt you will prefer it when it shall be exhibited to you." Washington, too, expressed his admiration for "the grandeur, simplicity and beauty of the exterior . . . [which] give it preference."

Dr. William Thornton's vision of the Capitol. *Library of Congress/Prints and Photographs Division*

Thornton completed more drawings, among them two additional floor plans and an elevation of the west façade. In March he traveled to George-town to meet with the commissioners, but the journey was a formality. Thir-teen months after it had begun, the contest concluded when, on April 5, 1793, the commissioners wrote to Thornton. Their letter opened with the happy words, "The President has given his formal approbation of your plan." He had won.

Despite Dr. Thornton's inexperience, Washington, Jefferson, and the commissioners had finally found what they wanted in his design. Jefferson, the student of classical architecture, was gladdened to see the dome, the columns, and colonnades. There was a balcony, like the one at Federal Hall, suitable for inaugurations. The ever-practical Washington admired the room arrangement, commenting upon "the propriety with which the apartments are distributed—and the economy in the mass of the whole structure."

Thornton's monumental conception embraced their ideas and something larger, too. The artist in Thornton imagined a building that could be a visual and literal focal point for the new American government. Here was an unpre-cedented opportunity to apply his protean mind—one intimate with the best science ("natural philosophy") of the day and wholly converted to the human values the democratic experiment represented. He wanted to make a building that spoke to him as a convert to the American cause; Jefferson and Washington adopted it because they recognized in his design a shared vision.

VII.
Autumn 1919 . . . Hotel E . . . Charlottesville, Virginia

THE UNCERTAINTY HAD PASSED: Kimball had a new job.

The preceding two years had been an exhausting roller-coaster ride. The head of the department of architecture at Michigan, Sidney Lorch, refused to reappoint him in the fall of 1917 after Kimball's sabbatical year; his jealousy of Kimball's busy writing life contributed to the dean's dislike of his younger colleague. Upon learning of his dismissal, Kimball decided to fight for his job, and took the next train to Ann Arbor. He went straight to the president of the University of Michigan, who then interceded, restoring Kimball's appointment. The outraged Dean Lorch repaid his unwanted associate for going over his head by assigning him thirty-four hours of class instruction per week.

The following year had proved memorable, too. Having somehow found the time to complete his book, *A History of Architecture*, Kimball noted, "Its appearance just kept me from getting fired again." He was invited into the pages of the 1918 edition of *Who's Who in America*, and made historian of the American Institute of Architects. Yet once more his Jefferson work proved most valuable, as *Thomas Jefferson, Architect* brought him to the attention of the University of Virginia. On May 2, 1919, he received a telegram, hiring him at a salary of $3,000. He was to be the first director of the new McIntire School of Art and Architecture.

Kimball could not believe his good fortune. He had got out from under Dean Lorch. His appointment made him head of a new department that was his to shape. *And* he had been given the title Supervising Architect. There were buildings to be built at the university, the first an outdoor theater that he had already begun to ruminate upon, planning a Greek-style amphitheater. It would have to be classical since he saw a crisp, modern, cosmopolitan classicism as very much of his time as well as Jefferson's. In fact, the curriculum he established emphasized the "architectural traditions of the South . . . based primarily on classic architectural forms." Surely Jefferson would have approved.

* * *

KIMBALL EMERGED AS THE PREEMINENT SCHOLAR of the founding of the
Federal City. Two major articles of his had appeared in 1918, one about the
President's House competition, "The Genesis of the White House," the other
devoted to L'Enfant, "The Origin of the Plan of Washington." His series with
Wells Bennett, "The Competition for the Federal Buildings," was published in
four issues of the *American Institute of Architects Journal* throughout 1919.

He chose to recount Washington's history from numerous vantages,
among them Hoban's, L'Enfant's, and Thornton's, as well as Washington's
and Jefferson's. But there was a single, consistent theme: American architecture had begun to come of age in the 1790s. George Washington wanted to
make a bricks-and-mortar statement with the "Federal City," seeing the capital as essential to the dignity of the great nation; Jefferson's angle of approach was compatible but more aesthetic. "The character of the colonial
buildings no longer satisfied the founders of the independent states of America," Kimball wrote. "For the buildings at Washington, a determined attempt
was made, under Jefferson's leadership, to secure designs which should be worthy of a great nation and conform to the best architectural taste of Europe."

Kimball shaped the multifold stories of the architects and builders into
one coherent narrative. A small migration of architectural talent had arrived
from Europe, including the Irish James Hoban. He would remain in Washington for the rest of his life, nearly four decades, choosing to work most often as a builder rather than an architect. The other competition winner, Dr.
Thornton, had taken a different approach. Thornton liked to think the big
thought, but quotidian details bored him. In the explanatory letter that accompanied his winning entry into the Capitol competition, he offered the
commissioners an almost incidental—but important—aside. When it came
to structural issues, he explained, "the architects may be consulted." And the
loser, Stephen Hallet, though outraged that a victory seemingly his had been
handed to someone else, had been hired "to study Doct. Thornton's plan of a
Capitol." The commissioners wished to appease Hallet and take advantage of
his professional training.

Kimball assembled the story of Hallet's contribution, too. The Frenchman
had harangued the commissioners, citing a variety of structural flaws in
Thornton's design. The untrained amateur, Hallet pointed out, had set the
columns too far apart to support the structures above—if built as Thornton
specified, Hallet claimed, the building would collapse. To address various
problems, Hallet produced revised drawings, which Jefferson described
as "Dr. Thornton's plan, rendered in practicable form." However, unable to

respect Thornton's design, Hallet was dismissed within a year when the commissioners discovered he had been further revising the design to suit himself. (Later, when arguing for additional compensation, he made a case for his ownership of his design, based on his "application to abstract Theory, the result of which [it is] mine by that inherent right which every author has to the fruits of his Genius." He may have made the first argument for intellectual property rights by an American architect.)

The story continued with Thornton back in charge. After moving to Washington in 1793, he had been appointed a commissioner in September 1794. He directed construction on the Capitol for a time but soon acknowledged that a professional successor to Hallet was required. Once again the good offices of John Trumbull proved to be the means by which an Englishman was hired in the person of George Hadfield. Kimball knew his work earlier, too, from his Massachusetts studies, since a Hadfield drawing resided in the Coolidge collection. Kimball reconstructed Hadfield's story, as well.

When patronage for his history paintings failed to materialize, Trumbull had accepted a diplomatic post as John Jay's secretary in London in 1794. "I would have been a beggar had I wholly relied on painting for my support," he explained. Trumbull assisted Jay in the negotiations that produced the Jay Treaty, but found time to renew old acquaintances, too, among them his Paris friends Maria and Richard Cosway. When the letter came from the commissioners asking him to "select, contract with, and send on" someone qualified to supervise the Capitol's construction, Trumbull recommended Maria Hadfield Cosway's brother, George. Hadfield had completed a distinguished apprenticeship in architecture, training at the Royal Academy, then working for six years in the office of James Wyatt, a prominent London architect. When Trumbull sought him out, he had recently returned from four years in Italy as the recipient of the Academy's first Traveling Scholarship in Architecture.

The timing proved propitious as Hadfield had just been refused membership in London's Architects' Club. One voter had placed a black ball in the ballot box, automatically excluding him. Although no reason had been given, the snub damaged Hadfield's London prospects. At Commissioner Thornton's personal request, Trumbull offered him the post of superintendent with its salary of £300 plus traveling expenses. Hadfield accepted.

On his arrival in Washington, Hadfield discovered that the foundations begun under Hallet differed from Thornton's plans. Like Hallet, he attempted to remedy structural problems. He spent three years in his post before he, too, was dismissed. One of his successors would confide the explanation to his diary: Despite being "a man of correct tastes, of perfect theoretical knowledge and of bold integrity," Hadfield had too little direct experience in "the practical execution of great work [and] he was no match for the rogues then employed in the construction of the public buildings or for the Charlatans in architecture who had designed them."

The "Charlatan" the writer had in mind was Thornton. As an architect, he straddled two camps, personifying the oxymoron "professional amateur." Despite winning the Capitol competition, he chose not to leverage his public success into an architectural career. He never regarded himself as an architect, and rarely signed or annotated his drawings. Building didn't interest him, really; he wished to retain his upper-class Englishman's distance from "trade." His plans for the Capitol reflected "the amateur's indecision," wrote Kimball, "[as well as] a vagueness in structural matters, and [a] pedantic dependence on academic rules." Even so, his design had an imposing grandeur, as Kimball also pointed out, one derived in part from Thornton's experience with European architecture. Despite all the criticisms, a consensus would emerge, as the brilliant Benjamin Latrobe later observed, that "[The Capitol] is one of the first designs of modern times."

Thornton's winning design was one of amateurism's last and greatest gasps, but it is also true that, as George Washington observed, "The plan is nobody's, but a compound of everybody's." Eventually the many drawings bore a variety of signatures, including those of Hadfield, Hallet, and Hoban, as well as Thornton. They all made contributions to the building and, in a larger sense, helped produce a new discipline, that of architectural design. The work in Washington, wrote Kimball, signaled the shift to "the professional architects—hitherto lacking—who henceforth assumed the leading role."

The architects who came to the Federal City demonstrated an ability to relate the disparate parts of a building to one another in an aesthetically pleasing way, even if often in a manner notably derivative of others. They were sensible of an architectural aesthetic in which the art of design informs the craft of building. And as Kimball's nascent research would soon demonstrate, the immigration of Latrobe (he would arrive in 1796) and the presence of Charles Bulfinch, already at work in Boston, would assure that true architecture would have an important place in the new country.

In a sense, Thornton had the last word about the Capitol when he offered a casual remark even before the cornerstone was laid in 1793. The building, he predicted, "would not probably be finished in thirty years." Kimball would cite the words in his article "William Thornton and the Design of the

Kimball's new job took him to the heart of Jefferson Country to the "Academical Village," as recorded here in 1856 by draftsman Edward Sachse. *The University of Virginia Library*

United States Capitol," which appeared in the inaugural issue of *Art Studies*. As Kimball well knew, Thornton's unintended prophecy came true. His Capitol was not quite complete when Thornton died in March of 1828. And Thornton then was a man remembered less for his architecture than for his "well-earned reputation for letters and taste; he was a writer, a painter, and a poet."

IN THEIR NEW ACCOMMODATIONS in Charlottesville, Marie and Fiske Kimball felt as if they had been transported back to Thornton's time. Certainly their new house was a Jefferson dreamscape come to life: The University of Virginia had been a brainchild of Jefferson's. It consisted of a central building for the library flanked by two matching rows of professors' dwellings (the ten domiciles he called "Pavilions"), which faced one another across a two-hundred-foot-wide green. Jefferson had wanted these buildings to be "models of taste and good architecture, & of a variety of appearance, no two alike, so as to serve as specimens for the Architectural lecturer."

When the Kimballs arrived, they settled into a brick support building in the West Range behind the Pavilions. Designed by Jefferson as a dining hall, Hotel E had later been converted to a chemistry lab. Now it was remodeled to become the Kimballs' quarters. It was comfortable, even if it hadn't the prestige of the Pavilions, which were inhabited by ladies and gentlemen of higher social caste than the Kimballs.

At first, Marie disliked genteel Charlottesville. The reserved Southern culture seemed strange, and Kimball, his behavior boisterous, his speech occasionally profane, seemed always to draw attention to himself. Once at an
uproarious party Fiske dared to roll in a barrel down the slope of the near-
sacred ground of The Lawn. By then the Kimballs had begun to gain acceptance, and one faculty wife excused his transgression with the remark, "After
all, he is only an overgrown boy."

Despite the breadth of his responsibilities, Kimball was just thirty years old.
He habitually rose at five o'clock, using the early hours for his research and
writing before addressing his teaching, administrative, and other university
duties. He established a strong art and architecture department, fulfilling Jefferson's own plan for the Academical Village to include a school of fine arts.

He also kept a watchful eye on the happenings on Jefferson's own mountaintop. The same year the Kimballs arrived in Virginia, Monticello went up
for sale. The mansion had been the summer home of wealthy New Yorkers
for almost a century, but it had become too expensive for its present owner,
Jefferson Levy, to maintain. Kimball followed the events as politicians, local
preservationists, and the historically minded plotted to purchase the home.
From across the valley, he watched and wondered whether there would be a
role for him to play.

CHAPTER 4

MR. LATROBE COMES TO AMERICA

"The profession of architecture has been hitherto in the hands of
two sets of men. The first,—of those who from travelling or from
books have acquired some knowledge of the theory of the art,—
but know nothing of its practice—the second—of those who
know nothing but the practice,—and whose early life being spent
in labor, & in the habits of a laborious life,—have no opportunity
of acquiring the theory."

—BENJAMIN HENRY LATROBE,
WRITING TO ROBERT MILLS, JULY 12, 1806

I.
July 16, 1796 . . . Mount Vernon . . . Overlooking the Potomac River

BENJAMIN HENRY LATROBE PREFERRED riding in a coach, but his route this
particular Sunday took him away from any well-traveled byway. His early departure brought him to John Mason's home near Colchester, Virginia, in time
for breakfast. He wasn't far from Gunston Hall where John's father, George
Mason, had died several years before, but by mid-morning Latrobe had
climbed back into the saddle and was headed for a different destination. Accompanied by his manservant, he pointed his borrowed horse eastward,
knowing he had some ten miles yet to travel, much of it through thick forest.

Latrobe felt a rush of relief when a water-powered gristmill came into view
about eight miles further on. Several times in the preceding weeks he had
lost his way on journeys into the wilds of Virginia, but seeing the mill meant

Benjamin Henry Latrobe, in Charles Willson Peale's portrait. *White House Historical Association/White House Collection*

he had found the entrance to George Washington's eight-thousand-acre plantation. Though the road remained rutted and uneven, Latrobe soon noted the neatness and orderliness of Washington's lands. "Good fences, clear grounds and extensive cultivation strike the eye as something uncommon in this part of the World," he observed.

The Englishman had come to America four months earlier seeking a new beginning. His marriage six years before had brought him the happiest moments he had known; his wife's death while giving birth to a stillborn child less than four years later had left him bereft. His surviving son and daughter had been sent to live with relatives, and Latrobe found himself profoundly alone. To make matters worse, his once-promising London career seemed at a standstill due to a pause in construction attendant to the war with France. Having packed his surveying instruments, drawing tools, and his immense library of some 1,500 volumes, he had boarded the *Eliza*, a ship bound for Virginia.

He had stepped ashore at Norfolk, after a rugged fifteen-week winter passage. While the North American landscape was still new to him, Latrobe had seen a good deal of Europe. Born in Fulneck, Yorkshire, within walking distance of the emerging industrial city of Leeds, Latrobe had spent his adolescence studying in Germany, then traveled to Paris and Rome and other capitals. He had worked in London for a dozen years, too. But all that was now behind him.

A large white house came into view a mile later. To a man who had designed two stately mansions near London after establishing his own architectural practice in 1792, the house presented "no very striking appearance." Yet having visited the homes of other Virginia gentlemen, some of which were built of logs, he recognized Mount Vernon as "superior to every other house I have seen here." He headed not for the front door but to follow a pathway to the south, past a kitchen garden to the stables. There he produced a letter from his chief Virginia friend, Bushrod Washington. A lawyer whose acquaintance Latrobe had made in Norfolk soon after his arrival, Washington had been pleased to write a letter of introduction to his uncle on his new friend's behalf. A slave went to deliver the missive, leaving Latrobe to wait.

"I walked into the portico next to the river," he would confide to his diary that night. He saw before him a dramatic waterscape on which "Nature has lavished magnificence, nor has Art interfered but to exhibit her to advantage." Overlooking the Potomac from an elevation more than a hundred feet above its waters, the vista took in a broad bend in the river that seemed to embrace Mount Vernon. From the tall piazza that lined the rear of the house, Latrobe gazed several miles upstream to the north, whence the river had flowed past the new Federal City. Three or four miles south it turned out of sight, continuing on its way to the Chesapeake Bay. On the opposite bank more than a mile away Latrobe saw Maryland's wooded hills, dotted here and there with the open land of plantations. Washington had taken good advantage of what he himself termed the "Vistoes."

Latrobe barely had time to take in the grand prospect as, "in about 10 Minutes, the President came to me."

Though his hair was dressed and powdered, George Washington wore a plain blue coat; he had come to pride himself at wearing clothes of American manufacture. He had grown accustomed to unannounced arrivals, welcoming thousands of them over the years, but Latrobe was more promising than most. Washington shook his visitor's hand, greeting him as a friend of his nephew's. Offering his guest a seat, he drew up a chair himself. Their formal conversation began with pleasantries, with talk of common friends, but Washington soon discovered a great breadth of knowledge in his guest and they talked for more than hour until Washington made to excuse himself. He explained he must tend to correspondence "which not withstanding [my] distance from the government still presse[s] upon [me]." But the conversation took a new turn, and their exchange continued for another hour.

Seated in matching, bottle-green Windsor chairs, the two men found much common ground despite the fact their personal histories shared little. Latrobe, at thirty-two, was exactly half Washington's age. He had grown up the son of a Moravian minister, dispatched at age three to a boarding school in Yorkshire, then to a *Pedagogium*, or high school, in German Silesia, at age twelve. He continued his studies at a Moravian seminary in Saxony before being dismissed when he admitted to being skeptical about certain church doctrines, labeling himself an "indifferentist." By then, however, he already had a sound knowledge of Latin, ancient Greek, several modern languages (including German, French, Italian, and Greek), geometry, algebra, history, and geography, as well as evangelical training in the Bible and theology. As an adult he had gained broad knowledge of geology and botany.

Although Washington's formal schooling had ended at age twelve, Latrobe found his host's observations "the well expressed remarks of a man who has seen and knows the world." Latrobe observed him carefully. "Washington has something uncommonly majestic and commanding in his walk, his address, his figure and his countenance. His face is characterized however more by intense and powerful thought, than by quick and fiery conception. There is a mildness about its expression; and an air of reserve in his manner lowers its tone still more. . . . He did not at any time speak with very remarkable fluency:—perhaps the extreme correctness of his language which almost seemed studied prevented that effect." Washington, long conscious of the limits of his formal education, always considered his words carefully.

At last the aging president rose. He excused himself with the words, "We should meet again at dinner." Having just been issued an invitation to stay for the main meal of the day, Latrobe found himself with the leisure to examine the great man's house.

HE APPROVED OF WHAT HE SAW, noting that "everything . . . is extremely good and neat." But Latrobe was less than overawed, remarking that Mount Vernon was "by no means above what would be expected in a plain English Country Gentleman's house."

This appraisal came from a man possessed of expert knowledge. Upon leaving off his studies in Germany thirteen years earlier, Latrobe had acted the Grand Tourist on his journey back to England, making stops in Paris (where he, like Jefferson, admired the Halle aux Bleds) and Rome (the Pantheon in particular struck his fancy). Settling in London, he took a job to learn engineering in the office of John Smeaton, a fellow Yorkshireman and a man known for his pioneering work in civil engineering. He helped Smeaton build bridges, canals, and lighthouses for a few years, then spent several more working for architect Samuel Pepys Cockerell. By the time he departed for America,

Latrobe had become a superb architectural delineator, an experienced engineer, and a man immersed in the design currents of the day. No one within three thousand miles of Mount Vernon could make the same claim.

As for Washington, he had taken possession of a modest house in 1754 and proceeded to reshape it with little regard to theory or a larger historical perspective. Instead, he brought to the process the same considered approach he employed elsewhere in his life. He listened with care to what those around him had to say and he had strong instincts of his own. He wanted elements that, he said, would "please the eye." In the absence of any means of exercising strict control over construction—he was often absent and the drawings he left behind were skeletal—he delegated considerable responsibility to the various tradesmen who executed the work for him.

He rarely chose to rely on architectural books; just one was to be found on his library shelves. Instead, he became a keen observer of buildings, developing for himself a sense of what was "correct." As a member of the Virginia gentry, he had come to know many of the great houses of the Tidewater, among them Gunston Hall, John Tayloe's Mount Airy, and the Lees' Stratford Hall. Before the Revolution, he and Martha had traveled two or three times each year to Annapolis to visit friends and enjoy the cosmopolitan air of the Maryland capital. He had traveled up and down the American coast, living for extended periods in Cambridge, Philadelphia, and New York.

The *experience* of what he saw guided his revisions to Mount Vernon. In his decades there, the house had remained in works the entire time, with major renovations undertaken in the late 1750s, when Washington contemplated marriage to Martha Dandridge Custis, and in 1774, just as he was emerging as a national figure. The modest house George inherited after his brother Lawrence's death had consisted of four rooms and a passage on the main floor with four smaller rooms above. The very different structure Latrobe viewed was worthy of a great man, one grand in scale with twenty-odd rooms in an era when most Americans lived in houses of two first-floor rooms with unfinished sleeping quarters in an attic.

The first house had been built of wood, a material that had gone out of favor among the Virginia gentry. But when Washington decided to raise the roof of his house in 1759, he elected not to start again but to apply a new skin to the exterior. His visitor noted the walling surface immediately.

"It is a wooden building," Latrobe observed, "painted to represent champhered rustic and sanded." Washington had seen such siding on a trip to New England and instructed his carpenters to bevel the edges of the wood pieces, giving them the appearance of rusticated blocks, a style of stonework in which the joints between the cut stones are deeply recessed. Fine white sand dashed upon a thick coat of paint enhanced the illusion. In looking at the rusticated siding, Latrobe could not help but compare and contrast, as his two major domestic commissions in England, Hammerwood Lodge and Ashdown House, had both been built of stone. If the faux stone appearance of the rusticated wood siding did not deceive him for a moment, he appreciated the intention.

Washington wanted his house to be "in the newest taste," but the duration of his various renovations at Mount Vernon was such that tastes changed. In the early days, he was influenced by William Buckland's work, which Washington had seen at neighboring Gunston Hall. Later, he saw more of Buckland's signature style when dining with the Edward Lloyds, because Buckland had finished their mansion before undertaking the Mathias Hammond house across the street. Although the talented Mr. Buckland never came to work at Mount Vernon, the chief carver on Buckland's crew at Gunston Hall and Mount Airy did. William Barnard Sears had become something of a fixture at Mount Vernon.

After taking a "stroll . . . about the lawn," Latrobe entered the house for the first time. There he found Mrs. Washington and her granddaughter Miss Custis in the hall. He took to the lady of the house immediately. "She retains strong remains of considerable beauty," he remarked. He found her to be as sociable and unaffected as her husband. "I introduced myself to Mrs. Washington as a friend of her Nephew, and she . . . gave me an account of her family in a good humoured free manner that was extremely pleasant and flattering."

When he got around to paying attention to Nelly Custis, he found himself enraptured. "Miss Eleanor Custis . . . has more perfection of form of expression, of color, of softness, and of firmness of mind than I have ever seen before, or conceived consistent with mortality," Latrobe rhapsodized. "She is every thing that the chissel of Phidias aimed at, but could not reach; and the soul beaming through her countenance, and glowing in her smile, is as superior to her face, as mind is to matter." He was smitten.

They soon sat down to dinner, the custom at Mount Vernon being to dine at three o'clock. Washington seated his guest on Mrs. Washington's left, with Eleanor Custis on her other side. The president occupied a chair near the middle of the table, and they were joined by the son of the Marquis de Lafayette, George Washington G. G. Motier Lafayette. In exile from France during his father's imprisonment following the French Revolution, the teenaged Lafayette resided with the Washingtons, together with his elderly tutor. Several seats

Mount Vernon's covered piazza had no clear historic precedent, and its columns were too far apart to suit the prescription of any ancient architect. Yet for all its vernacular awkwardness, the piazza captured Latrobe's fancy, as he would produce several sketches of it from different angles, including this one with Mrs. Washington, along with her lovely granddaughter Nelly.
Maryland Historical Society, Baltimore, Maryland

remained empty, as other guests were expected. Latrobe thought the conversation lagged at dinner, and he "felt a little embarrassed at the silent reserved air that prevailed."

They were soon joined by the late arrivals, Washington's former secretary, Tobias Lear, and his three boys. "The President retired in about 3/4 of an hour," and Latrobe, too, prepared to take his leave. But Washington unexpectedly returned and inquired whether pressing business prevented him from staying longer. Latrobe allowed that none did.

"Sir," said Washington, "you see I take my own way. If you can be content to take yours at my house, I shall be glad to see you here longer."

THE LIFE OF THE HOUSE flowed naturally onto Mount Vernon's piazza. The fourteen-foot-wide porch extended the full ninety-six-foot length of the house, allowing the Washingtons and their guests to linger, talking, reading, or simply taking in the sweeping vista of the Potomac and the Maryland hills beyond. Or, as in Latrobe's case, to work in his sketchbook, a favored pastime of his.

At six o'clock coffee was brought. Latrobe and Washington resumed their thoughtful exchange, talking well into the evening, conversing on matters ranging from the nutritional value of Indian corn to the technology of the modern plough. The majestic riverscape faded with the light, and Washington proposed going inside. There the conversation continued until "the President left the company about 8 o'clock. We soon after retired to bed."

In the morning Latrobe rose with the sun. He walked the grounds near the house, continuing to work in his sketchbook. His habit was to sketch first, using a pencil. Later he could fill in the outlines with India ink, then brush in the modeling with a leaden, blue-gray color. Only then would he add brighter tones, using layers of color washes.

When he sketched Washington's Mansion House, he saw a building "of the old school" laid out on a five-part Palladian plan. The main body of the mansion was flanked by curved rows of arches which formed mirror-image arcades linking the main dwelling to matching subsidiary buildings on either side, one for the kitchen and the other a servants' hall. The suburban London house he himself had designed back in England, Hammerwood Lodge, drew upon the same five-part precedent, but Washington's effort lacked the verve and coherence of Palladio's great villas. Latrobe saw a building that reflected less Palladio's *Four Books* than an attempt by Washington to adapt American imitations, the five-part Palladian houses Washington had seen, among them Mount Airy and the house his acquaintance Mr. Buckland had built for Mathias Hammond in Annapolis. Washington's version wasn't entirely symmetrical, with windows that didn't quite balance one another and an off-center cupola. It had the look of a place that evolved slowly, irregularly, over time.

Writing in his journal, Latrobe caught the essence in a sentence: "The center is an old house to which a good dining room has been added at the North end, and a study &c. &c., at the South." Implied in his words is the tale of the simple cottage that Washington had inherited and, over forty years, greatly expanded into his mansion complex. The general had tinkered with porticoes and cupolas, added arcades and a piazza. Latrobe characterized what he saw as a "building . . . in a very indifferent taste," but he intended no harsh judgment. It was a truthful recognition that Washington's house was old-fashioned, with a cupola that harkened back to the Baroque style of the Governor's Palace in Williamsburg, a building completed in 1722. On the inside, the rococo carving done by William "Barney" Sears was based upon plates in Abraham Swan's *British Architect,* a book published in 1745.

Not that Barney Sears's work wasn't worth admiring. Even by London standards, he was a gifted workman. He had arrived in America a convict, found guilty of stealing clothing, and was sentenced to a seven-year indenture to George Mason, which had enabled him to master the carver's craft under the watchful eye of William Buckland. He then worked at Mount Vernon, as well as at the parish church attended by Mason and Washington, where he demonstrated both a gift for carving and the wit to recognize his talent. According to his assistant, a former Mount Vernon slave named Sambo Anderson, one of the vestrymen dared challenge Sears's fee for carving a pulpit topped by a dove. "Well, Gentlemen," Sears responded, "if you refuse to pay my price, I will take it down, put breath in it, and set the bird to singing." His work was so lifelike that his threat seemed just possible and his invoice was paid in full.

Although he admired aspects of Mount Vernon, Latrobe thought about houses very differently from Washington. For almost a dozen years, Latrobe's professional experience had disciplined him to think like a designer. He conceived a project first as an *idea*. As he began considering a design, he would bring to the process a historical aesthetic, as well as his knowledge of building materials and technology; he would imagine a building that was respectful of the past yet also imaginative *and* practical. He would weigh its parts individually; he would combine them so they related to one another and to the structure as a whole. In collaboration with his client, he would produce a detailed plan. Only then would construction commence, a common understanding having been reached that meant few decisions were left to the workmen or the client as the structure rose.

Washington took his house seriously—as a visitor years before had remarked, "It's astonishing with what niceness he directs everything in the building way, condescending even to measure the things himself, that all may be perfectly uniform." But the house he built didn't come out of one man's mind, nor even from one architectural book. There were numerous visual references to English pattern and building books since most of the builders who worked for him owned one or more architectural volumes. Those same builders also arrived with mental images captured at other building sites. And their tools, too, implied design ideas. Hand tools like molding planes shaped specific profiles. Flat fillets; concave and convex curves shaped by hollows and rounds; beads, ogees, and other shapes all lent themselves to assemblies of contoured surfaces for skirting boards, chair rails, panels, cornices, entablatures, capitals, and columns. The workers brought with them some book knowledge, but also the memory of what their eyes had seen and their hands had shaped at other places, at other times.

Mount Vernon was an architectural event in its own right, not least because it belonged to the singular George Washington. In his mature years, the squire of Mount Vernon was ever conscious that he was on stage, that he was an actor in a theater piece of national and even international importance; his

When Washington decided to enlarge the mansion at Mount Vernon in 1773, he himself
sketched his vision. Compared to the artistry Latrobe would bring to his drawings, the
elevation seems shockingly amateurish, leaving all but the most basic decisions to
the builders. *Mount Vernon Ladies Association*

house, then, was among the stage sets where he had to perform. To suit his
personal needs and to serve political ends, Washington had created a property
that, like him, was sensible and practical while being majestic and imposing.

At ten o'clock on Monday morning, Latrobe prepared to leave. Washington bade him farewell; he enjoyed the man's company, as not many visitors
rivaled Latrobe's lively, wide-ranging intelligence or his technical expertise.
They parted with a handshake, two tall men who could look one another
in the eye. Washington invited Latrobe "to call again if [you] come again into
the Neighbourhood." He wished him good morning, and Latrobe departed.

Benjamin Henry Latrobe recognized he had been in the presence of "one
of the greatest men that Nature ever produced." He was also struck by the
fact that this same man had "treated me as if I had lived for years in his
house; with ease and attention." They had talked at length about farming, a
subject of consuming interest to Washington as well as his livelihood, since
he refused any compensation as president. They had discussed engineering
projects such as the canal Latrobe was investigating for several Richmond investors. But Latrobe chose to explain his mixture of feelings about Washington in terms of a family anecdote.

Some twenty years earlier, Latrobe's youngest brother, then age six, had
glimpsed King George III. The king was processing through Saint James' Park
in his carriage on his way to the House of Lords. Latrobe confided in his journal that, after the great personage had been pointed out, the boy "could

scarcely believe that the person he saw could be the king; and being assured that he really was so, he cried: '*Good lord, papa, how like a man he looks!*'"

II.
Late Summer 1796 . . . Captain Pennock's . . . Norfolk, Virginia

LATROBE HAD NOT THOUGHT OF Captain William Pennock for months. Then, one afternoon at the Eagle Tavern in Richmond, he overheard "many oaths and imprecations" directed at "a frenchman . . . at Norfolk, who had given Captn. Pennock the most preposterous design, which he had ever seen." His dinner interrupted, Latrobe listened attentively to the further report of the gentleman, a city councillor in Norfolk, one Colonel Kelly. "Captn. Pennock had been mad enough to attempt to execute it," Colonel Kelly continued, "and that having carried up part of the Walls he was now perfectly at a stand[still], as none of the Workmen knew how to proceed."

Suddenly it dawned on Latrobe. He didn't regard himself as French (though his surname certainly was, having descended to him from French Protestants who moved to Ireland three generations earlier), but—*of course!*—he was the very "frenchman" referred to. And Pennock, knowing no better, had obviously attempted to raise from bricks and mortar a house using the little floor plan Latrobe had sketched for him. The notion was absurd: The sketch was plainly insufficient; many more drawings would be required. But to Pennock and his fellow Virginians, a single sheet had, at least at first, seemed entirely normal.

The episode had started innocently enough, Latrobe remembered. As he had noted in his memorandum book at the end of March, "The friends to whom I was recommended have been extremely kind to me, and I have loitered my time away at their Houses, doing odds and ends of little services for them."

His little service for Captain Pennock, though hardly a commission, had offered him his first chance on American soil to exercise his architectural imagination. He was a bit rusty, just two weeks into his American life, and still recovering from his prolonged and fearsome sea journey. He had tuned a pianoforte that week for a new friend (as a trained musician, Latrobe as a younger man had considered making music his profession). And just a day or two earlier he had laid out a staircase for another new acquaintance. Still, he admitted, "I have been very idly engaged since my arrival."

He could afford to be. He had brought with him both cash and credit, along with the promise of more funds from a legacy his mother had left him. Born in Pennsylvania, Anna Margaretta Antes Latrobe had bequeathed her son property in her home state, which an uncle would soon set about selling for him. But money alone was not enough to salve the sadness in his life. He missed his late wife and his two small children. He wanted to be busy, to exercise his skills, to leave his imprint on his new country. But Norfolk had not appeared to be the place to do it, as the city had yet to recover from a major conflagration ignited by the British bombardment in 1776, and the cityscape Latrobe saw seemed to him ill-built and unhealthy. He had resolved to ready himself to depart for greener pastures and, he had been advised, the growing city of Richmond might offer him more attractive prospects.

Back in April, though, before his departure, he had fulfilled his end of a "trifling Wager" he had made with William Pennock. A wealthy merchant and shipowner, the captain had bet him that he could not design a substantial house for a narrow lot on Norfolk's Main Street. The structure could be no more than forty-one feet wide and, Pennock insisted, its ground floor was to consist of no fewer than three rooms plus a handsome staircase and a backstair for service access. A final requirement added interest to the game. "The essential requisite," Latrobe was told, "[was] that the front door . . . should be in the Center." For the neoclassicist Latrobe, a man for whom symmetry was a virtual incantation, that sealed the challenge.

Once he settled down to put it on paper, Latrobe had produced a solution in short order. "On leaving Norfolk . . . I gave [Pennock] the drawing, drawn to a very small scale." A mere bagatelle, the floor plan was enough to win the wager, but provided little real satisfaction at the time since, Latrobe understood, Pennock "had no idea of executing the plan."

Upon learning months later in the Eagle Tavern that the plan had actually been put to use, Latrobe wrote to offer his further services. His letter crossed with a reciprocal one from Pennock asking for further guidance, and he soon made arrangements to travel to Norfolk.

Latrobe was taken aback by what he found. "No part of the plan has been accurately set out," he complained. "The front was totally altered . . . The Chimneys occupied double the space requisite for them; and in general . . . the original plan has been [undone] by the blunders committed by the workmen . . . their prejudices and obstinacy, and . . . their ignorance."

The siting was all wrong, too. The house had not been set back on a small rise to take advantage of the water views as he had suggested. It was being constructed almost "upon the street," aligned with all the others where it admitted the dust, noise, and smells of the seaport. The bricks and brickwork were bad and the joiner in charge "wedded to the heavy wooden taste of the last century." Latrobe didn't say it in so many words, but he thought the place a disaster.

He resolved to do what he could ("It was with much difficulty that I could repair the mischief already done"), but his first American commission, if it could be called that, had been inadvertently sabotaged by the unskilled artisans hired to construct it. It was hardly an auspicious beginning and, sadly, an omen of his time in Virginia.

III.
December, 1916 . . . Looking for Latrobe . . . Bel Air, Maryland

THE CLUES HAD BEGUN TO ACCUMULATE during his Sachs fellowship. Three months earlier, Kimball had found the Latrobe scrapbooks that contained Jefferson's and the other entries in the Federal City competitions. A month later, he had come across drawings of the Capitol by Latrobe at the Office of the Superintendent in Washington. Another lead had taken him to the home of a descendant, H. Latrobe Roosevelt, who allowed him to photograph his modest collection of Latrobe drawings in Washington. Kimball had a hunch there was much, much more: He was coming to believe that Latrobe, in addition to his government work, had had "a great private practice in architecture and engineering."

Just before Thanksgiving, Kimball had returned to Baltimore hoping to find the evidence to prove it. He learned from one of his new contacts that still another descendant, Ferdinand C. Latrobe II, possessed "by far the largest body of [Latrobe] papers." Unfortunately, his source also informed him that the man known as Ferdie "has generally refused to let anyone examine them." But there was a genetic imperative at work, since Ferdie's grandfather, John H. B. Latrobe, had not only donated the competition drawings to the Maryland Historical Society but, over a period of many years, attempted in his lectures and papers to keep his father's name from slipping into obscurity. Before his own death in 1891, John H. B. Latrobe had spoken of his late father "as a person of very extraordinary accomplishments in literature, science and art, as well as a thoroughly educated architect and engineer." In the intervening generation, Ferdinand C. Latrobe Sr. had maintained the family tradition of revering the past, leading the celebration of Baltimore's sesquicentennial during one of his seven terms as Baltimore's mayor.

The break Kimball was counting on came when Latrobe contacted him at his Washington apartment overlooking Rock Creek. At twenty-seven, young Ferdie Latrobe was just beginning to take the measure of his great-grandfather's inheritance and, having gotten wind of Kimball's work on Jefferson, he agreed to allow him to examine the materials that had come to him at the time of his mother's death. In his tantalizing description, he mentioned to Kimball some twenty volumes of manuscript books that had belonged to his great-grandfather. "[He] was good enough," Kimball reported, "to invite me up to his country place, where they are, for . . . as long as proved necessary to study them." Kimball eagerly accepted the invitation, and the date was set.

Although snow had begun falling when he left Washington the morning of December 18, Kimball boarded the train for Baltimore. He had such confidence in the importance of what he would find that he had set aside three days and three nights to spend at the Latrobe country house in Bel Air, Maryland. His host met him at Baltimore's Penn Station and, through deepening snow, they made the treacherous thirty-mile drive, reaching Bel Air at midday.

As soon as social niceties allowed, Kimball set to work. To his great joy, he found a vast collection of materials; to his chagrin, he realized the allotted time would be insufficient to get more than a slight familiarity with the letters, diaries, and drawings. Despite being given "the assurance [the documents] would always be accessible to me," he set to work with an almost manic intensity, getting no more than a few hours of sleep during his stay. He immersed himself in the "16 quarto letter books, 1803–17, comprising perhaps 8,000 pages, many pocket diaries, and about a dozen large sketch books filled with architectural drawings and water colors." He read most of the diaries and some of the correspondence, marking about 150 letters for transcription, which Ferdie Latrobe had offered to have done.

Kimball's enthusiasm proved infectious. During the visit Ferdinand Latrobe promised to send the collection to Kimball in order that he, as he had done with the Jefferson drawings, could continue his research and write a book about their author. Latrobe even agreed to "guarantee the margin of expense of a publication relating to his ancestor the architect, say from $500 to $1000."

Better yet, Benjamin Henry Latrobe appeared to have been everything Kimball had suspected and more. As an architect, the Englishman had built houses, a bank in Philadelphia, the cathedral in Baltimore, and for many years had worked as the nation's Surveyor of the Public Buildings, making major contributions to the evolution of the Capitol and the President's House between 1803 and 1817. As a hydraulic engineer, he planned river improvements and canals and had designed and overseen the construction of municipal water systems for Philadelphia and New Orleans. He built a dry dock for the Navy Department and even designed a prison for Virginia. His use of steam engines at his waterworks projects and in the Navy Yard ranked him as America's first great steam engineer.

Dr. Kimball smelled something important, not only for himself but for everyone involved in the study of old buildings and the men who built them. Kimball was carried by his own energy but also a larger academic wave. Until late in the nineteenth century, the discipline of American history had not existed as a distinct field of study. The first history professors were appointed at major universities only in the 1870s; the American Historical Association (AHA) was founded in the following decade. The doctrine called "scientific history" had emerged, its practitioners aiming to substitute objectivity for the informed storytelling of traditional narrative history. Instead of using political history to shape the recounting of the past, the new notion was to fortify the retrospective view with a range of cultural factors such as economics, sociology, aesthetics, psychology, and literature, and their influence on the patterns of history. Rather than relying on fond reminiscences ("fantasy spinning," Kimball called it), there was to be a systematic analysis of documents and data. As the AHA's statement of purpose expressed it, the organization had been created "for the promotion of historical studies, the collection and preservation of historical manuscripts and for kindred purposes in the interest of American history and of history in America."

The new historians took a page from the lab books of their scientific colleagues, looking to establish standards for research and training. Historian Henry Adams, John Adams's great-grandson, saw history in a Darwinian light: In the wake of *Origin of Species* (1859), Adams wrote, history ceased "to be a mere narrative, made up of disconnected episodes having little or no bearing on each other." When Kimball walked briskly onto the scene, he wanted to identify a larger scheme, and sought a unity in studying the architectural past. For him, a tale about a given building was empty of real meaning without an examination of the artifact. The hands-on approach was reinforced by the growing interest in the preservation of antique buildings (the Mount Vernon Ladies Association, which took possession of Washington's house in 1858, had been among the first to embark on a restoration effort). In Kimball's time, the conservators of early buildings, borrowing techniques from archaeologists, had begun to document the vertical history of individual sites by studying the material remains of historic structures. By measuring, taking photographs, and making detailed drawings, a graphic record of the historic past could be produced.

Although Kimball was preoccupied with the mountain of manuscript materials around him, he couldn't help but overhear Ferdie Latrobe's succession of calls. The house phone sat in the hall outside the room in which Kimball worked, and his host's broker kept calling. The stock market, which had peaked the previous month, was in a precipitous decline, driven by the war scare. The Kaiser's navy had begun attacking U.S. shipping, and fears were rising that American troops would be dispatched abroad. The broker was telling Latrobe that his inheritance was rapidly shrinking, but Kimball could do nothing for Ferdie Latrobe. And his time was limited so, never happier than when exploring a new avenue into the past, Kimball kept working. He made page after page of notes, transcribing passages, assembling chronologies, planning articles he wished to write.

The richness of the Latrobe archive represented to Kimball nothing less than an enormous doorway to the past, one that Ferdie Latrobe had thrown open to him. Instead of having to rely on new, measured drawings of historic structures, he had original documents. "After an examination of the house as it now exists," he had written in his first article on Monticello, "the drawings may then be traced backward without a break . . . so as to reconstitute the architectural history of the building and to permit a study of its sources and its significance." With Ferdie Latrobe's collection, he would be able to do for Benjamin Latrobe what he had done on Jefferson: Many of the drawings at hand had been drafted by Benjamin Henry Latrobe himself, others by delineators working under his supervision. Kimball found letters to clients and, in some cases, their responses; as he read them, he could almost hear conversations conducted more than a hundred years earlier.

When his three-day, three-night visit came to an end, he rejoined Marie in Washington. He had one big idea—he hoped to write *the* book on Latrobe—but first there was more research to do. He sensed that the project, at least in strictly architectural terms, could be even more significant than his work on Jefferson. He resolved to begin publishing his findings and his first article about Latrobe would appear the following December in the *Michigan Technic*, a journal of the university's engineering school.

Kimball didn't mince any words as he laid out his claim to the new scholarly territory in his essay, "Benjamin Henry Latrobe and the Beginnings of Architectural and Engineering Practice in America." He announced the breadth of his findings, stating boldly, "The first established professional here [in America], either in architecture or in engineering, was Benjamin Henry Latrobe, who was in a unique degree a master of both."

Kimball prepared to make the case. Many of B. H. Latrobe's buildings had been demolished and not a few of his designs had never been built. Unlike Palladio's Veneto, Jefferson's Central Virginia, or Charles Bulfinch's Boston, no single locale contained a great corpus of his work, since Latrobe had designed major buildings in England, Richmond, Washington, Baltimore, Philadelphia, Pittsburgh, New Orleans, and Kentucky. But Kimball was ready for the challenge, the hard work, and the travel. He was confident that in Latrobe, a man he now knew was immensely talented, ambitious, and dynamic, he had found another essential figure in the evolution of American design.

IV.

Winter 1797–98 . . . Quarrier's Court . . . Richmond

AT THE FOOT OF SEVENTH STREET, Latrobe's Richmond home and office was a short walk from the site of the new penitentiary. Word of the gaol, his first public commission in America, had reached him on June 25, 1797 in a letter from Virginia's Governor. It seemed the fulfillment of many hopes.

His design had been selected unanimously by the Governor and his Executive Council, chosen over entries from Samuel Dobie, George Hadfield, and Thomas Jefferson. A movement to humanitarian penology had made the building necessary, as Virginia, following Britain's lead, had established a new penal code that eliminated the death penalty for all but first-degree murder, substituting imprisonment, labor, and solitary confinement as punishments for other felonies. Latrobe's winning design resembled Newgate Prison, a building by George Dance the Younger that he had seen in his London days. He varied the scheme, combining a rectangular front section with administrative offices and cells for women prisoners with a prison area to the rear consisting of a semicircular row of cells enclosing a large open court, which could be supervised from a central keeper's house.

The building's cornerstone memorialized the lofty goals of architect and politician alike:

THE LEGISLATURE

OF THE COMMONWEALTH OF VIRGINIA

HAVING ABOLISHED THE ANTIENT SANGUINARY CRIMINAL CODE

THE FIRST STONE OF AN EDIFICE

THE MONUMENT OF THAT WISDOM

WHICH SHOULD REFORM WHILE IT PUNISHES THE CRIMINAL

WAS LAID ON THE 7TH DAY OF AUGUST

IN THE YEAR 1797, AND OF AMERICAN INDEPENDENCE THE 22ND

BY JN WOOD ESQ. GOVERNOR.

Latrobe envisioned public buildings as permanent, meaning they needed to be fire-resistant. Masonry materials were not unusual—brick or stone walls had become de rigueur for the seats of Virginia plantations—but wood still supported the internal structure of virtually all American buildings. Timbers shaped into beams and joists fit into the pockets in the masonry walls, providing a horizontal framework for wood floors, partitions, and other flammable elements to be attached to them. The roof rose atop wooden rafters.

Latrobe wanted to do better, so he specified barrel vaults—arched ceilings, like half-barrels—for the cells. Built of brick and stuccoed, the all-masonry cells met his standard for fire resistance. He used arches, arcades (series of arches), and lunettes (half-round windows) to give the penitentiary a Roman look. Symbolically, he added festoons of chains so the prison would look forbidding. In one of his drawings, he even added a black and threatening sky above the penitentiary, giving the image something of the theatrical impact of the gouaches of Clérisseau and Piranesi's prints.

Latrobe wanted the penitentiary to be a fine and highly visible building but he also saw the project as an opportunity to establish a level of professionalism in America in the practice of public architecture. He expected his thorough plans would set a precedent: The architect should be the principal construction supervisor. And, since he wanted to get paid for his trouble, "I stated the terms on which I would execute it." His payment scale was the standard one in England, for which an architect, in return for his design and supervision, was entitled to a fee equal to 5 percent of the construction cost. Latrobe spelled out the arrangement and the Executive Council made no objection. But Latrobe soon saw his high hopes compromised.

First, he found himself embroiled in a series of petty disputes with the building superintendent. The man questioned every estimate, suspicious of the unfamiliar arrangement in which he was second-guessed by a foreigner whose principal skill seemed to be drawing pictures, not constructing buildings. Next, when he readied his first bill, Latrobe was shocked when "individuals of the council with . . . whom I was in habits of friendship, advised me not to adhere to my charge of 5 p. cent *for it would not be allowed.* After a great deal of most unpleasant wrangling, I was then offered *1000 dollars or nothing* for my services for 15 months in the actual direction of the work." Suddenly, Latrobe found, the rules had changed.

He kept working on the building, but a bitterness stayed with him. "Had I not been able to live independently of my profession, I must have starved in conducting this work," he explained. His independent means were not such that he could continue indefinitely working for so little. With a major civic commission in works, he felt as if his American career ought to be set in motion; all of a sudden, he wasn't so sure.

His frustration was tempered by the fact that many well-placed Virginians invited him into their homes and society. Despite their hospitality, however, he had begun to find their company lacking in the energy and curiosity of his London companions. He felt they spent too much time betting on horse races and gambling. None but Bushrod Washington had become an intimate friend. "He can feel with me, and I believe loves me," Latrobe explained to an acquaintance in Philadelphia. Yet even that affectionate friendship fell short of meeting Latrobe's need for stimulation, for "[Bushrod] is only a Lawyer, and I have the itch of Botany of Chemistry, of Mathematics, of general Literature strong upon me yet, and yawn at perpetual political or legal discussion." Latrobe knew loneliness and, harder still, he felt intellectually alone.

There had been other professional opportunities. In addition to "Captain P's" and the penitentiary job, he had received a commission for an important house for John Harvie in Richmond. But construction once again had not gone according to his plan, with Harvie insisting upon changes Latrobe could not accept; and the workers had, as usual, proved ignorant. Latrobe felt the end result, its wings unbuilt, was "garbled and disgraced." He added, "I disdain it."

He had put another house on paper, this one for John Tayloe, one of the wealthiest men in Virginia, whose iron furnace Latrobe had visited. Yet when Tayloe had begun his in-town house in the Federal City earlier that year, he had adopted a design by William Thornton, not Latrobe's. Commissioned to examine the Appomattox River for navigational possibilities, Latrobe conducted a survey of the often shallow and rapids-filled river. After delivering his report, he heard no more. A later survey for the Dismal Swamp Canal Company also came to nothing.

Latrobe was not a man to give up. "His mind and hands," as Kimball would later observe, "were never idle." In the face of his disappointments, Latrobe devoted himself to a flurry of drawing and designing over the course of these Virginia months. Knowing that few or none of the structures he put on paper would ever be realized in bricks and mortar, he was driven by the belief that the drawings would be of use in attracting new customers, perhaps in another place and time. He had begun to accept that Virginia was not destined to be his permanent home.

He organized three albums. In one he bound the plans for the Virginia State Penitentiary. The second held the results of his flirtation with the theater in Richmond; for five weeks, beginning December 1, 1797, he had devoted himself to creating an ambitious plan for an up-to-date theater building. He had little hope it would be built, so his title sheet read, "Designs of a Building proposed to be erected at Richmond in Virginia to contain a Theatre, Assembly-Rooms, and an Hotel." The third album bore the title "Designs of Buildings erected or proposed to be built in Virginia."

These portfolios represented something else, too. Latrobe found he had to retrain himself in order to succeed in his adopted country. His new work was very different from his London days, when he labored for Cockerell and Smeaton. He spent little time in Virginia with other trained architects and engineers, and he very much missed the professional give-and-take. Instead, he had lived for many months alone on an island that he purchased from his friend Bushrod (thus its name, Washington's Island). It was in the middle of the James River, southwest of Richmond, with a panoramic view of the city dominated by the Jefferson-Clérisseau Capitol, which overlooked the landscape from its perch atop Shockhoe Hill. Even after moving downtown to Quarrier's Court to supervise construction at the penitentiary, he felt isolated.

His American circumstances had conspired to make Latrobe both master and pupil. Unlike most designers of his time in America and Europe, he had been unable to refer to the pages of books for inspiration. His library of 1,500 books, laboriously boxed and shipped from England, had never arrived, since the ship on which they traveled had been captured by a French privateer. Latrobe was forced to draw upon his remarkable visual memory; often, his drawings displayed his rich imagination.

Latrobe realized that few of his new countrymen recognized the need for the kind of architectural skill he had to sell. When he did manage to find American customers for his designs, the level of building expertise he had taken for granted in England was rare or even unknown. He worked to master the art of teaching his customers to see; equally important, as he observed, he needed "*to make the men*" who would make his buildings, to train the tradesmen in the crafts required to construct buildings as he envisioned them. The evidence of his disappointment was at hand: He could lay claim to just three buildings in Virginia in three years, and in each case, Latrobe acknowledged, "my intentions have been entirely overthrown."

But during his months on his island, he had devised a means of expressing the power of his imagination; the drawings in his portfolios had provided him with that outlet. As he noted inside the cover of the third portfolio, "During my residence in Virginia . . . my *fancy* was kept employed in building castles in the air." He painted an elegant watercolor for that album's frontispiece, which showed the Pennock and Harvie houses on terra firma, but above were ten unbuilt projects suspended in the clouds, unrealized dreams floating on air. Inside the album were plans for a grand masonry country house worthy of an English aristocrat; a slightly more modest domed villa; a church; and garden temples that he once had hoped might adorn the landscape garden of some Virginia gentleman. He illustrated each in his most professional fashion with elevations, sections, and even perspectives of the various projects.

The portfolio offered a thirty-four-page sampling of what he could do, but there had been a more immediate satisfaction in executing the drawings, too, particularly those for the Captain William Pennock House: They gave him the chance to correct the wrongs done to his first Virginia commission. He drew the presentation drawings in the portfolio not for Pennock but for himself and, perhaps, later publication. He knew how Robert Adam and his brothers launched themselves in London with their books; he hoped one day to do the same.

Two of the sheets devoted to Pennock's house featured plans of each floor and a front elevation of the three-story house. They revealed Latrobe's cleverness in giving the house a symmetrical front while enclosing a compact, asymmetrical plan. They were beautifully executed, but remained essentially two-dimensional diagrams, practical line drawings made to convey information. He drew them with basic tools—a square, two rulers (one with an angled or beveled shape), a pointed instrument that scored or impressed lines on the paper to be inked, and a compass to pick up measurements for transfer.

On the third sheet, he added a third dimension. Labeled in his copperplate script "View in Perspective of Mr. Pennock's Hall and Staircase," it contained a tour de force of the architectural illustrator's art. In executing this drawing, Latrobe drew upon the theatrical effects he mastered as a watercolorist. He offered an exhilarating vignette of life in the Pennock house. His picture invited the viewer to observe the stair hall just inside the front door. Two guests have arrived and are making their way upward to the main floor, bound for the drawing room. They climb a flying staircase; at the landing above, the lady of the house waits to greet her company, the curved rear wall of the room embracing her from behind. The ceiling is lightly ornamented, with a rosette at its center; the checkerboard pavers on the ground anchor the rising space.

Using no more than India ink and a pale watercolor palette, Latrobe showed his new American friends a new kind of architecture. The illusion offered by his perspectives seemed so real that at least one contemporary would describe such drawings as "architectural charlatanism"; the drawings were so vivid that they seemed too good to be true. And the house itself was not the standard, center-hall mansion well known to the Virginia gentry with a long, low, narrow passage. Captain Pennock's hall seemed to rise upward, its curvilinear shapes dramatized by the play of light from the windows. The experience it promised was unprecedented. Latrobe was manipulating more than wood, plaster, and brick; he employed in his composition a visual vocabulary that consisted of air, space, light, and shadow. What he created on the page differed from standard-issue English Neoclassicism, too, as he was finding his own voice, independent of his English masters.

Even with friends like George Washington, Latrobe had found it difficult to launch a career in his adopted land. But he had devised a way to do it by himself, using paperwork plans of a brilliance and persuasiveness never before seen in America.

In his perspective drawing of Captain Pennock's entry passage, Latrobe deceives the viewer, having removed an interior wall in the foreground to make the view possible; the close vanishing point produces a pitched ceiling and steeply sloping floor. But the drawing anticipates much of Latrobe's later work and his ambition to create inspiring spaces on compact plans, relying less on ornament than was customary and more on a harmony of openness and curving lines and planes. *Library of Congress/ Prints and Photographs Division*

V.
April 1798 . . . A Journey to Philadelphia

TO LATROBE, THE AMERICAN METROPOLIS had seemed inevitable but, somehow, unattainable. He had family nearby, as his mother's brother lived in Pennsylvania. He had heard a great deal about the place, prompting him to confide in a friend, "My affections, my vanity, my ambition all coincide to point out Philadelphia as the only situation in which I ought to reside." Still, he had difficulty persuading himself to travel there, explaining, "By some inchantment I find myself unable to stir from Virginia."

At last, in March of 1798, he embarked on his first journey to Philadelphia, his purpose twofold. Publicly, he let it be known that in relation to his own prison design he wished to acquaint himself with the Walnut Street

Gaol; it was a 1774 structure that had recently been enlarged and updated as the Pennsylvania state prison. Privately, still stung by the paltry payment terms of "a Salary of £200.0 Per Annum" for his work at Virginia's "Penitentiary house," he went in pursuit of another job. Word had reached him of a new Quaker school to be built in Philadelphia, a commission he wanted to win.

The journey took him through Fredericksburg, Baltimore, and Wilmington, among other places, but the city on the Schuylkill that rainy April was unlike any other in America. It was the nation's wealthiest city and remained its capital, as the government was not scheduled to move to the Federal City for two more years. Silversmiths, dealing as they did in goods with assayable values at a time when American currency was in flux, produced work in the newest London styles for rich and powerful patrons, as did furniture-makers, painters, craftsmen, and artisans of all sorts. As a fashionable place, Philadelphia drew men of talent and aspiration; some met with great success, others with ill fortune. Latrobe witnessed both when, on one of his first days in the city, he made his way to an incomplete house, one designed by Pierre Charles L'Enfant after his Federal City dismissal.

L'Enfant had designed a grandiose marble and brick pile for the former senator, financier, and China trader Robert Morris; its unfinished state resulted from the spectacular collapse of Morris's empire, which landed him in the very gaol Latrobe had come to examine. Latrobe had been curious to see the Morris house, having "frequently been told in Virginia . . . it was the *hand*somest thing in America." When he caught sight of it, however, he quickly dubbed it "the monster," adding, "Indeed I can scarcely at this moment believe in the existence of . . . its complicated, unintelligible, mass."

The enormous house—it was some 120 feet long and at least 60 feet deep—was set on its own square between Walnut and Chestnut Streets. "I went several times to the spot and gazed upon it with astonishment," Latrobe reported. "It is impossible to decide which of the two is the maddest, the architect, or his employer." He was shocked by the ostentatious display of wealth in a taste that he called "irresistibly laughable" and "violently ugly." Although Morris's and other Philadelphia buildings he saw were out of sync with true classical design, Latrobe was nevertheless gratified to see buildings on which money had been lavished to pay for fine white marble and the workmen to carve it. He could not help but think to himself that opportunities must lie in a city where such wealth could be put in the service of architecture.

Latrobe arrived with letters of introduction from well-connected Virginia friends. One of them brought him into the presence of the new vice president, Thomas Jefferson, a man who, Latrobe had been told, shared his passionate belief in the power of good architecture. Another letter, addressed to Samuel Mickle Fox, elicited a dinner invitation. Philadelphia had become the new nation's financial center, and Fox was president of the powerful Bank of Pennsylvania.

At Fox's dinner table, Latrobe listened absent-mindedly as Fox regaled the guests with his plans for the bank's future. Disinterested in financial matters, Latrobe grew attentive only when Fox mentioned the proposed construction of a new "Banking house." He soon found himself distracted again as the conversation swirled around him. He fell to sketching, producing a simple sketch of how he envisioned Mr. Fox's new bank might appear. When the evening ended, he handed the drawing to his host as a courtesy. It was the work of but a few moments and he had not "the remotest expectations of its ever being executed."

At the end of his two-week stay, he judged the journey to have been a mixed success. He held out little hope for his prospects at the Quaker school, but he had toured the gaol and dined with its director. He had made contact not only with Jefferson, but with other companions who provided the kinds of intellectual company he so sorely wished for in Virginia. He soon wrote to one of them, "I shall be the happier and the better throughout my life for having spent a fortnight among you." The company reawakened his desire for scientific inquiry, and he set to work on a learned paper concerning Virginia geology that he hoped one day to present to the American Philosophical Society in Philadelphia, America's chief scientific association.

In addition to examining L'Enfant's domestic folly for Robert Morris, Latrobe had visited the future capital the Frenchman had laid out. His route to Philadelphia had taken him through the Federal City, where he had the good fortune to meet Dr. William Thornton. Thornton had been so kind as to escort him personally around the Capitol and Latrobe had, with reservations, been quite impressed. On his return trip, Latrobe had made a point of stopping again "in the Fœderal City, during which time I rambled over the Capitol."

Back in Richmond, he felt Philadelphia's pull more than ever; it was the finest city he had seen since London, and he wondered whether his future awaited him there. But he had a job to complete in Richmond and no prospects of one anywhere else—until, that is, he received a letter from Philadelphia in July. The sender was Samuel Fox.

The shareholders, Fox advised, had appointed Latrobe architect for the new headquarters of the Bank of Pennsylvania. When he read Fox's words, Latrobe required a moment to grasp what the message conveyed. But there it was: Fox had written not only to give him word of his quite unexpected appointment, but to press him to draft corrected plans and to draw up necessary building instructions in order that construction could commence.

He must go Philadelphia, Latrobe realized, but he knew he must not until he had "finished every thing that could possibly be done this Season at the Penitentiary house." Certainly he owed the Virginians that much. But *the Bank of Pennsylvania!* The feelings of surprise, elation, and . . . yes, perhaps, even vindication . . . were inevitable. After all, he had just been handed the most important private building project of the day.

VI.
1798 and After . . . A Masterpiece Emerges . . . The Bank of Pennsylvania

ONE LITTLE PEN-AND-INK STUDY HAD WON HIM THE JOB. He had tossed off his drawing on the Philadelphia visit but, as Latrobe knew very well, what Mr. Fox had bought was really less a building than the rendering of a momentary reverie. The true challenge was now at hand, and Latrobe sat down to the work of designing the Bank of Pennsylvania.

He did not believe in starting with the face of a building. Instead, he sketched the location of the rooms on the main floor of the structure, drawn as if seen from above. "[First] your *plan*, that is, your distribution should be settled," as he advised a Virginia friend.

His initial doodlings were just that, crude outlines of the spaces. Latrobe used no straightedge and made no attempt to work to scale. His aim was to devise an approximate scheme that accommodated the uses to which the building would be put. He worked to anticipate which were to be public and which private spaces, and to imagine the flow from one to another. One sketch led to a second version, and then a third. When Latrobe learned that the Bank in its temporary quarters in Carpenters' Hall had suffered a major

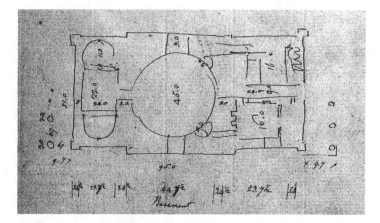

By the time he drew this preliminary floor plan for the Bank of Pennsylvania, probably in
November 1798, Latrobe had decided upon the basic arrangement.
Maryland Historical Society, Baltimore, Maryland

robbery in early September, he felt added pressure to complete the plan and
travel to Philadelphia.

He incorporated certain agreed-upon elements consistent with the drawing he had left with Samuel Fox. The main façade, looking east onto Second
Street, was to have a temple front, just as the Virginia Capitol did. Visitors to
the Bank would enter a vestibule through a central door on the entrance
porch. A long, windowless hall then would lead past offices to the left and
right for the president and cashier and into the central section of the building. There, within the square footprint of the middle third of the structure,
was to be a circular banking hall. Filling the rear third of the plan would be
the stockholders' meeting room, a space longer than it was wide, running per-
pendicular to the structure's main axis. Its core was square, but its north and
south ends semicircular. Unlike Richmond's focal building, the Bank of
Pennsylvania would have a matching portico to the rear, which would function as a porch overlooking the enclosed garden and provide private access
for bank officials.

Latrobe refined the room sizes. He worked on one pen-and-ink drawing in
the back of a sketchbook. The sheet wasn't large, only 7 by 10 1/4 inches, but
it incorporated estimated dimensions. He had determined the rotunda would
be 45 feet in diameter; on the plan he jotted "45.0" at the banking hall's center. The columns? Their diameter, in feet, was to be "3.0."

He drew a similar schematic of the upper floor, and it revealed more of the
three-dimensional geometry of the design. The banking hall would rise two

full stories; the one-story stockholders' room to the rear would have apsidal ends. He studied these plans, and "devoted the greatest share of . . . attention to the economy of room and convenience of . . . public use."

Latrobe increased the size of the paper on which he worked when he went to the next step. He had established the precise dimensions of the building, 53 feet wide and 148 feet long. That enabled him in drafting the main floor plan to use a one eighth-inch scale (with one inch on the drawing to represent eight feet of the proposed building). He produced plans for the basement and second levels next, resolving the location of fireplaces, chimney flues, staircases, windows and doors, and the bank vaults.

Latrobe believed "the elevations must grow out of the plan," so having drawn the fundamental features to scale, he set to work on the front and sides of the building: He established the size and pattern of the openings and the floor levels. The work was painstaking, as exactingly drawn elevations were required for each of the four sides of the building.

Sectional drawings came next. Latrobe was inventing a big, complicated stone box by drawing flat pictures on paper, and the sections in particular revealed mistakes and inconsistencies. Imagining his building guillotined along a designated plane, he drew the resulting cross section, which showed the details of construction. The curves of the banking room's domed ceiling and of the shareholder's room's half-domed ends appeared along with the vaulting in the cellar below. Thanks to his intimate knowledge of the interrelationship of his various views—Latrobe constantly referred back to the floor plans and elevations, adding vault lines, amending and correcting oversights—he was able to explore the building's parts from within and without. By making such extensive preliminary drawings, he came to know very well how the Bank of Pennsylvania was to be built.

THE TECHNICAL DRAWINGS TOOK TIME, as did Latrobe's work at the penitentiary. He had packing to do and farewells to make, but as the leaves fell from the trees, he planned his departure. On November 30, he wrote to Governor Wood to tell him of his imminent journey.

On arriving in Philadelphia in early December 1798, Latrobe's first task was to complete the presentation drawings for the Bank of Pennsylvania. The design had progressed well and his first set of elevations, floor plans, and sections were in hand. While Latrobe was confident that *he* knew what he wanted the Bank of Pennsylvania to look like, he also realized that for the

uninitiated, his geometric drawings would look like fragments. For the annual shareholders' meeting on February 1, Samuel Fox needed more in order
to present the building Latrobe proposed; for that, a perspective drawing of
the sort he had done of the Pennock entrance hall would be necessary. Only
this time Latrobe would illustrate the exterior of the building. The bankers
were concerned with the impression the bank would make on the world, and
that would begin with its appearance on the streetscape.

Latrobe walked from his room on Twelfth Street to the proposed site, examining the neighboring buildings and the configuration of the streets. As
was his habit, he made sketches in his memorandum book. Then he returned
to his living quarters, in the home of his friend William Maclure, a well-to-
do merchant and himself a recent arrival from Scotland. At Maclure's he set
out his drawing tools and went to his reserve of Whatman wove, the finest
English watercolor paper. The bright white paper was expensive, and he used
it only for presentation drawings. He selected one large sheet, moistened it,
then stretched it taut over his drawing board; this would prevent the later oc-
currence of the watercolor wrinkles he called "cockles." Folds he made at the
perimeter of the paper enabled him to attach the sheet to the edges of the
drawing board with tacks or adhesive.

While his previous drawings had been exacting records of two-dimensional
planes, this time Latrobe would offer Mr. Fox and his partners the illusion
that they were seeing the building from a point of view diagonally across the
street. Thus he made Second Street the main axis of the drawing, rising at a
low angle from the lower-right corner of the sheet and running to the opposite side. He then selected a point roughly a third of the line's length from
the left-hand edge, and extended a second line, rising just above the horizontal to represent westbound Lodge Street. The near corner of the building
would be set in the oblique angle where the lines intersected; that same angle
would be the drawing's point of convergence.

Working from the plans and elevations at hand, he began transferring
some of the basic horizontal and vertical lines. This time, however, the building's horizontals would not be parallel to one another; the further the lines of
the foundation and the roof were from the near corner, the closer they became. By using the convention of the vanishing point, Latrobe could give his
three-quarter view of the Bank a surprisingly lifelike quality. As he sketched
in the building, he used a hard graphite pencil so he could correct mistakes,
as well as vary the weight of the line.

The dramatic perspective of the Bank of Pennsylvania helped to sell Samuel Fox on the design—as Latrobe explained, it "has a good effect as a piece of scenery." Note the tall man on Lodge Street: Might it be Latrobe himself? *Maryland Historical Society, Baltimore, Maryland*

Unlike the Roman-inspired portico at the Virginia Capitol, the one he drew for the Bank had the proportions of a Greek temple. During Latrobe's London years, Greek antiquity had begun to be understood in a new way. Thanks in part to M. Clérisseau's old friend, Johann Joachim Winckelmann, the Greek was appreciated as distinct from the Roman. That Greek culture had preceded the rise of the Roman Empire was an insight new to his father's generation, but Latrobe was ready to put it to use. He thought the bold scale of the Greek temple with its large columns and the tall assemblage of moldings above (the entablature) very tasty; he also liked its relative simplicity of ornament.

From his own study of books devoted to Greek architecture, Latrobe had come to disagree with Palladio's notions that there were "fixed rules for the most minute parts of the orders. The Greeks," Latrobe opined, "knew of no such rules, but having established *general* proportions and laws of form and arrangement, all matters of detail were left to the talent and taste of individual architects." The implied freedom suited him, too, as he was unafraid of hybrids. Rather than copying an older building, as Jefferson had chosen to do, he felt confident in taking a more eclectic approach. That meant that while he knew all the windows and doors in ancient Greek structures had horizontal heads, he complemented his Grecian temple façade with three

Roman arch-topped principal windows on each side of the Bank. And the central section of the building was dominated by a Pantheon-like dome, enclosing a distinctly Roman rotunda.

Once satisfied with the appearance of the building, he set about inking over the pencilled lines. He used India ink because of its stability. His English training had introduced him to translucent watercolors and, after the ink had dried and he had erased any visible pencil lines, he dampened the whole sheet again before applying a translucent wash to selected areas. When it dried, the wash would appear suffused with a soft radiance, highlighting the areas left untreated, which remained bright and reflective. To indicate modeling he added other shading, too, with graded neutral washes to indicate shadows and the position of the sun.

The tinted drawing was becoming an effective illusion, but Latrobe added one more pictorial element: people. He sketched a Quaker man, waiting with arms crossed on the portico, and a fashionably dressed couple who conversed nearby. He drew two women parading down Lodge Street, one in a Quaker cap. The street, two flanking buildings, a few trees, and the Bank—their sum was an atmospheric landscape. Function was no longer the watchword, for now Latrobe was looking to display his building to best advantage, to appeal to his client's tastes.

When he regarded his finished watercolor drawing, he looked at a pretty picture, one created using the techniques of the watercolorist. The earlier drawings would be of practical use in executing working drawings to guide the builders, but he fully expected that this perspective would remain with the client. He knew, too, that this would not be the final design; for one thing, he himself wasn't yet sure what configuration the dome should take. He, along with Fox and company, would have to resolve a number of issues before the design became final and he could begin the working drawings.

Those would be done on coarser paper, stock with ragged edges and a duller finish. He would need to draft many working drawings to guide the workmen. After his experience in Virginia, he knew an umbilical was necessary to connect his pen to the hands of the workmen; he would be asking them to perform tasks and produce forms unfamiliar to the average Philadelphia craftsman. If Latrobe wanted the men to execute the building as he envisioned it, he would have to show them not only how it was to look but how the pieces were shaped, how they went together. His working drawings would make that possible, and there would be times, he knew, when he would work at a larger scale, drawing building parts at quarter-, half-, or even actual size.

First, however, his presentation drawings would have to persuade Mr. Fox to proceed.

SAMUEL FOX LIKED WHAT HE SAW. The design was quickly finalized, with the addition of a cupola and upper story windows. On February 26 a contract was signed with the masons, who, to Latrobe's relief, were headed by a recently arrived Scotsman trained abroad. Fox and Latrobe were in attendance as the cornerstone was laid on April 5, 1799. The cellar arches were completed by July. The bank opened for business on June 29, 1801, but by the time Fiske Kimball learned of the Bank of Pennsylvania, the building was gone, having been demolished in 1867.

His article "The Bank of Pennsylvania, 1799" in the *Architectural Record* told the building's story for the generations who could no longer visit the edifice. "Among the works of art long since swept away by the ruthless, unexampled growth of cities in America," Kimball wrote, "none was more beautiful than the masterpiece created by Latrobe in his first monumental work on our soil—the Bank of Pennsylvania." He hastened to add, lest his readers fail to realize they were in the presence of an important rediscovery, "No photograph or drawing of it has ever been published."

A Latrobe descendant, Charles H. Latrobe, son of B. H. Latrobe Jr., was responsible for introducing Kimball to the building. Charles had gifted the perspective drawing his grandfather had done for Samuel Fox to the Maryland Historical Society in 1897. The drawing hung in the Society's galleries—and it had stopped Kimball in his tracks. As he concluded in the *Architectural Record*, it represented nothing less than "our first competent example of preliminary perspective drawing." Perspective drawings hadn't seemed important before—typically, when the advertisement had been placed for the President's House, the commissioners asked for site plans, elevations, and sections, but made no mention of perspectives. They didn't know what to ask for; only later did American patrons realize what they were missing.

The shards of the story were there for Kimball to reassemble. In Ferdie Latrobe's collection at Bel Air he found a twenty-eight-page manuscript inside an album labeled "Family Journal." Written by John H. B. Latrobe, the "Memoir of Benjamin Henry Latrobe" knit family recollections into an abbreviated life of Latrobe. Despite the fact that John Latrobe (1803–1891) had yet to be conceived when the Bank of Pennsylvania was built, the "Memoir" included such vignettes as the making of the dinner-time sketch for Samuel Fox. John's role as family historian was made possible by the fact that as a child he heard his father's stories firsthand and worked in his office as a teenager. Later he would be an inventor and a lawyer specializing in patent law, as well as a writer recounting the events of his father's life as the man himself had told them.

For Kimball, though, the life facts were less compelling than what the building represented. "This was the first attempt on this side of the water to substitute Greek detail, with its superior refinement, for academic or Roman forms—a step quite in consonance with modern ideas, but then entirely new in America." Kimball noted, too, that "in construction the building was quite as novel as in design, for it was vaulted throughout in masonry. . . . There was nothing anywhere in the states comparable to the great domed banking room and the suites of fireproof offices which Latrobe provided." He made bold claims for Latrobe but, because of the voluminous Latrobe archives, he had the substantiation to back them up.

In Latrobe's architectural drawings Kimball also saw a recognizably modern way of working. Washington had given his workers at Mount Vernon little more than a crude elevation to guide them; in contrast, Latrobe's freehand sketches made clear that he developed the program of a building first, then prepared scaled floor plans and elevations. The extravagant presentation perspectives came next, and Kimball saw in them some of the most beautiful architectural renderings he had ever encountered. As an art historian, Kimball recognized Latrobe was not merely a draftsman but a master of the line and a gifted watercolorist, one who used shading and light effects to make the buildings seem almost real.

Samuel Fox proved to be everything his Virginian predecessors had not been. He took a chance on Latrobe who, for all his training, wasn't yet a master architect; he had executed only a few commissions in England and his Virginia work hadn't met even his own expectations. But Fox gave Latrobe almost complete creative freedom, underwriting a fully vaulted building. It had been Fox who insisted the Bank be constructed of Pennsylvania marble, and the building set a new standard for stonework in America, not only with its vaulting but with the quality of its ashlar (cut and squared stone) masonry. Mr. Fox's building cost a great deal of money—$228,000 was a mighty sum for the time—and the price tag, Kimball wrote, "lay the architect open to criticism." Yet Latrobe had fewer disputes in constructing the Bank than on any other project in his career. He was compensated reasonably well, too, receiving a fee of $4,000.

The Bank of Pennsylvania excited those who saw it both as a homage to the past ("a neat specimen of the Ionic order," remarked one contemporary, "taken from an ancient Greek temple") and as a building well adapted to its uses. Latrobe himself, Kimball reported, valued most "the unaffected praise" of a layman. Writing in his journal in 1806, Latrobe recalled that "walking up second Strt. I observed two french Officers standing opposite to the building and looking at it without saying a word. I stept into a shop, and stood close to them. After some time one of them . . . exclaimed several times, *Si beau! Et si simple!* He said no more, and stood for more than quarter of an hour longer before he walked away with his companion."

The Bank of Pennsylvania was much admired in its time, but for Latrobe the French soldier's unguarded utterance—*So beautiful! And so simple!*—was "the highest encomium, and the most flattering I ever received, relative to the Bank of Pennsylvania."

VII.
January 26–27, 1801 . . . The Waterworks . . . Centre Square, Philadelphia

LATROBE HAD A SURPRISE FOR HIS CRITICS. For nearly two years, his ears had been filled with their insults. A man of delicate temperament despite his thick, imposing frame, his nervous stomach turned somersaults when he heard such published attacks as the one that described his plan as "a confused and enormously expensive project of '*aerial Castles*.'" But he would quiet their querulous voices. His Waterworks *would* work, of that he was certain, and this night he would prove it.

Even before he had been consulted, Latrobe had known something had to be done. The vile taste and odor of much of Philadelphia's water had repelled him on his first visit to the city. With no municipal supply, the drinking water was drawn from shallow wells dug down to a bed of sand ten to thirty feet below grade. Some of those wells produced potable water but most did not, since the city also lacked a system of sanitation. As Latrobe observed, runoff and waste from privies found its way into "bog hole[s], sunk into the ground at different depths. Many of them are pierced to the sand."

Enlightened and influential Philadelphians had for years been considering a plan to divert water from the Schuylkill River about four miles upstream. To employ gravity as the Romans had done almost two millennia earlier, the plan called for the water to be directed into a proposed canal that would bring it to the city. The length of the aqueduct and the irregular terrain presented problems that, in the absence of trained engineers, proved problematic to surveyors more familiar with measuring the land than reshaping it. Latrobe's new patron, Samuel Fox, and the other members of the Watering Committee charged by Philadelphia's governing councils, approached him soon after his move to the city, hoping he would have a solution.

And here he stood at Centre Square, twenty-five months to the day later, ready to demonstrate that they had indeed consulted the right man.

Back in 1798, he had required just two days to draft the proposal he delivered on December 29. Titled "VIEW OF THE PRACTICABILITY AND MEANS OF SUPPLYING THE CITY OF PHILADELPHIA WITH WHOLESOME WATER," the document drew upon his knowledge of municipal systems in Europe. As an apprentice in Smeaton's engineering office, he had come to know pumping stations in London, just as Jefferson had studied the fourteen waterwheels of the Machine at Marly. Latrobe had little choice but to draw upon European precedents, as there were none in the United States to follow.

Instead of diverting water upstream, Latrobe proposed building a settling basin at the riverbank adjacent to the city. To create the basin, his plan called for two parallel earthwork walls to extend into the river, terminating at a masonry wall facing the opposite shore. A gate in the end wall would be opened at ebb tide, when the water was less brackish and muddy, to allow flow into the basin. When the basin filled, the gate would be closed and the sediment allowed to settle; then a sluice on the landward side of the basin would be opened to admit water to a 200-foot-long canal. From there it would flow through a 400-foot-long tunnel to be dug and blasted into the bank that rose precipitously from the river. At the tunnel's end, a deep well, lined with eighteen inches of brick, would rise to the surface above. It was a major engineering project requiring substantial excavation just for the canal, which was to be more than a dozen feet deep and forty feet wide.

And that was but half of what Latrobe had proposed.

Atop the well would stand the Schuylkill Engine House, with a steam engine inside to raise the water the forty-eight feet from the tunnel below to street level. Latrobe's detractors, some of whom had invested in the earlier

canal scheme, derided his approach, one of them asserting "*steam-engines . . .
are [the] machines of all machinery that are least to be relied on, subject to
casualties and accidents of every kind.*" But the Watering Committee had
few such reservations.

From the Schuylkill Engine House the water supply was to flow through
another tunnel, one buried just below the streets. This tunnel would extend
almost a mile to Centre Square at the intersection of Philadelphia's central
roadways, Broad and Market Streets. There, a second Engine House would
contain pumps to raise the water again, this time to a 7,500-gallon reservoir
in the building's attic. Finally, gravity would be employed to carry the supply
of fresh water to the city through a network of wooden distribution pipes.

The plan had been adopted, and now the tunnels and the Centre Square
pump house stood ready to be tested. Just this afternoon Latrobe had instructed the workers to leave the street hydrants open. It was of no moment
to them, and they complied. Only Latrobe, three of his friends (among them,
perhaps, Mr. Fox?), and one workman knew for certain that this was to be the
night of the ultimate test.

Latrobe had been reminded almost daily that his waterworks was due and
overdue. His initial proposal had been overly optimistic, calling for completion in July 1799, in time for summer and the yellow fever season. "Yellow
Jack" epidemics in the 1790s had killed thousands of Philadelphians and, according to the latest thinking, might be the result of the city's tainted water.
But now the project was late *and* way over budget, both factors that added to
the fusillade of criticism. Still, Latrobe felt ill-used. What he was doing was
unprecedented, so how could he have known? And he felt entirely confident
the system would be all that he had promised. A preliminary test of the
Schuylkill Engine House had been successful, and Latrobe hoped and believed that he was on the verge of vindication.

Once night arrived and the city drifted toward sleep, Latrobe issued another order. The fire was kindled beneath the boiler at the Centre Square station. Hours would be required to raise steam in the wooden boiler, which had
been assembled of white pine planks and lined with iron. Large, rectangular
flues passed through it, radiating the heat from the fire to the water in the
tank before venting the smoke into the brick chimneys. As the fire began its
work, Latrobe settled in for a night of high anticipation, of watching coal being fed into the firebox and periodically opening the cocks at the top of the
steam gauges to check for rising pressure.

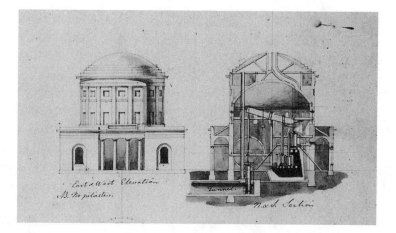

"Sketch for a design of an Engine house and Wateroffice in the City of Philadelphia March 1799. BH Latrobe archt." *Maryland Historical Society, Baltimore, Maryland*

DARKNESS SHROUDED THE SCENE, but during those hours any Philadelphian who happened by might have caught a shadowy glimpse of the Centre Square building. He might have thought it odd to see smoke billowing from the top of the Engine House, but hurrying home on a cold January night, he probably would not have worried about it. And certainly a passerby would not have known he was an unwitting witness to a historic merging of industrial technology and architecture, as well as civil and hydraulic engineering.

Beneath the street was the tunnel, which extended back to the Schuykill Engine House; the steam engine there had already filled the upper tunnel with river water. The countless gallons had been drawn up through the well, which had been dug at great danger, as the treacherous soil had collapsed once during construction. The completion of the earthworks below—the lower tunnel, the canal, and riverside basin—amounted to a major engineering feat in itself.

In the moonlight, the silhouette of the building in Centre Square resembled no other in Philadelphia. The base was rectangular, just one story high. An upper level rose from the center of the base like the second layer of a wedding cake, but this structure was cylindrical rather than square. At the very top, the coal smoke did not appear to emerge from a chimney but from the apex of the dome that capped the second-story drum. Blurred by darkness and not yet complete, the composition was an exercise in pure geometry, a hemisphere atop a cylinder stacked upon a cubic podium.

The drawings Latrobe had presented the Watering Committee revealed a building that, to the student of architectural history, took its shape from Roman temples used as tombs. It was a structure with four faces at ground level, each looking out with a certain hauteur at the cityscape around it. Though the immense columns were not yet in place, the openings at the center of the east and west façades would be recessed porticos, executed in the bold Greek Doric Order.

Latrobe could claim both Roman and Greek ancestry for his design of the building's exterior, but inside, where he and his companions waited, antiquity had been superseded by modernity. The large steam engine, rising from the basement, filled the circular core of the building; the surrounding space in the first-floor structure contained compartments for waterworks workers. The great machine had been installed under the supervision of its designer, James Smallman, who had formerly worked for James Watt and Matthew Boulton, whose firm monopolized steam engine production in England. Suspended horizontally from the building's heavy wooden frame at ceiling level was the working beam of the engine, which would pivot at its center on bearing blocks when the engine was in operation. Connected to the working beam was the piston rod, which was to be driven by the steam cylinder. The other end of the beam, seesaw-like, would drive the piston rod that operated the pump. A third rod would crank the sixteen-foot wooden flywheel that, weighted by its cast-iron rim, would moderate the fluctuating speed of the reciprocating steam piston into a smoother motion. The assemblage of pieces—many of wood, some of cast iron, others of both—filled the room. There were the engine's thirty-two-inch steam cylinder, the three smaller cylinders of the pump, the pipes that ascended to (and descended from) the wooden reservoir in the attic, the immense flywheel, the working beam, the firebox, the boiler, and the masonry chimney that corbeled to the center of the dome. This was not the technology of antiquity, but Latrobe had designed a classical building to house the steam works, one that would "combine ornament with utility."

As dawn approached, the steam had risen in the boiler and the four men inside the Engine House prepared to start the engine. The process involved more than simply opening a valve, as steam alone would not provide enough power to bring the engine to life. Start up required manpower, too, to overcome the inertia of the heavy engine and the double-acting pump which would move water on both the up and down strokes.

When the moment arrived, the steam valve was opened, producing a hiss as the steam gained entry to the cylinder. But it was not the piston in the main cylinder that set the giant mechanism in motion; it was a large pry bar, attached to the flywheel. And it was muscle power, applied to the bar, that moved the flywheel, at first almost imperceptibly. As steam was fed into the engine, men strained at the bar, but the bar had only just begun to move in its arc when it had to be repositioned on the circumference of the sixteen-foot wheel. More pushing produced further rotation.

The seesaw motion of the working beam also began, and, in turn, the beam drove the up-and-down motion of the pistons in the pump. With more pushing, the flywheel groaned another increment, and the bar was repositioned again. The start-up was arduous, with one man monitoring the steam that fed the cylinder, while the others barred the engine, turning the wheel a half cycle, once around, and then again, as the mechanism began to move faster and more easily. The rods and linkages rose and fell, accompanied by the groans of the wood and the clanking of the metal parts. The noises in the Engine House included the gasps and hisses of the steam entering and escaping the cylinder. Gradually, the inertia of the great mechanism was overcome. As the thrust of the steam cylinder took over, the flywheel seemed miraculously to have a momentum of its own. The barring, once needed to maintain the engine's motion, became unnecessary.

The engine had begun to run. With the cylinder powering the beam and the pump, the machine lumbered along, soon reaching its expected speed of about twelve revolutions per minute. The working beam rose and fell; the spokes of the flywheel turned, faster than the sweep hand on a watch but hardly a blur to those watching. To Latrobe it was a moment to cherish—but another sound would prove even sweeter.

Amid the engine's din, Latrobe listened for the *whoosh* of water. Yes, he could hear it, the fresh water drawn from the Chestnut Street tunnel sloshing into the tank overhead, producing an audible wave action as the stroking of the pump delivered gallon after gallon in rhythmic bursts. The steam engine was running, the pump was pumping, and the water system was ready to function. But the ultimate proof he wished to offer the townspeople of Philadelphia, the doubters and the believers alike, remained to be demonstrated.

The cistern in the attic was filling, meaning that water soon could be released to the 18-inch pipe connected to the distributing chest buried on the east side of the building. The chest could hold some 250 gallons, but when the water flowed into the chest, Latrobe knew, it would quickly flow through holes in the sides that led to the water mains on Broad, Market, Arch, Race, and Chestnuts Streets. Those mains were of white oak and yellow pine logs, joined at their ends with iron hoops. The inside diameter had been bored to

6 inches, while subsidiary branches to come would have inside diameters of 3, 3 1/2, and 4 1/2 inches. For the time being, upright pipes that rose three feet above street level would provide access to the water. Each had two cocks, one of 3/4-inch bore for common use, the other of 2 1/2-inch bore for use in watering streets and in case of fire.

At sunrise, the white marble Centre Square Engine House in its parklike setting emerged from the gloom. The building bore little ornamentation, as Latrobe had chosen simple recessed arches for its openings and minimal architectural detail. From it a new noise emerged, too, as a loud, awkward-looking utilitarian steam engine chugged and hissed and billowed smoke. But on nearby Broad Street, water—at first a trickle, then a stream—had begun in the early morning hours to emerge from the hydrants. The flow had grown steadier as the system filled, and other hydrants on other streets also produced a flow.

The early risers that day in Philadelphia were greeting by streams of fresh, clear water running in the gutters of their fair city—compliments of Mr. Latrobe.

VIII.
1804 . . . Mr. Peale's museum . . . The Old Capitol, Philadelphia

CHARLES WILLSON PEALE PAINTED so many early American worthies that it is no surprise to find that he painted a portrait of Benjamin Henry Latrobe. As active members of the American Philosophical Society, the two men had become friends. The Society had elected Latrobe to its ranks in July of 1799, and he found himself free to explore a wide range of his interests at the nation's principal association of men engaged in scientific inquiry. He wrote about and debated geology and flora and fauna with a coterie of men with hungry minds, among them Mr. Peale.

The man in the portrait looks confident—and for good reason. He had just enjoyed what would be the best half-decade of his life. His Bank of Philadelphia received universal acclaim as a work of architecture worthy of the world's attention and a prototype of the American Grecian style. Even as he sat for Mr. Peale, his Philadelphia Waterworks just a few blocks away delivered ample clean water to the entire city. Latrobe got national recognition for perhaps the most notable engineering feat yet achieved in America, with its two steam engines and some 30,000 feet of wooden pipes.

In his private life, the widower Latrobe had also found new happiness. On May 1, 1800, he had married Mary Elizabeth Hazlehurst, the daughter of a prominent Philadelphia merchant (his benefactor, Samuel Fox, may have played a role in this, too, as the bride's father, Isaac, was a longtime friend and business associate of Fox's). Mary Elizabeth had proved of generous and affectionate spirit, welcoming Latrobe's two children from his previous marriage as if they were her own. While their firstborn had died at two months of age, she had since presented her husband with a healthy son, John Hazlehurst Boneval Latrobe, in 1803, and a daughter, Julia, in the July just past. To Latrobe, a man who valued domestic happiness above even his work, Mary Elizabeth had been nothing short of a godsend.

The conventions of portraiture having changed since he painted his friend Mr. Buckland thirty years earlier, Peale surrounded Latrobe with no symbolic books or building fragments. The head and shoulders of Latrobe himself dominated the modest canvas, some 19 inches wide and 22 inches high. In his pose, Latrobe has shifted his spectacles to the top of his head, where they are half obscured by the tendrils of his curly hair. His glasses were a fixture, as he was unable to read or draw without them ("I am only half alive without their assistance," Latrobe once explained, "having worn them incessantly since my 17th Year"). He wears a green coat, its brown edging a match for his auburn hair and dark brown eyes.

Latrobe was poised to take on great projects. By 1804 he had been appointed engineer of the Chesapeake and Delaware Canal. He had been hired to redesign the Chestnut Street Theatre. Just as his Bank had been the first Greek Revival building in America, Sedgeley, a fine country house he designed for a Philadelphia client, had been the first American example of the Gothic Revival. Another pending project was a Roman Catholic cathedral for the Baltimore Diocese, and its monumental plans were taking shape in his mind.

He had assembled a staff, including a copying clerk, draftsmen, and even pupils. For individual projects, he had clerks of the works to be on-site at ongoing projects, especially those outside Philadelphia. His American doldrums seemed so clearly at an end that he wrote to Christian Ignatius Latrobe back in England, "I have had to break the ice for successors, and what was more difficult . . . destroy the prejudices which the villanous Quacks in whose hands the public works have hitherto been, had raised against the profession." With his older brother, a clergyman and perhaps his closest confidant,

Benjamin Henry felt no need to mince words. "Here [in America]," he concluded, "I am the only successful Architect and Engineer."

WHEN KIMBALL BEGAN RECOUNTING LATROBE'S LIFE HISTORY, he could not help but agree. While Latrobe hadn't overstated his importance in his own time, much of the physical evidence to support his assertions had disappeared in the nineteenth century.

A success and a revelation in 1801, the waterworks had become outmoded. After a newer, larger system went into operation in 1815, a proposal was made to adapt the Centre Square Engine Station as an observatory for the American Philosophical Society. But no one came up with the needed funds and the building was demolished a decade later, to survive only in engravings and the handful of Latrobe's drawings that Kimball encountered. (Much later, Philadelphia City Hall had risen in its place.) The Bank met a similar fate, demolished in 1867. For years the rumor circulated that its marble had been reused in constructing a new post office in Portland, Maine, but Kimball got to the bottom of the tale. He determined that the surviving stone had been recycled—but in the foundations of a new building complex in Philadelphia, "which thus mark the grave," reported Kimball, "of this artistic masterpiece." The Pennock House was long gone, too, as was the Virginia Penitentiary.

Kimball's relationship with Benjamin Henry Latrobe never quite blossomed into the kind of intimate scholarly love affair that some writers have with their subjects. Kimball could have written the basic text on Latrobe, just as he had done with Jefferson; he considered doing so, again and again, over a period of several decades. While on his Sachs Fellowship, he had prepared a book outline, proposing to tell the story of Latrobe in fifteen chapters, three of which, Kimball hoped, would be "chapters to be used as articles." Essays on the Bank, the Baltimore Cathedral, and a summary of Latrobe's accomplishments did make it into print in scholarly journals, but Kimball came to an impasse when Ferdie Latrobe, despite his promises, refused to allow him access to his ancestor's papers after the snow-bound December visit.

Kimball hypothesized that he had somehow become linked in Ferdie's mind to the painful recollections of the tumbling stock market, but Ferdie never explained his refusal. Thirty years later, Kimball confided in a friend,

"No one can write the final book on Latrobe until Ferdie's papers become publicly available. If that happened I might be intrigued to do it myself." Instead, Ferdie Latrobe worked at his own study of his great-grandfather's work, though his draft manuscript, prepared with the assistance of a former editor at the Baltimore *Sunday Sun*, would never see publication. The closest Kimball got to having the last word was his profile of Latrobe for the *Encyclopaedia Britannica*.

Latrobe's legacy included his use of historic elements at a time of immense cultural transformation. In the case of the Centre Square Engine House, he used ancient forms to house the foremost symbol of the industrial revolution, the steam engine. Latrobe not only brought a sense of history to his work, pulling from his nearly photographic memory Greek, Roman, and even Gothic forms but, as Kimball pointed out, he also had the special genius of thinking in three dimensions, and even four, imagining the passage of time and the movement of light. As he explained to Jefferson, architecture was to be understood in terms of light, of what he called "determinate shadows." He built the first masonry vaulted monumental interior in the United States. He was an engineer and an artist.

Little wonder that Charles Willson Peale wanted to take his portrait for his hall of fame at the museum he had established in Philadelphia. He captured Latrobe in a philosophical moment, seeming to be aware of the onlooker yet lost in thought. Or perhaps he's just lost without his glasses, waiting for his friend, the diminutive Mr. Peale, to finish his work.

CHAPTER 5

THE SEASONS OF MONTICELLO

"The private buildings are very rarely constructed of stone or brick; much the greater portion being of scantling and boards, plastered with lime. It is impossible to devise things more ugly, uncomfortable, and happily more perishable . . . A workman could scarcely be found here capable of drawing an order . . . The first principles of the art [of architecture] are unknown, and there exists scarcely a model among us sufficiently chaste to give an idea of them."

—THOMAS JEFFERSON,
NOTES ON THE STATE OF VIRGINIA (1787)

I.

Autumn . . . The Thorntons Come to Visit

THE SATURDAY DAWNED WARM AND AGREEABLE, a day in early fall that seemed tailor-made for the journey. Two carriages, readied by half-past ten o'clock, departed the home of James Madison, bound for Charlottesville, Virginia.

The date was September 18, 1802. Mr. Madison, then in service as his nation's secretary of state, rode in the first carriage, leading the entourage out of his plantation acres. Along with Madison were his wife, Dolley, and the guests they had entertained for the previous fortnight. For Dr. William Thornton and his wife, Anna Maria, it would be their first visit to Mr. Jefferson's.

Thomas Jefferson, age seventy-eight, as recorded by portraitist Thomas Sully at Monticello.
West Point Museum Collection/United States Military Academy

Though his Capitol was far from complete—only the north wing was in use—Dr. Thornton had made powerful friends in Washington. He had earned George Washington's confidence and, even after the president's retirement, Thornton "received from him many invitations and many attentions." His visits to Mount Vernon had ended with Washington's unexpected death in December 1799, but Thornton had continued to serve as a commissioner of the Federal City until the June just past. Then the board had been dissolved and Thornton found himself at a professional crossroads.

He had found a new direction, thanks to his Washington neighbor, James Madison. Thornton had helped develop an early steamboat a decade earlier, and his notebooks and correspondence contained uncounted sketches for labor-saving devices. Given Thornton's reputation as something of an inventor, Madison put his friend in charge of the Patent Office. Just a year and half into his presidency, Thomas Jefferson, another friend of Thornton and himself an inveterate tinkerer, approved the appointment with alacrity.

The carriages, rocked by Virginia's notoriously bad roads, jounced the passengers inside as they wended their way south and west; a rainy summer had left the roads even more rutted than usual. The temperature rose in the afternoon but the speed at which they traveled seemed to slow to a crawl. On reaching Charlottesville, a growing courthouse town with a few taverns, shops, but as yet no church on its fifty-acre grid, they continued on, traveling to its outskirts on a winding road that meandered over hills and through up-land valleys. As the light of the autumn-shortened day waned, the riders observed flashes of lightning that illuminated the peaks of the Blue Ridge Mountains to the west. They could only hope the rains would hold off long enough for them to reach their destination.

Mrs. Thornton left a record of her life: Seven bound volumes in her hand survive in the Library of Congress. In one of her diaries, she recounted that September carriage journey, which came to a halt as the thunderclaps grew closer. "It was quite dark before we reached the foot of the mountain, and had it not been for the lightening [that] played almost incessantly we should not have been able to have seen the road at all; at last, we became so much afraid that we alighted."

A frequent visitor to Monticello, Madison knew a shortcut so, rather than following the "Roundabouts," the concentric roads that spiraled around the mountain, he hurried his fellow travelers from the carriages onto a woodland path. As Mrs. Thornton reported, "[We] walked the remainder of the way to the house, which I suppose might be about 3/4 of a mile, [and] the exercise of ascending the Hill and the warming of the evening fatigued us much."

Along with her companions, the small figure of Mrs. Thornton—short of stature, she weighed barely one hundred pounds—first approached Monticello after dark. She glimpsed it as the flashes of lightning produced an almost stroboscopic effect, outlining the mass of the building against the night sky. In truth, only after dark could the circa 1802 version of Monticello be said to have resembled a finished house. While the envelope of the building was largely complete, essential elements were still to come. The party approached the east façade, where the columned portico that would one day be the building's frontispiece was notably missing. Had they arrived from the west, they would have been greeted by the silhouette of the dome, but the glass oculus would not be installed for another three years.

With the impending storm, they chose not to dawdle outside and, as Mrs. Thornton reported, "[In] about a ¼ of an hour . . . it began to rain violently." The sense of relief at reaching their destination was tempered, however, by the state of the house. The main hall they entered, intended to be a grand and welcoming space, had bare brick walls and its window openings were boarded over. The floorboards had yet to be nailed to the supporting joists beneath. While the Thorntons had been warned to expect an unfinished house, Mrs. Thornton was distracted by the loose planks that shifted and rumbled as they walked across them.

"I cou'd not help being much struck with the uncommon appearance &
which the general gloom [that] prevailed contributed to increase." Even by
the standards of the day, the lighting was poor, as just "one dull lantern" lit
the cavernous space of the large room. They went through to the shadowy
dining room, which was illuminated only by the light that splashed through
the archway that framed a smaller, bow-shaped room where some of the company sat at supper. They saw members of Jefferson's extended family, half-
hidden in the shadows, seated in the outer room. "The appearance," observed
Mrs. Thornton "was singular & unpleasant."

Although born in France, Anna Maria Brodeau had spent much of her life
before her marriage in Philadelphia, where her mother ran a school for privileged girls. She lived comfortably and well, dressing in the latest fashion with
an admitted tendency when she traveled "to take too many clothes . . . at least
for [this] part of the world." The Thorntons' adopted home of Washington,
D.C., certainly wasn't Paris or even Philadelphia, remaining little more than a
settlement, one that bore a passing resemblance to a carefully planned garden
where most of the seeds had yet to sprout. But central Virginia? At Mr. Jefferson's, she suddenly felt as if she was very far indeed from civilization.

In recording her impressions in her diary, Mrs. Thornton sought to describe in a genteel way the rugged and rather unwelcoming experience of arriving at Monticello. The best the gracious lady could muster was, "Every
thing has a whimsical and droll appearance."

MRS. THORNTON'S BEMUSED RESPONSE to Monticello is hardly surprising.
She had arrived during a period when the house was in the midst of a major
renovation. Yet, as Madison or any other regular visitor to Monticello might
have told her, the house was always abuzz with construction activity. It would
remain so for virtually all of the fifty-six years of its builder's habitation.

Back in the spring of 1769, the twenty-six-year-old Jefferson had overseen
the first foundation work and brickmaking on his hilltop. His father had died
when Thomas was fourteen, leaving as a legacy some 5,000 acres. The son
might have chosen any of dozens of other fine settings on which to build, but
the mountain had been his "favorite retreat" as a boy. His daughter, Martha,
later told a friend, "Here he would bring his books to study, here he would
pass his holiday and leisure hours. . . . [H]e determined when arrived at man-
hood he would here build his family mansion."

As for Mrs. Thornton, she wasn't entirely persuaded that siting the house at the crest of the hill had been such a good idea. She allowed that "there is something grand . . . in the situation," but reservations remained. She felt the setting was "far from convenient or in my opinion agreeable—it is a place you wou'd rather look at now & then than live at." She recognized the choice was unconventional, since most of the grand houses she knew were near navigable rivers or well-traveled roads. But Jefferson had a grand vision of embracing the entire landscape when he sited his house on a hill that stood almost six hundred feet above the Rivanna River, which wound through the countryside below.

While he made up his mind early about its location, rather longer was required to determine exactly what his home would look like. Certainly Jefferson began musing on the house well before breaking ground, and as he worked at the plans for the main house, he supervised construction of a small outbuilding, which would later be little more than a decorative pavilion at the perimeter of the west lawn of the mansion complex. The house design emerged in desultory fashion, as Fiske Kimball would find in examining the remarkable collection of drawings on Boylston Street in Boston. Perhaps ten early sketches from 1768 and 1769 survive, each representing an attempt by Jefferson to initiate his house design. Three sketches in particular suggest how he floundered as he tried to make the most basic of decisions. The footprint in the first is square, in another it is rectangular, while the third was cross-shaped (cruciform).

Jefferson's design of Monticello had begun in earnest when he paged through James Gibbs's A Book of Architecture, probably for the umpteenth time. It was the same canonical work of English Palladianism that would inspire James Hoban's President's House and various elements of Buckland's design for Mathias Hammond. On one special day, however, Jefferson saw a shape he liked in one of Gibbs's square plans and he copied it, varying the scheme only slightly. After considering for a time, he finally decided the arrangement of spaces didn't quite suit his needs. On another day he tried stretching its elements into a rectangle. When that didn't please his eye, he began anew.

The drawing process took time since Jefferson was also teaching himself architectural drafting. His father, Peter Jefferson, had been a surveyor, and Thomas, like George Washington, had inherited his father's instruments. Earlier, he had mastered the mathematical tools of the surveyor's trade, and they would prove valuable to him as he planned his landscape. But the discipline of drawing buildings posed a different challenge, and he learned to plot his building designs on paper by making reference to his books, including his

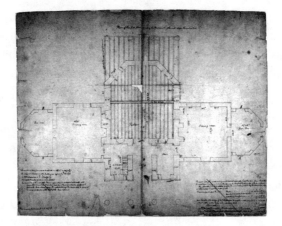

The plan for Jefferson's first Monticello, as of circa 1772, with a west-facing portico covering the semi-octagonal parlor. The two semi-octagons at the extremes of the building were added to the plan a few years later, and it was the north "bow room" in which Mrs. Thornton first glimpsed the diners upon her first arrival at Monticello.
Massachusetts Historical Society

Palladio and another volume by James Gibbs, *Rules for Drawing the Several Parts of Architecture.*

For his next attempt, he copied another plate from Gibbs's *A Book of Architecture.* This one illustrated an octagonal pavilion with smaller, square structures attached on either side. It proved not to be the solution he wanted, so he moved on to a three-room cruciform plan. Dissatisfied with that, he tried subdividing the rooms on either side of the large middle room.

Before he was able to devise a suitable plan, Jefferson's life was thrown into disarray when Shadwell, his mother's house and his own domicile at the time, burned to the ground on February 1, 1770. Lost in the flames were the young lawyer's legal papers, correspondence, accounts, and other records. But the coup de grâce was the loss of most of Jefferson's books. Until he could reconstitute his library, he—like Latrobe almost thirty years later—had to go it alone. The absence of architectural books seems to have worked to his advantage, as he was left with the surviving earlier sketches, which no doubt were at Monticello, perhaps in the nearly finished pavilion. In the end, like molecules bonding to form a new compound, a distinct plan emerged, one descended from but different than its printed precursors. It would be the basis of the first Monticello, the home that Jefferson's builders constructed between 1770 and 1782.

His working plans emerged slowly as the design evolved. Construction progressed as he refined and rethought aspects of his house, and more than a few changes in the plans resulted from problems that presented themselves as the walls of the building rose. But the evolution represented not only a design transformation: The designer himself went through a key transition, too. He had begun by working as his contemporaries did, picking a plan from a book he liked. While most gentlemen amateurs of his era simply went about building houses based upon favored plates, Jefferson didn't settle for mere imitation. He moved chimney flues, repositioned arches, and changed the fenestration. He adjusted the dimensions, computed and recomputed the number of bricks that would be required, and shifted staircases. He spotted mistakes and omissions and corrected them. On the exterior, the result would be a tall, gable-roofed structure with entry and garden porticos on the opposite façades; the central block would be flanked by two shorter, hip-roofed wings. Inside, the ground floor of the central block would contain the entrance hall and main parlor, with a dining room in the north wing and the master's bedroom to the south. The scale was generous, but it was not to be a large house, consisting of four main rooms down and one upstairs.

Though indebted to Gibbs's plates, Jefferson combined familiar elements in a new way, adding two porticos and a semi-octagonal room to a cruciform shape. In the course of his design development, he planned a house that was unlike any other. Jefferson emerged from a self-administered apprenticeship with a capacity for independent thinking; it could be said that he earned himself a place beside a handful of others in America, among them Buckland and Latrobe, deserving of the appellation "architect."

Not that Mrs. Thornton would have agreed. The early steps in the process had required many years and, in fact, Jefferson's architectural style would require more decades to ripen. As Anna Maria Thornton remarked in her wry way to her diary, "He is a very long time in maturing his projects."

A DAILY ROUTINE PREVAILED IN MR. JEFFERSON'S HOME. The first bell rang at seven o'clock, announcing the time had come to prepare for breakfast. One hour later, the guests and family were summoned for the meal. Despite the prescribed regimen, Mrs. Thornton found Sunday to be a more agreeable day. She was introduced to the rest of the guests and the family members. She remarked in particular upon Jefferson's daughters, thinking Martha Jefferson Randolph, "[who] had five very fine Children . . . a very accomplished sensible woman" and describing Mary Jefferson Eppes as "very beautiful but more reserved than Mrs. Randolph."

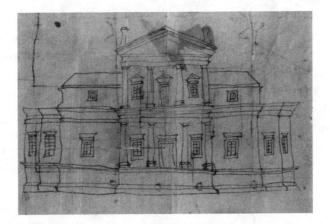

Jefferson didn't have a great gift for freehand drafting, as this sketch of the first Monticello's façade indicates. The design is loosely based on the Villa Cornaro, a work of one of Jefferson's favorite sources, Andrea Palladio. *Monticello/Thomas Jefferson Foundation, Inc.*

Her solicitous host kindly gave Mrs. Thornton a tour of his house. They were friends, known to one another from Washington society, and the usually reserved Mr. Jefferson felt comfortable with this charming lady with whom he could exercise his rusty French. He explained how the house had been altered over the years as his life had undergone significant changes. One momentous event had been the arrival of his newlywed wife, Martha Wayles Skelton Jefferson, in January of 1772. If Mrs. Thornton thought her trip to Monticello arduous, the newly married Mrs. Jefferson had had to wade through two feet of snow, only to find the accommodations consisted of a one-room pavilion with no fire burning in the hearth.

Over the next decade, Jefferson had developed the plan, enlarging the house, adding rooms at each end. The family—Martha, familiarly known as Patsy, arrived barely nine months after the wedding—moved into the north wing of Monticello in 1773. Jefferson worked at a scheme for adding dependencies for the kitchen, pantry, food processing, stables, and carriage house (also known as the "chariot house" in Jefferson's notes). Those spaces would be half-buried in the hillside, invisible from the mansion but well ventilated and lighted, opening from the downhill slopes on either side of the house.

Though far from finished in its first incarnation, the house had certainly been habitable when Jefferson's life was transformed by his wife's death in 1782. The next fourteen years saw little construction progress, but during that time, he experienced more of the world than he ever had before and, absorbing a new range of architectural possibilities, he rethought the entire program at Monticello. After his time as minister to France and secretary of state in Philadelphia, he returned to Monticello determined to transform his house. He would lower the roof from the original scheme and double its depth to produce what would appear to be a one-story house but actually contained thirty-five rooms on the first floor, mezzanine, and attic story.

He confided his plan to his French friend, but even with her new understanding of the process, Anna Maria Thornton remained flummoxed. "Mr. J. Has been 27 years engaged in improving the place, but he has pulled down and built up again so often, [and] . . . a great deal of money has been expended both above & below ground, but not so as to appear to the best advantage."

During Jefferson's five years of service in Paris, his journeys around France, England, the Lowlands, Germany, and to northern Italy had fed his voracious appetite for architecture. He had added more than a book a day to his library; he had accumulated countless recollections of buildings and gardens and landscapes in his mental collection of images (a resource that, for any architect, can never be underestimated). But the experience of one particular building powered his rethinking of Monticello.

Construction at the Hôtel de Salm had been well under way when Jefferson arrived in Paris in 1784, and the building was completed during his tenure as minister. He watched its progress from a terrace overlooking the Seine. As he confided in his friend Madame de Tessé, "I was violently smitten with the Hôtel de Salm, and used to go to the Tuileries almost daily to look at it." Though he paid a modest fee for a chair in the Tuileries, he complained that the attendant was "inattentive to my passion [and] never had the complaisance to place a chair there, so that sitting on the parapet, and twisting my neck around to the object of my admiration, I generally left it with a *torti-colli*." Jefferson's reinvention of Monticello was thus informed by the stiff-necked memory imprinted in his brain at the Tuileries.

When he began the renovation in 1796, he ordered that all walls above the ground story be demolished, in order to mimic the one-story appearance of the Hôtel de Salm. One-story houses were all the rage in Paris, and the configuration suited Jefferson. The upper levels became private spaces and the staircases small—which pleased him, believing as he did that grand stairs were a great waste, amounting to a loss of "space that would make a good room in every storey." Here again Mrs. Thornton's personal experience with the stairwells left her doubtful. "To [go to] bed we had to mount a little ladder of a staircase about 2 feet wide and very steep."

Jefferson replaced the upper level of the two-story portico, which had never been completed, with a central dome, one very like the one that topped the Hôtel de Salm. And Jefferson specified that it be constructed like the flattened dome at the Halle aux Bleds. He showed Dr. and Mrs. Thornton his architectural drafts of the new scheme, which might have put them in mind of their most recent experience with domestic buildings in Washington, the Tayloe house. Mrs. Thornton, having closely observed the completion of that design of Dr. Thornton's, recognized the unreality of Jefferson's expectations when he assured her that the work would be finished at Monticello by the following summer. She had the firsthand experience to appreciate how unlikely *that* was.

Jefferson did have reason for his optimism. Four years earlier he had at last found the man he needed to complete his house after years of watching lesser men come and go. An Ulsterman, James Dinsmore became a naturalized citizen in Philadelphia on June 5, 1798, no doubt under the auspices of then-vice president Jefferson. For many years Jefferson had difficulty delegating responsibility, but as had happened with George Mason and William Buckland, he was able to place great trust in Dinsmore, enabling work to proceed apace even during his long absences in Washington. Jefferson described Dinsmore as a "house joiner . . . of the very first order both in [his] knolege in architecture, and practical abilities . . . a more faithful, sober, honest and respectable man I have never known."

Torrential rains would delay the scheduled departure of the Thorntons, so it wasn't until the following Friday that Anna Maria and William Thornton resumed their travels. After spending almost a week at Monticello, she concluded, "Nothing is compleated, nor do I think ever will be."

II.
Winter . . . Visiting the "Phylosopher"

THE TWO YOUNG MEN FROM BOSTON ENCOUNTERED NONE OF THE SNOWS characteristic of their native New England, but arriving on February 4, 1815, they experienced a Central Virginia cold snap. On the last leg of their journey, George Ticknor and Francis Gray observed a barren winter landscape. Their driver had to clamber down at one crossing to ford the creek, hammering through ice to lead the horses safely across. From their

While she hardly fell unreservedly in love with the place, Mrs. Thornton did paint a
watercolor of Monticello's garden façade in which the place appears in a favorable light.
Private Collection; photograph courtesy of Old Salem, Inc.

coach seats the young men observed a less fortunate animal, an enormous
horse whose carcass had been abandoned on the stream bank.

As they neared their destination that Saturday, Francis Gray noted the
wildness of the approach to Mr. Jefferson's home. "The forest had evidently
been abandoned to nature; some of the trees were decaying from age, some
were blasted, some uprooted by the wind and some appeared even to have
been twisted from their trunks by the violence of a hurricane." Eager to reach
the warmth of Monticello, George Ticknor observed as they followed the
curving drive that "the ascent of the steep, savage hill" seemed to go on and
on. Finally, when they emerged from the trees, they could admire the
panoramic view from the summit of the mountain. As Ticknor told his father
in a letter he penned a few days later, "The prospect is admirable."

The only child of a wealthy and educated Boston family, George Ticknor
was something of a prodigy. After graduating from Dartmouth at sixteen, the
earnest and self-assured young man studied law. Though he passed the bar
and opened an office on Boston's Court Square, Ticknor by age twenty-three
had determined lawyering was not for him. He had set his sights instead on
the life of a belletrist. Recognizing that a professional man of letters needed
exposure to the world, he resolved that, "hav[ing] trifled away some of the

best years of my life, I must spend some years in Italy, France and Germany." This trip was to be a dress rehearsal. Along with his friend Mr. Gray, he would visit America's greatest men, in part to obtain letters of introduction to their European counterparts.

Perplexed at finding neither bell nor knocker, Ticknor and his companion opened the glass doors and admitted themselves to the house. Once inside, they knew immediately that this was no ordinary dwelling. "On one side hangs the head and horns of an elk, a deer and a buffalo," Ticknor observed. "Another is covered with curiosities which Lewis and Clarke [sic] found in their wild and perilous expedition. On the third, among many other striking matters, [is] the head of a mammoth. . . . On the fourth side, in odd union with a fine painting of the Repentance of Saint Peter, is an Indian map on leather . . . and an Indian representation of a bloody battle, handed down in their traditions."

The visitors were soon joined by Colonel Thomas Mann Randolph, Jefferson's son-in-law, who directed them into the dining room. They handed over their letters of introduction, and Randolph left to deliver them to Mr. Jefferson in his private study (Jefferson called it his *cabinet*, having adapted the French convention of a private dressing room off the bedroom, turning the space into his sanctum sanctorum, where he retired to read, write, and think). One of the letters, brought from Quincy, Massachusetts, was addressed in the hand of John Adams himself. Jefferson's old friend had written to recommend these lads as among the "most exalted" of Boston's young scholars, advising the recipient that they desired "to see Monticello, its Library, and its Sage."

While they waited, Ticknor examined the dining room. "Here again we found ourselves surrounded with paintings that seemed good," he thought. Gray noticed two drawings hung of the new Capitol in Washington, "one of them very elegant." Hanging nearby was a meticulously executed rendering of Monticello's west front drafted by a young protégé of Jefferson, Robert Mills, who had labored as a delineator for Jefferson during his presidency. Nearby hung an engraving of Washington's Mount Vernon.

Jefferson appeared in short order. Having met Adams in Boston and, in recent days, James Madison, both visitors were surprised at Jefferson's six-foot, two-and-half-inch stature. "He is quite tall," recorded Gray, ". . . his face streaked and speckled with red, light gray eyes, white hair, dressed in shoes of very thin soft leather with pointed toes and . . . grey worsted stockings, corduroy small clothes, blue waistcoat and coat, of stiff thick cloth made of the wool of his own merinoes [sheep] and badly manufactured, the buttons of his coat and small clothes of horn, and an under waistcoat flannel bound with red velvet. His figure bony, long and with broad shoulders, a true Virginian." Jefferson, retired since 1809, had the eccentric look of a man who dressed for his own comfort.

Straightaway he invited Ticknor and Gray to be his guests for a few days. They accepted, and he excused himself to arrange for their baggage. That left the Bostonians once again with leisure to regard the house. The museum-like room through which they had entered—the "Indian Hall," Jefferson called it—was the same space that just a dozen years earlier, on Mrs. Thornton's visit, had boarded-up windows, bare brick walls, and loose floorboards. Now it was plastered and decorated. The room in which they waited this time was, according to Ticknor, "a large and rather elegant [parlor] . . . which, with the hall . . . composed the whole center of the house." A master painter from the Federal City had come and gone between 1805 and 1808, spending roughly two years painting the interior of the house. Curtains made of printed fabric Jefferson had purchased in France had been hung. Ticknor noted the "tessel-lated" floor, a parquet "formed of alternate diamonds of cherry and beech, and kept polished as highly as if it were of fine mahogany." The house no longer had the air of a construction site, as it had when the Thorntons had arrived on that rainy night thirteen years earlier. But Gray could not help but notice its shabby-genteel aspect, observing chairs with leather seats that "were completely worn through," the stuffing "sticking out in all directions."

When Jefferson returned, he and the young men talked away the after-noon. Jefferson's habit was to direct the flow of conversation to subjects most familiar to his guests; he was by nature curious, more interested in learning from others than in hearing the sound of his own voice. He found he shared with these intelligent young men a deep affection for "ancient authors," and sitting before a fire crackling in the large fireplace, the conversation wan-dered through the literature of Greece, Rome, and England. With the men lounging in comfortable chairs, a workman arrived to fix a broken window in one of the glazed doors that overlooked the garden. It was odd, Gray thought, that the man was replacing the glass with a wooden panel. Jefferson ex-plained in his low, mild voice that the large size of the panes meant no re-placement was to be had nearby, but had to be ordered from Boston.

Jefferson put great stock in buildings that were "light and airy," and his house boasted large windows and many skylights. These were not standard notions; the window sash had to be made to order in Monticello's millwork shop, and the roofs often leaked. Nor was Jefferson content with familiar room configurations, favoring instead tall ceilings and the angular shapes of half-octagon plans. Even on that cold winter day, the slanting late afternoon light cascaded into the parlor through the ten-foot-tall windows and door. Hanging on the wall were two pier mirrors, each four feet wide by nine feet high. Jefferson had brought them from his domicile in Paris, the Hôtel de Langeac, and they sent the light caroming around the room. Shadows played off the decorative cornice based on a Roman temple dedicated to Jupiter that Jefferson had found in a plate in a book. The room—indeed, the entire house—reflected Jefferson's delight in amalgamating antique details into spaces reminiscent of those he had encountered in Paris. His was a mind fascinated by spatial drama; in Monticello he created a theater and test lab where he found a special joy in employing light to reveal the surface textures and dimensional character of his house.

Young Ticknor and Gray observed the seventy-two-year-old Mr. Jefferson at one of the happiest moments of his life. His house was effectively finished. His only surviving child, Martha, presided over his table as the lady of the house. His grandchildren and even great-grandchildren were regular visitors, and their combined presence in his elegant home represented a dream realized. There was an expectant sense of relief, too, since any day he anticipated hearing that he would be able to staunch the rising tide of his debts. He had always bought too many books and spent too much on his house, but he had a solution. It did represent a great sacrifice, because he would have to bid his library farewell, but his financial pains would be eased just as he hoped to embark on a new project. It was one in which he might immerse himself, one he hoped would be a great legacy to his beloved state.

He had warmed quickly to his much younger guests. He anticipated a companionable dinner, joined by daughter Martha and her husband, Colonel Randolph, as well as two of their children, Thomas Jefferson Randolph and his eighteen-year-old sister Ellen. Jefferson looked forward to the evening's conversation and hearing more of what his guests had to say.

"I have seldom met a pleasanter party," Ticknor reported later, "[and] the evening passed away pleasantly in general conversation."

GEORGE TICKNOR DESCRIBED MONTICELLO as built "of brick . . . I suppose, in the French style." While he was uncertain of his knowledge of architecture, young Ticknor was a man of ideas, and he found Mr. Jefferson shared his pre-occupation with books and learning.

On his forthcoming journey to the Old World, Ticknor was especially keen to visit German universities, reputed to be the best in the world (as one contemporary French professor enthused, "The Germans begin where we leave off!"). To make the most of his German visit, Ticknor had devoted the previous summer and fall to learning the language. He had labored to trans-late the entirety of Goethe's novel *The Sorrows of Young Werther,* having bor-rowed a copy from John Quincy Adams's library. He needed a mastery of the German tongue to take full advantage of the two-hundred-thousand-volume library at Universität Göttingen, which, Ticknor had been told, made the collection he knew at Harvard seem like a mere "closetful of books."

It was Sunday morning, their second day at Monticello, when Jefferson welcomed Ticknor and Gray into his library. Not every visitor received such an invitation; Mrs. Thornton, in fact, had complained that "the president's bedchamber is only separated from the Library by an arch, he keeps it con-stantly locked, and I have been disappointed much by not being able to get in." Jefferson had eventually offered her entrée back in 1802, and had gra-ciously displayed for her page after page of fine engravings of ancient sites that appeared in the grand volumes imported from abroad with which he supplemented his own architectural thinking.

On that cold February day in 1815, the three men were surrounded by books. More than six thousand filled to overflowing Jefferson's private quar-ters, the suite of rooms at the south end of the house that included his bed-room, *cabinet,* and three other rooms with walls lined, floor to ceiling, with tightly packed bookcases. Their host pointed out volumes he particularly treasured, including Greek and Latin classics, a rare volume of Chaucer, and Milton's *Paradise Lost.* There were biblical works, too, as well as innumerable tomes on the law. Many histories were devoted to North and South America ("The collection on this subject is without a question the most valuable in the world," observed Gray). As Jefferson pulled one book after another from the shelves, it was easy to see how he could find himself with twenty or more spread around him on the floor, as one elderly slave, Isaac Jefferson, described him. "Old master [would] read fust one, then tother. Isaac has often won-dered how old master came to have such a mighty head."

A superb library was the sine qua non for a man of the Enlightenment. A library like Jefferson's embraced human knowledge; it was a resource that embodied the age's desire to try to understand the world. Ticknor noted with interest Jefferson's cataloguing system, one he had adapted from the Renaissance philosopher Francis Bacon. The arrangement of books on his shelves followed the organizing principles of the three *faculties:* Memory (that is, history); Reason (philosophy); and Imagination (fine arts). The system was a perfect paradigm of the way Jefferson looked first to the past; next to reason and logic; and then, spicing the mix, to his taste for the artistic. It was quintessential Jefferson, at once embracing a universe of knowledge, endeavoring to tame it, and employing it.

While Ticknor had been perfecting his German the previous year, Jefferson had also been occupying himself with an educational assignment. For decades he had tried to persuade his fellow Virginians that the Commonwealth needed a state university, having attempted as Virginia's governor back in 1779 to enact legislation establishing publicly funded schools and universities. For years he had regaled visitors to Monticello with his plans and written regularly to friends and confidants about his notions. But only recently had his hopes shown signs of coming to life.

The previous spring Jefferson had been made a trustee of the Albemarle Academy. A favored nephew of his, Peter Carr, whom he had helped raise from the age of three, had been named board president. Though the future academy was supposed to be merely a secondary school, Jefferson had immersed himself in its planning and had, as usual, a larger vision for its future. In August he had drafted a ground plan, a square with buildings on three sides; the fourth he left open to the horizon. Jefferson envisioned not one educational edifice. He had already coined a term for what he had in mind—he called it an "Academical Village," advocating that "in fact an university should not be an house but a village." His plan featured nine professor's dwellings, three per built side, linked by a string of student dormitories. The two-story professor's houses were to have classroom spaces on the ground floor and living quarters above. He sketched a sample elevation, too, with one professor's pavilion at center, flanked by a half-dozen dormitory rooms on either side.

Jefferson had great hopes for his project but that day, as he and his guests talked of books and education, his sense of expectation could not help but be tinged with sadness. These men had a high appreciation for the volumes he had worked to assemble over more than four decades; but all three of them knew of the proposal before Congress that the collection be purchased by the nation to replace the library lost to fire the previous summer when the

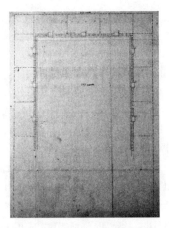

Jefferson's preliminary ground plan for what was then to be known as Albermarle Academy.
The University of Virginia Library

British had burned the Capitol. Jefferson knew something else, too, imparted in a letter he received that very day: The purchase had been approved, so now the departure of the books had become certain.

In return for $23,950, most of which would go directly to his creditors, his library would go to the Federal City. His 6,487 volumes would constitute the reborn Library of Congress; they would include several editions of Palladio's *Four Books*, a book by French architect Philibert Delorme (it explained the curved framing technique Jefferson first saw at the Halle aux Bleds and had used for the dome atop Monticello), and forty-three other architectural books. That day, however, Mr. Jefferson chose not to confide the news to his company but to enjoy the pleasure his library afforded the young men, just as it had him for many years.

After a time they rose from their chairs in the library and Jefferson took his guests into his most private quarters, his bedchamber and *cabinet*. It was Francis Gray who remarked upon the polygraph. It was a clever device of recent invention, the brainchild of John Isaac Hawkins, an English immigrant who had found a place in the workshop of Charles Willson Peale's museum. The labor-saving machine produced a simultaneous duplicate of a letter as it was composed. The writer would hold a pen in hand and apply it to paper, writing a letter or perhaps copying a drawing or musical notes. A second pen, which was connected to the first by a mahogany and brass structure of flexing arms and sliding frames, would simultaneously record on a second sheet of paper the movements the writer made. The original polygraph had been balky and awkward, but Peale, believing it had an important future, had adapted springs, pulleys, rollers, and other mechanisms in an attempt to perfect the device.

In his tinkering, Peale had had two invaluable consultants, men of similarly scientific inclination. One was Benjamin Henry Latrobe, then living in Philadelphia. Latrobe had done Peale the service of sketching "a very extensive building" to house Peale's natural history museum, the first in America. It was never built—the Pennsylvania legislature, to which the painter-turned-scientist had appealed for funds, instead granted him the use of several rooms in the old statehouse. But Latrobe had bought Peale's first prototype polygraph. Another was soon purchased by their mutual friend Jefferson, who at the time had recently assumed the presidencies of both the nation (after the deadlocked election of 1800) and the country's foremost scientific association, the American Philosophical Society. The three men had exchanged numerous letters about the device as each worked to improve its efficiency.

The polygraph that stood on the table near the fire in Jefferson's bedchamber was often used; as he told his companions, he composed all his letters upon it. In the years to come, George Ticknor would often be the recipient of letters penned on that very machine, Jefferson's half of an exchange between men whose friendship, born this February in Virginia, would develop into a bond between educators committed to changing the old ways.

Their visit that morning came to an end when Mr. Jefferson excused himself to take his accustomed exercise, and rode to his mills along the Rivanna.

MANY MONTHS WOULD ELAPSE BEFORE ALBEMARLE ACADEMY—which, by then, Jefferson had reformulated as "Central College"—was empowered by the Virginia Legislature to raise money. The Board of Visitors included the three surviving members of Virginia's presidential dynasty, Thomas Jefferson, James Madison, and James Monroe.

Mr. Jefferson set things in motion. On April 8, 1817, together with two other board members, he surveyed a site called Monroe's Hill a mile west of Charlottesville's courthouse. A few days later he wrote to his trusted master builder, James Dinsmore, inviting him to help build the proposed college. On May 5, the Board of Visitors voted to approve Jefferson's preliminary plan for the open-ended square. The site had been laid out, a builder invited to bid, and construction of the first pavilion duly authorized.

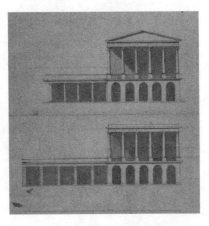

With a little help from his friends—in this case, Dr. William Thornton—Jefferson got the
work at the Academical Village under way. Though Jefferson wasn't entirely satisfied with
Thornton's rendering, he adapted it for the first pavilion to be constructed at the University
of Virginia. *The University of Virginia Library*

A key obstacle remained. When Jefferson sat in his *cabinet* in the days
thereafter, he understood that his rough sketches simply would not be sufficient. He might have turned to his drafting table, affixed a sheet of his coördinate paper to the board, and set to sketching more plans. But he felt
paralyzed. His library had departed and gone to the Federal City, and without
architectural plates to refer to, he felt ill-equipped to take on the task himself. As he confided in John Adams, "I cannot live without books."

The challenge he faced made Jefferson feel the books' absence acutely. The
architectural conceit of the Academical Village was, he had advised Virginia's
governor, that the professors' pavilions should be "models in architecture . . .
exhibiting . . . the purest forms of antiquity, furnishing to the student examples of the precepts he will be taught in that art." Until replacement copies of
certain key books arrived, he felt unable to fulfill his own charge.

He found himself turning to the polygraph to draw upon the kindness of
friends. First he wrote to Dr. William Thornton. Though he had chosen to
remain an architectural dilettante, Thornton had kept up an on-again, off-
again practice through the years. Most recently he had designed for Martha
Washington's granddaughter a fine Georgetown house, Tudor Place, completed just the previous year.

In his letter to Thornton, Jefferson described the overall scheme for Central College and drew a likeness of the ground plan. "This sketch will give
you an idea of it, the whole of the pavilions and dormitories to be united by

a colonnade in front of the height of the lower storey of the pavilions, under which [the students] may go dry from school to school." He asked for Dr. Thornton's help: "Will you set your imagination to work & sketch some designs for us, no matter how loosely with the pen, without the trouble of referring to scale or rule; for we want nothing but the outline of the architecture, as the internal must be arranged according to local convenience."

Thornton's reply from Washington arrived promptly, and included a sheet containing two studies of possible façades. The doctor proposed that the central pavilion have a pediment supported by a Corinthian order, that the others be flat-roofed with Doric columns. The voluble Dr. Thornton offered many, many other suggestions, too, regarding the planning of the university, not all of which were welcomed. Perhaps because of his many gifts, the doctor came across at times as an irritating know-it-all.

There were elements Jefferson liked, but he knew immediately that he needed more than Thornton's single sheet. The next day he dispatched a request to Benjamin Henry Latrobe. "This letter is that of a friendly beggar," began Jefferson. As he had done for Thornton, he described the overall conception in both words and a freehand drawing, then asked for an architectural consultation. "A few sketches, such as shall take you not more than a minute apiece, mere expressions of a first trait of imagination will greatly oblige us."

Jefferson and Latrobe had a bond of professional respect developed during Jefferson's presidency when Latrobe had served as the nation's first Surveyor of the Public Buildings, leaving an indelible mark on Washington's architecture. Never a man to take a drafting assignment lightly, Latrobe would oblige his friend over the coming months, but his drawings took a good deal longer than the "minute apiece" Jefferson had recommended. As a result, the first pavilion undertaken was loosely based on Thornton's drawing. But Latrobe's thoughtful suggestions about the conception of the Academical Village and a master sheet of numerous drawings received that October would have a larger impact. His general notion of colossal (two-story) columns would be used in seven of the pavilions; at least two of the professor's houses and perhaps as many as four would be based specifically on his designs.

Just as important, a principal central building would be added to the scheme at Latrobe's suggestion. It would be an example of what Jefferson called "spherical" architecture, a domed building that was a half-scale homage to the Pantheon in Rome. The Rotunda would be, in Jefferson's words, "a temple of knowledge"—not a temple in any religious sense, but home to the

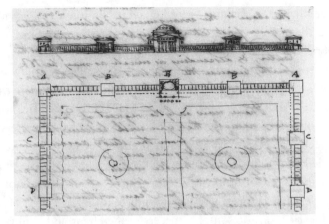

Latrobe's master sheet that would be the basis for the faces of least two pavilions has been lost, but this earlier sketch, limned on a letter dated July 24, 1817, played an important role in determining the Pantheon-like look of the "principal building."
Library of Congress/Prints and Photographs Division

university library. In working with Latrobe, Jefferson became the medium between an ancient architect and a contemporary one, much as he had been with Clérisseau in devising the design of the Virginia Capitol. He filtered the sketches of Latrobe (and Thornton) through his own sensibilities; added his plans for many of the buildings; and produced an educational precinct that was new and modern, yet echoed its ancient sources.

The Virginia Assembly, after much lobbying by Jefferson, determined in 1819 that the Central College would be chartered as the University of Virginia. Jefferson directed progress by letter and regular site visits, but he could survey the nascent university from his own hilltop not so far away. He watched what he had come to call the "hobby of my old age" become a school that, in the winter of 1825, would welcome its first forty students and five professors.

IN THE WEEKS BEFORE THE UNIVERSITY'S first students arrived, George Ticknor returned to Charlottesville. In spirit, he had never left Jefferson's companionable hearth. They had continued their conversations on paper, corresponding and even exchanging favors from afar. Jefferson's references had gained Ticknor access to the Marquis de Lafayette and other old friends in Europe. During his years abroad and, later, in Boston, Ticknor had secured replacement copies for Jefferson of many of his departed books.

In December 1824, Ticknor arrived merely as an interested friend and observer, but that wasn't Jefferson's fault. Years earlier he had asked Ticknor to assume one of the original professorships, "that of . . . Ideology, Ethics, Belles-Lettres, and Fine Arts." Despite Jefferson's pleas—"I have some belief," he wrote to Ticknor, "that our genial climate would be more friendly to your constitution than the rigors of that of Massachusetts"—Ticknor had declined the offer. Even after the younger man assumed a dual professorship at Harvard lecturing in Spanish and French and in belles lettres, his Virginia mentor tried once more, persuading the other members of the Board of Visitors at his university to authorize Ticknor's hiring at a salary of $2,000 per annum, double what Harvard was paying him. But money wasn't a particular concern for Ticknor, the son of a successful merchant and banker, who remitted almost half his salary back to Harvard's straitened coffers. He again chose to remain in Boston.

Despite his refusal to relocate, Ticknor's interest in Jefferson's experiment never waned. Unlike at Harvard, where the curriculum was rigidly prescribed, Virginia students were to be given a choice as to which lectures to attend. The very idea of students making such decisions for themselves was a revelation, but one that Ticknor found congenial; he thought Harvard hidebound and parochial in comparison to German universities. Jefferson's idea of an aristocracy of the mind made sense to him—that is, given educational opportunities, the natural aristocrat would distinguish himself by his intelligence rather than his family's means. Ticknor hoped Jefferson's "noble plan" might bring fresh ideas to American higher education.

When Ticknor finally accepted Jefferson's long-standing invitation to return to Virginia, he wished to renew his acquaintance with Jefferson in person, as the two men had developed a great sympathy for one another in the course of their long-distance correspondence. He arrived at Monticello on a Tuesday shortly before Christmas. He was accompanied by his wife and another prominent Bostonian, lawyer and congressman Daniel Webster. They would remain for five days, but Jefferson promptly gave Ticknor the tour he had come for.

"The University," Ticknor wrote to a friend during his Virginia visit, "is a very fine establishment, consisting of ten houses for professors, four eating houses, a rotunda on the model of the Pantheon, with a magnificent room for a library, and four fine lecture rooms, with one hundred and eight apartments for students. . . . It has cost two hundred and fifty thousand dollars, and the thorough finish of every part of it . . . show[s], I think, that it has not cost too much."

Upon renewing his friendship with Jefferson in 1824, Ticknor thought him "very little altered from what he was ten years ago, very active, lively, and happy, riding from ten to fifteen miles every day, and talking without restraint, very pleasantly, upon all subjects." Certainly, Ticknor noticed his friend was aging—he had the lean look of advanced years, his posture no longer quite so upright, and he complained of the "minuteness" of the type in some of his books. But his mind remained as active as ever. "He reads much Greek and Saxon," Ticknor observed. "I saw his Greek Lexicon, printed in 1817; it was much worn with use, and contained many curious notes."

The young scholar, just embarked on his brilliant career, found much to admire in the old politician working at his last great public project. Their friendship offered Ticknor a view of the distance between old age and youth. "[Mr. Jefferson] said of himself the other evening, 'When I can neither read nor ride, I shall desire very much to make my bow.'" Ticknor was impressed— impressed enough to conclude, with the optimism of youth, "I think he bids to enjoy both yet nine or ten years."

Jefferson, ever the tactful and cheerful conversationalist, allowed his friend to believe the best, and that is what Ticknor saw. As he said of the Academical Village, "It is . . . an experiment worth trying, to which I earnestly desire the happiest results; and they have, to begin, a mass of buildings more beautiful than anything architectural in New England, and more appropriate to an university than can be found, perhaps, in the world."

III.
Summer . . . Death and Dissolution

IN JUNE 1826, Jefferson made his last visit to the Academical Village. The culmination of ten years of work, the University of Virginia had welcomed its first students a year earlier. Despite a continued shortfall of funds and a few disciplinary problems, the institution had assumed a form recognizable to the man who conceived its curriculum, hired the faculty, shaped its philosophy, and laid out its physical plant.

The "Old Sachem," as he was affectionately known to other members of the university's Board of Visitors, arrived for an inspection. He was greeted by William Wertenbaker, the student librarian, who welcomed him to the temporary library quartered in Pavilion VII. After assessing progress there, Jefferson made a second stop on his tour, visiting the dome room of the Rotunda, the library's eventual home. Books, as always, held a venerated place in Jefferson's universe.

His timing that day was excellent, as he was able to spend an hour observing an important step in the building process. Wertenbaker provided him with a chair where he sat, rapt, watching as the first of the Rotunda's capitals was set atop the column shaft at the southwest corner of the building's portico. The large chunk of white Carrara marble had been carved in the Corinthian order, and delicate acanthus leaves extended from its basketlike form. The capital had arrived from Italy, via the port of Boston, just days before.

One can only wonder at his thoughts; for once, Jefferson's voluminous notebooks and correspondence are silent, leaving us to consider this tableau. But it seems very likely that its portico, capitals, and the nearly completed mass of the Rotunda itself had to be redolent with plates from Palladio, remindful of days with M. Clérisseau, and evocative of Jefferson's many architectural aspirations. For once, in a life of active absorption, of endless notebook jottings, Jefferson merely watched and took in what he had helped accomplish.

IF, AT MOMENTS, THE LAST MONTHS of Jefferson's life seemed the best of times, mostly they were among the worst. Yes, the university had come to life and Monticello had finally been completed in 1823 with the assembly of the east portico. But the slightly stooped, gray-haired gentleman of eighty years who watched his workers finish the job knew all too well that his house had already begun to deteriorate around him.

He had no money for painting or other maintenance. His indebtedness had risen above $100,000, a sum greater than the market value of Monticello and all his other holdings put together. Colonel Randolph's financial difficulties had become perilous, leading Jefferson's son-in-law to become estranged from the family. And Jefferson's robust health showed signs of deteriorating, with recurrent dysuria (painful urination) relieved only by the laudanum prescribed by Dr. Robley Dunglison. A Scotsman Jefferson had brought from London to be professor of anatomy and medicine, Dunglison had become a friend and a regular visitor from Charlottesville, where he resided in Pavilion X at the Academical Village.

Jefferson had also lost the ready companionship of a cherished member of his family. At age five, Eleanora Wayles Randolph (known always within her family as Ellen) had been among the spectral figures half-hidden in the dining room shadows on the rainy night in 1802 when Dr. and Mrs. Thornton arrived. On his visit in 1815, George Ticknor found Miss Ellen a handsome and sophisticated young woman; he had been very taken by the eighteen-year-old, remarking on her intelligence and other good qualities when reporting back to John and Abigail Adams. But it had been another visitor, Joseph Coolidge Jr., who had taken her back to Boston as his wife.

Jefferson's bittersweet parting with his favorite granddaughter had transpired early in the summer of 1825. Coolidge had arrived a year before that, bearing a letter from George Ticknor recommending him as a "gentleman of education and fortune . . . and [an] amiable and excellent character." Jefferson had taken a great liking to Coolidge, and he regarded Ellen and Joseph as an excellent match. Still, the old man felt acutely the absence of the granddaughter about whom he had once observed that, had she been a man, she would have been a great one. Ellen had been his chess partner—they often played beneath Monticello's trees in the summertime—but, having taken their vows in Monticello's parlor, she and her husband had departed on their wedding trip, traveling to New York, Lake Champlain, and through New England. As one of her sisters confided in a letter to Ellen in the weeks after she left, their beloved grandfather had been known to gaze at Ellen's accustomed chair in Monticello's parlor. When he did, someone would hasten to sit in her seat to distract the old man. But no one presumed to be able to take her place.

Jefferson had found a means of expressing his affection for his granddaughter when he learned that personal possessions of hers sent separately to Boston had been lost at sea. Among other items that went down with the packet from Richmond was a lap desk made specifically for her by Jefferson's gifted slave joiner, John Hemings. Jefferson wished to replace it but Hemings, his eyesight failing, felt unable to duplicate his earlier effort. Jefferson then decided upon a substitute. He chose the lap desk he himself had used for a half-century, the very one on which the document he called "the great Charter of our Independence" had been written. "[The desk] claims no merit of particular beauty," he wrote to Ellen and Joseph, "[But] its imaginary value will increase with years."

In an irony of timing, the gift would arrive at the home of Mr. and Mrs. Coolidge just after their return from visiting an eighty-eight-year-old widower residing on the second floor of his house in Quincy. Like Jefferson, John Adams was living out his last days surrounded by two generations of his family. He was lame and nearly blind, but, reported Ellen, "as far as his mind is concerned . . . he seems to have preserved the full vigor of his intellect . . . all the sprightliness of his fancy, all the vivacity of his thoughts and opinions." The couple delivered a letter from Jefferson. It would signal the last exchange of the long and unique correspondence between Jefferson and Adams, men who had been allies, opponents, then trusted confidants.

Such was the tissue of continuity and coincidence that accrued before the death of Jefferson and Adams within a few hours of one another on the afternoon of July 4, 1826.

FOR ELLEN'S BROTHER, THOMAS JEFFERSON RANDOLPH, their grandfather had nurtured high hopes. Twenty years earlier, Jefferson had arranged for his eldest grandson to reside with Charles Willson Peale and his family when he went to Philadelphia to further his schooling. On returning, Jefferson's namesake had assumed increasing responsibility for the management of Jefferson's estates. Even after young Jeff's marriage, he remained an intimate member of his grandfather's inner circle, as he and his bride took up residence in the Dome Room, the generous space beneath Monticello's dome, until the arrival of children made the accommodations too cramped. Then Jeff and his family had moved to a neighboring Jefferson farm, Tufton.

In January of 1826, Jeff settled his own father's overwhelming debts when Colonel Randolph's home and slaves were dispersed at public sale. Jeff managed to keep the plantation in the family, securing both the title to the property and, less happily, the enmity of his father (although his grandfather, mother, and sisters all approved of his actions). He continued to manage Monticello and Jefferson's various holdings, but what his grandfather himself termed his "embarrassed affairs" were in a desperate state.

The trust Jefferson had in his grandson's judgment was made explicit on March 16, 1826, when he named Jeff Randolph executor of his will and trustee of his estate, which he bequeathed to his daughter (and Jeff's and Ellen's mother), Martha Randolph. The following day he signed a list of codicils for specific bequests. Five slaves with trades, including John Hemings, were to be freed; his remaining books were to go to the University of Virginia; a walking staff was intended for James Madison, watches for the grandchildren, &c., &c. But all his papers he entrusted to Jeff. They were kept in Jefferson's *cabinet,* stored in a set of low wooden presses, neatly classified, bundled, and filed chronologically. The overflow of the 40,000 letters, journals, diaries, and other papers was stored in boxes nearby.

When the eighty-three-year-old patriarch died a few months later, Jeff and his mother knew they had no alternative: They would have to sell the contents of Monticello to satisfy creditors. The place was full of objects presumed to be of some value but, even more important, the slaves could be sold for ready money. Advertisements were placed, announcing the "Executor's Sale" would commence on January 15, 1827.

The sale took days, with uncounted items (few records survive of the sale) reaching the auction block. Aside from some of Jefferson's personal effects that were withheld, the family had to bid against the general public for items they wanted. Among the goods sold were farm animals, equipment, and grains; 130 slaves; furnishings and household goods; and "various other articles curious and useful to men of business and private families." A surprising number of lots of furniture and other household goods were bought by Jefferson's relations, since few items other than the slaves sold for high prices.

For the family, it was an exquisitely painful process. Even Jeff and Ellen found themselves bickering about who would get Grandfather's filing table, with its octagonal top, tripod base, and eight drawers (four of them square, four triangular). Ellen wanted it for her own use, while Jeff "said it was the only thing in the house he would bid against Joseph [Coolidge] for." For both grandchildren, the table held happy memories of the library at Monticello. Their mother, Martha, decided it would go to Boston.

Jeff got the revolving bookstand and his grandfather's writing device, the polygraph. Martha managed to retain most of the furniture that had been in her father's bedroom, even though she didn't have the money to pay for all of it. She also arranged for the tall clock from Jefferson's private suite, a highly accurate timepiece he used to assist him in his astronomical observations, to be purchased as a gift for Dr. Dunglison.

While the sale netted nearly $50,000, after back interest payments had been made, the estate's total indebtedness was reduced by only a third. The decision had been made to try to sell Jefferson's paintings and sculptures in a city where their value was more likely to be recognized. Whatever hopes the family held for a significant return were dashed when only one painting, a portrait of Ben Franklin, found a buyer at the exhibition Joseph Coolidge arranged at the Boston Athenaeum. A later auction would see more works sold, but long before that the heirs again recognized the inevitable: This time, it was Monticello itself that would have to be sold. In July of 1828 an advertisement appeared in the *Richmond Enquirer.* The asking price for "MONTICELLO, in the country of Albemarle, with the Lands of the estate adjacent thereto," was $70,000.

Martha Jefferson Randolph would depart that autumn, traveling north and eventually reaching Boston where she would live with the Coolidges. She was newly widowed (her difficult husband died that year); she had no funds and had been deprived of the home she had known since birth. Even after her marriage, she had regularly returned to Monticello when her father was in residence, reigning as the lady of the house since her mother's death in 1782. But she was philosophical, observing in her notebook that "there is a time in human suffering when succeeding sufferings are but like snow falling on an iceberg." She left orders that visitors who wished to see the house were to be given the tour, for which a price of fifty cents was exacted by the caretaker.

At that, it was a high price, as little remained to be seen. Visitors to the house reported it was a sad and abandoned place, like a book with many of its pages torn out. Without Jefferson's collections, the large proportions of the rooms looked cavernous. In the absence of the mind and personality that had bound the disparate decorations, furnishings, and spaces together, the house seemed merely eccentric with its too-small stairways, which made the upper levels almost inaccessible. A few tired pieces of furniture remained after the dispersal sale, among them Martha's harpsichord, abandoned in the parlor as unplayable, useful only for the mahogany of its case. Along with a few books and the two immense pier mirrors in the parlor, the built-in clock in the Indian Hall remained, although it no longer worked.

The house would not sell until 1831. Despairing of having to make extensive repairs as the empty house deteriorated, Jeff accepted an offer from Charlottesville apothecary James Turner Barclay for the house and 552 acres. The purchase price was $4,500.

WHEN JOHN H. B. LATROBE CAME TO VISIT IN 1832, the house had deteriorated still further. Barclay had planted the property with mulberry trees, hoping to raise silkworms. Jefferson's landscape was rapidly fading into memory as trees were chopped down and garden beds went to seed. As for the house, its terraces had collapsed and part of the roof had fallen in. Broken windows and rotting shutters added to the air of abandonment. "The first thing that strikes you," Latrobe reported, "is the utter ruin and desolation of everything."

Within two years, Barclay was gone and the house was for sale once more. The next owners, a New York family named Levy, would own the place for almost ninety years. They, too, would have a checkered record as caretakers. Uriah Levy, who purchased the house in 1836, held Jefferson in high esteem, having literally put the third president on a pedestal, donating a statue he had commissioned of Jefferson to the nation. In his eccentric fashion, he did well by the property, performing basic maintenance and leaving the house largely unchanged. For a time the house was in governmental hands—Levy tried to leave it to the nation and, during the Civil War, the Confederate States seized the property after classifying Levy, a U.S. Navy officer, an "enemy alien." After the war, a protracted legal battle enabled the Levy family to regain clear title and Uriah's nephew, Jefferson Monroe Levy, began his stewardship.

He inherited a house whose skylights had been shingled over. The "tesselated" parquet floor on which Ticknor had remarked was covered with grain, since the parlor had become a granary complete with winnowing machine. Cattle were stabled in the basement. Grass grew from the gutters. But Jefferson Levy, a lawyer who speculated on real estate and stocks, wanted a summer house. He proved to be an active owner, adding indoor plumbing and remodeling portions of the upper stories. He filled the house with furniture to his own tastes, rather than Jefferson's, including numerous French Victorian pieces, many in the style of the Second Empire of Napoleon III. He favored gilt mirrors and tasseled draperies, and slept in a gold Louis XIV bed on a dais. A billiard table was installed in the Dome Room.

He made the house available to visitors, humble and not-so-humble. Theodore Roosevelt stunned the Secret Service agents assigned to protect him when the president, an experienced horseman, elected to enjoy the Little Mountain's meandering approach on horseback, leaving his security men in his dust. Monticello had a small but steady stream of visitors over the years, and there was a campaign before World War I to compel Jefferson Levy to give the house to the nation. Yet Jefferson's role as architect of Monticello remained unacknowledged.

EVEN AFTER THE HOUSE WAS SOLD OUT OF THE FAMILY IN 1831, neither Ellen nor Jeff ever lost interest. Thirty years after leaving Monticello, she responded to an inquiry from Henry S. Randall, an early biographer of Jefferson's. She composed a long and memorable letter filled with warm and historically invaluable recollections of her grandfather. Jeff Randolph remained a frequent visitor to Monticello during Barclay's brief ownership and after. Even into his eighties, he regaled younger members of his family with stories of the place.

Among his listeners was a great nephew, a Massachusetts boy who also happened to be Ellen's grandson. As an impressionable lad of ten, Thomas Jefferson Coolidge Jr. visited old Mr. Randolph at his home, Edgehill, a house he had built in 1828 on the plantation that had been his father's. The boy and the octogenarian rode together in full view of Mr. Jefferson's Monticello. As an adult years later, Coolidge wrote, "I well remember being perched up on a large horse and his showing me the way across the deep ford of the Rivanna with the water up to our saddles." Memories of the time spent with Great Uncle Jeff Randolph, who despite his age remained "a fine hearty old Virginia gentleman," stayed with the boy from Massachusetts, "bring[ing] the household [at Monticello] quite close to the present."

T. Jefferson Coolidge's childhood trips to Albemarle County helped inspire in him a life-long interest in his great-great-grandfather. He was reminded of Monticello by the ink-and-wash rendering that Robert Mills had done for Mr. Jefferson in about 1803, which had hung in Monticello's dining room; Grandmother Ellen had gifted it to his father who had, in turn, presented it to him. The idea would occur to T. Jefferson Coolidge in early adulthood that he might build his own Monticello, which he proceeded to do. He constructed a replica, making certain climatic adaptations, in Manchester-by-Sea, a well-to-do coastal town north of Boston. Perhaps inevitably, the experience drew him back to Virginia, and he and his wife made the pilgrimage to Monticello in 1911.

While in Charlottesville that year, he made a discovery. Most of the papers that once filled the presses and boxes in Jefferson's *cabinet* were gone. Charged with the proper disposition of the unprecedented cache of correspondence, Jeff Randolph had tried to sell it to the nation many decades earlier. At first he had met with little interest since the Library of Congress in the years after Jefferson's death was regarded as an archive for congressional, not presidential papers. But over a period of more than twenty years, reams of Jefferson's official correspondence and other documents were sold to the Department of State. Other papers had made their way to other repositories, including the Massachusetts Historical Society, where Coolidge's father, T. Jefferson Coolidge Sr., had deposited correspondence, farm books, almanacs, and account books he had inherited. Only a small fraction of the papers remained in family hands when the younger Coolidge and his wife, Clara Amory Coolidge, arrived in Virginia.

Mr. Coolidge came both to see Monticello first hand and to visit his extended family. To his surprise, he learned more about the architecture of the house from his family meetings than from the building itself. In talking with two second cousins, Miss Cornelia Jefferson Taylor and Mrs. Mary Walker Randolph, both of whom were Jeff 's granddaughters, Coolidge learned that they, too, had inherited some Jefferson papers along with the house at Edgehill. In fact, they allowed that in their possession were a number of architectural drawings. Having constructed his Massachusetts Monticello by working from measured drawings made well after construction, his interest was immediately piqued. Eventually, he persuaded Cornelia and Mary to part with the portfolios of architectural renderings.

Relegated to Edgehill's attic for decades, the drawings had sustained damage from both water and mice. But the collection was largely intact when T. Jefferson Coolidge took it back to Boston in 1911. He would die suddenly, at age forty-nine, the following year; thereafter, his widow would deposit the drawings at the Massachusetts Historical Society. All of which enabled Fiske Kimball to embark upon his explication of Jefferson, as well as the other architects represented in the collection, who included William Thornton, Benjamin Henry Latrobe, James Hoban, and Robert Mills.

WHEN FISKE KIMBALL CAME TO CHARLOTTESVILLE for the first time in 1914, he had just begun work on the book that he was then calling *Thomas Jefferson as Architect*. His fee as its editor provided him with the ready cash to pay for the journey. "That summer, to see the buildings I was to write about," wrote Kimball, "I made a hasty trip to Virginia." He took Marie as far as Washington, where she planned to spend time with her brother and work at the Library of Congress, then he headed straight for the Academical Village.

He wanted to see the drawings there—for Kimball, the drawings would always come first—and next he made his way to Monticello.

His guide that sultry August day was not the absentee owner, Jefferson
Monroe Levy, but Levy's agent. A Charlottesville man, Thomas L. Rhodes
had lived on or near Jefferson's mountain all his life; he had spent the previous twenty-five years as caretaker at Monticello. He had led many notables
through the house, among them New York architect Stanford White. While
remodeling the Rotunda at the Academical Village after a fire gutted it in
1895, White had developed an admiration for Jefferson and, Rhodes told
Kimball, upon seeing Monticello the first time, he proclaimed "that every
proportion and detail [are] perfect."

Having overseen all the recent work done to both grounds and buildings,
Rhodes knew the property intimately. Kimball also recognized him as "a wor-
shiper of Thomas Jefferson," which, at times, had put him at odds with Levy.
While Jefferson Levy valued the Jefferson past at Monticello, he also wanted
to have a comfortable and impressive house that reflected his own needs and
tastes. Rhodes, charged with effecting Levy's plans, had attempted whenever
possible to carry them out with an eye to preserving Jefferson's architectural
fabric.

On that first visit, Kimball was in a hurry. He was due in Ann Arbor early
in September to assume his teaching responsibilities at the University of
Michigan. In a few short days in Virginia, he also needed to visit several
other buildings of Jefferson's that he knew only from the drawings. And he
hoped to rejoin Marie to review some of the Jefferson papers. Whatever his
time constraints, Kimball also wanted to test a premise that had occurred to
him in examining the Coolidge drawings. He was the first student of Jefferson to begin to understand the construction history of the house; specifically,
he believed that Monticello had been conceived as one structure and completed to another, larger design.

Once Kimball confided his theory, Thomas Rhodes proved the right man
to help him. Knowing the house better than anyone alive, Rhodes was able
to shortcut the inspection process. He directed the examination efficiently,
leading Kimball to discover evidence in the configuration of the basement
walls that confirmed the original structure had been half the size of the finished house. In a matter of hours, Kimball later noted, "I was able to verify an
inference from the drawings in Boston, that the house had been drastically
remodeled, doubled in width, after 1793."

The germination of that insight produced a much larger understanding of

Monticello. Kimball made a series of remarkable deductions when he reexamined the Boston drawings in light of what Mr. Rhodes's tour had revealed to him in Charlottesville. Many seemingly unrelated Jefferson drawings began to fit into a logical sequence. With one simple observation—*There must have been two Monticellos*—Kimball's understanding of Jefferson's architectural thinking had made an immense leap.

It meant that, in a sense, there were two Jeffersons, too. The first, a bookish Palladian, had moved beyond the vernacular brick boxes of his neighbors, a man who had begun, according to Kimball, "an epochal . . . return to canonical proportion and scholarly correctness of detail." The second Jefferson, just back from the Old World, had found "the strict Palladian ideal . . . no longer satisfied him." While his admiration for Palladio never wavered, he came to revere ancient Roman precedents. He matured, moving from imitations of Palladio and his post-Renaissance English followers Gibbs and Morris. He became an innovator who adapted ancient ideas in new ways.

As Kimball would later explain, Monticello was, at its "inception . . . a typical Virginia mansion of those days." As Jefferson reimagined it, however, "he brought about, ultimately, the transformation of the type."

WHEN THE LETTER ARRIVED IN AUGUST 1919, Marie and Fiske were packing. They were readying for the move to Charlottesville so that Fiske could assume his new duties at the University. The return address on the envelope—*The Metropolitan Museum of Art, New York*—was unexpected.

The secretary of the museum, Henry W. Kent, was the sender. "The Trustees of this Museum desire to give, annually, a series of important lectures by a scholar, which will be printed, if possible by a University Press," Kent began. "I write to ask if you would consider giving such a course; . . . if you would consider favorably the idea of the publication of the lectures; and if you would be willing and able to give them in spring of 1920."

The little genie that placed golden opportunities in Kimball's path had struck again, and the very day he received Kent's letter, Kimball responded. "Your kind letter interests me very much . . . and I may answer all three of the questions in the affirmative." Despite the many demands facing him at his new post at the Academical Village, he proposed delivering the lectures the following March.

The assignment seemed to have been tailored for Professor Kimball. He had begun to range well beyond Jefferson country in his research and writings, working on Latrobe and other early architects. He had begun shaping a comprehensive view of the entire history of American architecture in one chapter of his book *A History of Architecture* (1918), offering a capsule summary of American buildings from the Pre-Columbian up to Frank Lloyd Wright's.

With a characteristic burst of manic energy, Kimball set to work in early September upon arriving in Charlottesville. He drafted an outline for five lectures that quickly won approval from the Met, along with a note of encouragement from Mr. Kent. "Our real hope is that you are going to produce the notable and scholarly history of American architecture. We are not desirous of having it made 'popular.' . . . The course you are to give is designed as the 'scholars' course' [and] . . . there is the opportunity, we feel, to give the study of American antiquities a higher place than it has ever had."

Kent set high expectations, but no higher than Kimball established for himself. Kimball had no intention of rehashing the ideas of others; he had already expressed to colleagues—in person and in print—his dissatisfaction with much that had been written. The previous year a pair of articles had appeared in the *Architectural Review* bearing his byline in which he had begun to define his terms. He disliked the usual nomenclature, musing on the misuse of the word "colonial" which, oddly, had come to be applied to buildings built after the Revolution as well as before. Kimball felt such catchall designations as "Jacobean," "Georgian," and "Federal" carried a false sense of specificity. He preferred what he called "periodization," and advised Kent that his lectures would cover colonial architecture of the seventeenth century; colonial architecture in the eighteenth century; and the architecture of the early Republic. Having dealt in much of his previous writings with public architecture, Kimball also decided to focus his lectures on residential buildings, believing that "the general development of domestic architecture has not yet been adequately handled."

He established some ground rules for his research. Whenever possible, he would associate specific houses with their designer-builders; and he would seek to identify the architectural sourcebooks used. Both would be critical to his survey. Furthermore, he would elevate chronology as the first principle above all others. He would rely on historic documents to establish dates of construction for specific buildings, using "building contracts and accounts, inscriptions, and original designs, as well as inventories, wills, deeds, and other documents . . . to determine with sufficient and in most cases with absolute exactness the dates and original form of nearly two hundred houses between the time of settlement and 1835."

The goal was objectivity. Kimball canvassed every source he could find for certifiable construction dates, not merely hand-me-down hearsay. He omitted houses for which dates could not be documented. He assembled tables, arranging the houses of known date in order. Using them as the central structure—he was creating a sort of family tree, with houses suspended from its great branches—he collated an immense body of data, culled from hundreds of sources.

The lectures were a great success, and a book did indeed follow, an expanded version of the lectures titled *Domestic Architecture of the American Colonies and of the Early Republic*. Even in the absence of a darkened room and slides projected on a screen, one can almost imagine the dim echo of Dr. Kimball's booming basso while reading and inspecting the book's 219 plates of photographs and drawings culled from many sources. Kimball talks his reader through time, debunking the myth of the log cabin, describing the essentially medieval character of seventeenth-century colonial architecture. The tone is just short of conversational as he heralds the arrival in the eighteenth century of the "academic style," where the emphasis shifts from the functional (staying alive in a new and rather unwelcoming climate) to considerations of pure form, with the introduction of symmetry and classical elements (these more settled Americans began to be concerned with the appearance of their houses). At first, Kimball observes, the classical Orders were applied in "an isolated and ungrammatical" way, as they were borrowed essentially at random from books. Only gradually, he points out, did drawings become necessary as the buildings gained complexity. He follows the evolution of volumes (rectangular rooms are succeeded by octagonal, circular, and elliptical shapes); of massing (the roof pitches become less steep; domes and temple fronts appear); and of the details (doors and windows enlarge and assume different configurations as the Baroque gives way to the Adamesque and Roman and, eventually, to the Grecian).

Thomas Jefferson, Architect had established Kimball's academic bona fides when it appeared. "It portends well, above all, for the future of architectural writing in this country," a Columbia University professor had written of that book in the *Architectural Record*. "Its accuracy and detail, its scholarly completeness, its spirit of thorough investigation, its fine presswork, all combine to make it an edifying example for writers and publishers alike; and this all in addition to the great light it casts upon a fascinating subject which constitutes the first real chapter of republican architecture in the United States." The book has remained *the* basic reference on Jefferson's architecture for almost a century. But the big folio could have no broad public currency, having been privately published, its 350 copies gifted to a select list of libraries, institutions, friends, and family.

Domestic Architecture was a different matter. Kimball made the case that American architecture was a continuum; like Jefferson, he expected books, including this one, to be tools for architects. As he told his publisher, Charles Scribner Jr., he wanted to give its readers "references to the whereabouts of all such material which the architect needs." While it was of undoubted help to many architects, its true value to a larger readership of students of the past would become evident over the decades. The book is still in print and, as an important scholar a generation later would say, *Domestic Architecture* became the "scholarly basis for subsequent study of early American architecture."

The book also gave Kimball important visibility in New York, and helped secure him his next job. He had been charged with founding the School of Art and Architecture at the University of Virginia. During his four years in Charlottesville, he had continued to teach and conduct research, but he had also branched out from architecture to become curator of the University's Bayly Museum of Fine Arts. Demonstrating a previously untapped capacity for both museum work and administration, Kimball's range of accomplishments—which now included strong ties to the Metropolitan Museum, thanks to his *Domestic Architecture* lectures and book—had come to the attention of Elmer Ellsworth Brown.

As chancellor of New York University, Brown wanted to establish a new school devoted to the history of art, one that would link his university in Greenwich Village with the monumental Met Museum and the National Academy of Design uptown. Kimball seemed just the man to make the connections and, in 1923, Brown hired him to be the Samuel F. B. Morse Professor of the Literature of the Arts of Design at NYU. Kimball's move to New York further added to his already impressive résumé, as he would found the Institute of Fine Arts and NYU's Department of Art History.

Even in the much larger world of New York City, Kimball would find that Monticello remained a cardinal point on his intellectual compass. Shortly after arriving in New York in 1923, he and Marie had received an unexpected visitor. "One day old Jefferson Levy came puffing upstairs to our parlor floor apartment on Twelfth Street." Levy wanted to sell Monticello and had put the house on the market in 1919. In the interim, he had negotiated with a variety of groups and individuals interested in preserving the house as a monument to Jefferson, but no understanding had been reached.

"I was naturally interested in the preservation of Jefferson's place, Monticello, which was in the hands of [this] pompous and absurd old character. . . . He liked people to think of him as a descendant of Jefferson, when he was merely named from him. He took great credit for having 'preserved' and 'restored' Monticello. . . . But [then] he was a congressman from New York and passed for a rich man, [though] he had mortgaged Monticello to the eyes and was also deeply in debt."

While Kimball was not responsible for closing the deal (a new organization, the Thomas Jefferson Memorial Foundation, finally secured the deed late that year), he did become the object of one of the Foundation's first acts. He was appointed chairman of its restoration committee in early 1924. It was not a job per se, as Kimball volunteered to work without compensation, and years would be required to pay off the mortgage (Levy accepted $100,000 at the time of settlement, with the promise of $400,000 more; the last payment would be made to his heirs in 1940). Even in the absence of money to spend, Kimball immediately began planning the restoration and furnishing of the house. He also helped raise funds and, perhaps more important, persuaded the Foundation to adopt a policy, as he put it, "of admitting none but authentic furnishings, although this condemned the house for many years to barrenness." On the other hand, this stricture gave Kimball better ammunition with which to approach the Jefferson descendants, with a number of whom he remained on excellent terms. Over time, "loans and gifts of [Jefferson objects] began to come in to relieve this barrenness." When in 1936 funds finally became available, he and Marie (she had been named Monticello's curator) would mastermind the restoration of Monticello to the house that Jefferson knew.

IV.
Spring . . . Traveling through Time

BETWEEN 1809 AND 1815, THOMAS JEFFERSON made repeated trips to Forest, Virginia, some seventy miles southwest of Monticello. There he found respite at Poplar Forest, his home away from home. At the center of the 4,819-acre plantation that his wife, Martha Wayles Jefferson, had inherited from her father, Jefferson had constructed what was probably the first octagonal house in America amid a grove of poplars.

His admirers had become legion as he completed his second term as president (he left office in March 1809), and Jefferson found that Monticello had become one of the new nation's intellectual centers, a place that historian Merrill Peterson has called "a country philosophical hall." Over the years Jefferson would receive at Monticello not only the Thorntons and George Ticknor but thousands of other visitors and, in the tradition of Virginia hospitality, he welcomed all of them. His life had become an ongoing, forever-evolving dialogue on a wide array of subjects. Certainly, he liked that, but he also needed a break from time to time. His solution had been to begin construction in 1806 of his retreat at Poplar Forest, where he could be alone with his thoughts and his family for extended periods.

According to family recollections, he made the journey there in a carriage called a landau. It had two facing seats for passengers, with a hood that rolled open to reveal the burgeoning blooms and welcome the warm breezes. The source of locomotion was a four-horse team; their stately pace meant that three days were required to cover the distance to the hamlet of Forest on the outskirts of Lynchburg.

The tableau is a pretty one. His entourage is headed away from the bustle of Monticello. Mr. Jefferson is accompanied by his two favorite granddaughters, Ellen Randolph and her younger sister, Cornelia. He rarely played the forbidding grandparent with these girls or with any of his grandchildren. Stories abound of them running into his arms, of him rewarding them with kisses, of the great man chatting happily with them. "What an amusement do these little creatures afford us," a friend once observed to Jefferson as she watched the grandchildren at play at Monticello. To which Jefferson replied, "Yes, it is only with them that a grave man can play the fool." The trips to Poplar Forest offered exactly the sort of domestic scene Jefferson had dreamed of upon his retirement from public life: The old man and his grandchildren, bumping along in their landau with its top tied down, enjoying the spring day.

Looking backward from the vantage of the year 1856, Ellen Coolidge described the house at Poplar Forest to which they traveled. "It was of brick, one storey in front, and, owing to the falling of the ground, two in the rear. It was an exact octagon, with a centre-hall twenty feet square, lighted from above. This was a beautiful room, and served as a dining-room. Round it were

For many years, this elevation of Poplar Forest was believed to have been executed by
Cornelia Randolph, the most artistically inclined of Jefferson's grandchildren. More recently,
however, it has been attributed to John Neilson, an Irish builder (and draftsman) of great
skill who worked at Monticello and the Academical Village but, strangely, not at Poplar
Forest. *The University of Virginia Library*

grouped a bright drawing-room looking south, my grandfather's own chamber, three other bedrooms, and a pantry. A terrace extended from one side of
the house; there was a portico in front connected by a vestibule with the centre room, and in the rear a verandah, on which the drawing-room opened,
with its windows to the floor." By the time she wrote those words, the little
villa at Poplar Forest as she had known it existed only in memory, having
burned to an empty masonry hulk in 1845.

After a fashion, the building did survive. It was reconstituted by
nineteenth-century owners, and given a Greek Revival look quite different
from the Roman Classicism Jefferson favored. It was effectively forgotten,
with Jefferson scholars as late as the 1950s reporting that "the building is no
longer in existence." Kimball knew of it, of course, having traveled there first
during his whirlwind 1914 Virginia tour. The Corporation for Jefferson's
Poplar Forest, which now operates the property as an historic site, embarked
in the 1990s on a restoration of the Jefferson design. What they have on display today is not a Monticello-style museum. The bare brick walls on its interior attest to the fact it remains a work-in-progress.

Yet the idea of the house survives intact. The floor plan, the volumes of
the rooms, and the mass and detailing remain very much as Ellen's grandfather envisioned them. Poplar Forest is an exercise in solid geometry, with its
central cube installed within an octagon. It is a variation on the idea of a

house with a central rotunda that Jefferson, borrowing from Palladio and James Gibbs's *A Book of Architecture,* had worked and reworked over the years, notably for his entry in the President's House competition. When Jefferson called it "an octagon 50 f. in *diameter,*" his poetic license suggests the essential appeal the idealized structure had to the man Abigail Adams dubbed "the Phylosopher." It's an idea that seems cool, rational, and beautiful.

And practical, too, for Jefferson always had a taste for what he called "conveniences." One such was an early odometer he acquired during his second term as president; he put it to use coming and going from Poplar Forest. Attached to a carriage wheel, the device rang each time his landau covered another mile. The ringing bell would interrupt the conversation—perhaps he was talking, as Ellen reported he was known to do, "about his own youth and early friends, tell[ing] us stories of former days." He would record in his notebook the distance traveled. Tables in Jefferson's hand exist that record the elapsed distances between points on the route from Monticello to Poplar Forest.

Just as Jefferson liked to record in linear fashion the events of his life, he also liked to read history's timeline. He understood that life can be lived in the moment, to be sure; but he also valued both retrospective and prospective views as a politician, philosopher, inventor, and student of history. To consider Monticello, that exercise in architectural autobiography, is to be deflected away from the artifact itself in both chronological and geographical directions. Thanks to Kimball and the other scholars who have built upon his findings, Monticello must be seen as a narrative.

The story is a personal one, but its outline reveals the national revolution in architectural thinking that Jefferson fostered. He practiced his craft at Monticello as an individual; as a public man, he sought out Charles-Louis Clérisseau to aid him in designing the Virginia Capitol at Richmond, and later hired Dr. Thornton and Benjamin Henry Latrobe in the Federal City; later still, he solicited both Thornton's and Latrobe's advice in planning his Academical Village. And all the while, his architectural thinking hearkened back to the buildings of ancient Rome. More than anyone else, he helped make classical architecture the norm for civic buildings in the young United States, just as he helped establish the classical as the predominant manner for generations of stylish and desirable domestic buildings, too. In his native central Virginia, he created a building culture that defined the look of the region's architecture for a generation and beyond. Finally, Poplar Forest represents a late-in-life idealized vision of simple purity.

Jefferson's architectural accomplishments seem all the more remarkable given the subsequent eclipse of his reputation. Despite having done so much to shape American tastes, Thomas Jefferson, Architect, had almost entirely faded from memory when Dr. Kimball came along.

CHAPTER 6

MEANWHILE, IN MASSACHUSETTS

"The time has been within my own recollection when New England did not contain a single professed Architect. The first individual who laid claim to that character was Charles Bulfinch, Esq., of this city; to whose classical taste we are indebted for many fine buildings [and] . . . the first impulse to good taste . . . [in] Architecture, in this part of the Country."

—ASHER BENJAMIN,
THE PRACTICE OF ARCHITECTURE (1833)

I.
November 1790 . . . Trimountain . . . Boston

THE CLIMB TO THE TOP was short but arduous. The grassy knoll on which he stood capped the conical peak, which was barren of trees and littered with rocks. At an altitude of 138 feet above sea level, the summit could be reached only by climbing the steep sides, but once its acme had been achieved, the central peak of Trimountain offered a panoramic vista.

Standing atop the tallest point on the ridge that ran like a spine along the peninsula's north-south axis, Charles Bulfinch surveyed the town that he would transform. From his vantage, Boston's topography resembled a paint splatter, its principal landmass a peninsula with a jagged coastline that extended into the waters around it. Only a narrow spit of land, Boston Neck, saved the place from being an island. The Charles River defined the town's

Charles Bulfinch, Gentleman, painted in London, in 1786, by Mather Brown.
Harvard University Portrait Collection, gift of Francis V. Bulfinch

watery perimeter to the north and west, Boston Bay to the southeast. Like smaller spatterings, numerous islands dotted the nearby waters.

The appearance of the city had changed little in Bulfinch's twenty-seven years. The population had not yet reached 20,000 souls, having increased by only a few thousand over the preceding half-century. But Bulfinch himself had changed, his aesthetic appreciation transformed by his Grand Tour. He had left for Europe at age twenty-two, a Harvard graduate who already had spent several years working in the counting house of a wealthy merchant and family friend, Joseph Barrell. Trade had been paralyzed by the Revolution and, Bulfinch found, "My time passed very idly and I was at leisure to cultivate a taste for Architecture, which was encouraged by attending to Mr. Barrell's improvement of his estate . . . & the houses of some friends." The young man, who had taken to making pen-and-ink drawings of Corinthian columns at age ten, had discovered the designs of Robert Adam at the Harvard Library and the plates of Palladio's buildings on his own family's shelves. His musing on architecture was an enjoyable avocation he had pursued in his ample spare time until his mother gave him a £200 legacy she had received from an exiled Tory uncle. He promptly sailed for Europe.

Departing in June 1785, he husbanded the money carefully, staying with family in England and, armed with a letter of introduction from John Adams, found accommodations at Jefferson's Hôtel de Langeac in Paris. He journeyed south through France to Pisa, Florence, and Rome. He liked what he saw: "I was delighted in observing the numerous objects & beauties of nature &

art that I met with on all sides, particularly the wonders of Architecture." Taking the advice of Mr. Jefferson, he visited classical sites on his journey, among them the Maison Carrée in Nîmes. Together with John Trumbull and the Cosways, he followed Jefferson's lead in Paris, too, examining such modern designs as the city's new hôtels. In London he saw the new Somerset House, completed only the previous year, a striking neoclassical government building built by Sir William Chambers, Robert Adam's chief rival and Surveyor General to King George III. He also traveled to Bath, a Palladian city with its crescent-shaped rows of houses that had been constructed not one house at a time but in blocks. In coming to know the new urban elegance of Europe, where classical details had been melded into fresh, new forms, Bulfinch's frame of reference had been forever altered.

Back in Boston, from his hilltop aerie, he saw streetscapes dotted with foursquare dwellings that seemed to his new, sophisticated taste a generation or more out of date. Boston was a city whose character had been established generations earlier by Puritans and Royalists. Near the foot of the hills, the town looked more like a village, with boxy dwellings surrounded by generous yards with fruit trees and vegetable and flower gardens. As his gaze followed the landscape rolling toward the harbor, the view was of a medieval cross-hatch of lanes and alleys that met the water at the town dock and countless other quays and landings. But barely three years after his return from Europe, a demonstration was at hand of his very different vision.

When Bulfinch left home that day, he walked past his childhood home on Bowdoin Square, where his parents still lived. As he continued up the hill, passing an open four-acre field that belonged to his father, he had been able to raise his eyes to admire one of his first executed designs. A sixty-foot-tall column in the Doric order, the Sentry Hill Monument was a symbol of the city's heroic past, as one of the carved slate tablets affixed to its base proclaimed:

TO COMMEMORATE

THAT TRAIN OF EVENTS

WHICH LED

TO THE AMERICAN REVOLUTION,

AND FINALLY SECURED

LIBERTY AND INDEPENDENCE

TO THE UNITED STATES,

THIS COLUMN IS ERECTED

BY THE VOLUNTARY CONTRIBUTION

Bulfinch's Monument atop Sentry Hill, Boston, in an engraving from a Thomas Sully
painting. *Bostonian Society/Old State House*

OF THE CITIZENS

OF BOSTON.

MDCCXC.

As he continued up the slope, he walked through open pastures owned by Governor John Hancock, and into the six-rod precinct owned by the city of Boston. At the center of the ninety-nine-foot-square plot of common land stood the column, a symbol not only of the revolutionary past but of Bulfinch's plans.

On his return from the Old World in January 1787, he had known for certain he had no desire to return to the "business habits of buying & selling" with Mr. Barrell. As the grandson of one of Boston's wealthiest merchants, he didn't have to, and his marriage to heiress Hannah Apthorp in 1788 added to his standing as a man of property. He listed himself in the Boston directory as simply a "gentleman," but just months after his return to Boston, on November 5, 1787, he had formally submitted a plan for a new State House for Massachusetts. The legislative committee charged with the matter had not yet acted, but he had other building projects under discussion, too, including two church designs for the towns of Pittsfield and Taunton and another in Boston to replace one that had burned. Thus far, however, only the column on the hill neared completion, and it stood as tangible evidence that he could—no, that he *would*—introduce a new mode of design to his town and state.

The chill of winter had arrived early, so the pargeting of lime plaster that was to coat the column could not be applied until spring. Even so, the edifice of exposed brick was an extraordinary sight to Bostonians accustomed to seeing a tall wooden mast on that same hilltop. Since 1634, a series of wooden poles had stood at the summit. A pot filled with tar had been suspended from an iron bracket at the pole's top, with crossed sticks to function as a ladder along the shaft. The tar was to have been lit in the event the city was attacked, but the occasion had never arisen, and no flames had ever licked out from the iron pot as a warning beacon. Nevertheless, some of the townspeople had taken to calling the place "Beacon Hill."

The last of those wooden standards had been a sixty-five-foot-tall mast braced by timbers at the bottom that had blown down the previous year. Although John Hancock offered to pay for a new mast, Bulfinch proposed his grander alternative and even undertook to manage the subscription to raise money from his proper Bostonian friends. It was to be the first monument in the nation to the War of Independence, and the idea took hold quickly. Thanks to the social prominence of his physician father and his mother's merchant family, Bulfinch knew the rich and powerful in Boston, people with names like Amory, Coolidge, Derby, and Otis. They soon underwrote his scheme, just as they would soon become his architectural clients.

The column was in the Doric order and, when completed the following spring, it was to be topped by a carved wooden eagle. As Bulfinch himself knew, it was the work of a dilettante. His drawing skills remained rudimentary, and he had to rely on his growing library and his recollections of his Grand Tour for inspiration. Yet no one else in town had the vision he did of how to change the vista before him, to add buildings and streetscapes like those he had seen in Paris and London and Bath.

Over the next three decades, Charles Bulfinch would remake Boston.

II.
1794 . . . Cobble Hill . . . Charlestown

BILLED AS "THE GREATEST THAT HAD EVER BEEN PROJECTED IN AMERICA," the bridge had been completed in 1786, its £15,000 cost underwritten by eighty-four Bostonians. The Charles River Bridge had opened with great fanfare in June of that year when, cheered by a crowd of more than ten thousand citizens and accompanied by the pealing of bells and cannon salutes, a procession marched west across its 1,503-foot length to Charlestown.

The toll bridge, its builders hoped, would attract much traffic and enable Boston to become the central commercial hub for its region. It was the most remarkable engineering feat yet accomplished in the young country, but for Joseph Barrell, its significance was more mundane. It represented easy access to the city from his *villa suburbana*.

The bridge had lured him across the river in 1790 when, thinking his Boston properties overtaxed by the city fathers, he purchased two hundred acres of high land in Charlestown. He had imagined a new manse for himself, along with stables, farm buildings, barns, and dovecotes (the chicken houses of the day) to supply his table. On his parklike acres, he wanted a pleasure ground with an orchard, a fishpond, and a summerhouse. In the English manner, he gave his estate a name, calling it Pleasant Hill.

The timing seemed auspicious. In his business life, the omens were for a profitable future as he and his investors, including both Charles Bulfinch and his father, had just welcomed home ships from voyages to China, Russia, and the previously uncharted coastline of the Pacific Northwest. The trips had proven a great success, with one of the ships, the *Columbia*, becoming the first American vessel to breach the waters of a great river in the Northwest, to which it gave its name. The ships had been the first American vessels to circumnavigate the globe and, Barrell believed, they were harbingers of much successful trading to come.

Barrell's interests extended beyond his mercantile activities. He had joined the Sons of Liberty before the Revolution and served on numerous governing committees. Years before, he had commissioned John Singleton Copley to take portraits of himself and his wife. Though dressed in fine fabrics, the young man Copley portrayed had left his hair unpowdered; beneath a receding hairline, his unassuming countenance suggested a man with a thoughtful and appreciative regard for the world around him. Here, the artist seemed to say, was a man with power, influence, *and* taste.

While Bulfinch had not chosen to resume working in Mr. Barrell's counting house after his return from abroad, their friendship flourished. Bulfinch was just half Barrell's age, but having heard him expound on the beauties of architecture in Paris and London, Barrell knew to whom to turn for the design of

Pleasant Hill. He sought out the designer of the Sentry Hill Monument and asked for a plan.

Bulfinch was happy to oblige. In the years just before and after 1790, he engaged himself, as he liked to put it, "pursuing no business but giving gratuitous advice in architecture." The money in his wife's and his own family enabled him to be the gentleman designer; but Mr. Barrell's charge had a double appeal. Barrell had the money and, even more important, the desire to build a different kind of a house, one that would appear new and visionary to his fellow Bostonians.

The Charles River Bridge had made Pleasant Hill an easy destination. There was ample room for a carriage—the bridge was forty-two feet wide, supported by 75 piers of oak timbers. On his journeys there in the fall of 1792, Bulfinch could observe the house on Lechmere Point from the wooden roadbed atop the waters of the Charles. The brickwork of the structure's masonry shell had by then reached the second story. On his trips there early the following summer, he would find Barrell in residence; although the house was not yet complete, the eager owner moved in anyway. Six months after that, Bulfinch would find just one room unfinished, the carpenters and plasterers still at work.

That room—"my best room" Mr. Barrell called it—had proved to be the subject of a great deal of curiosity even before the house was completed. It exacted much comment because, as if to call attention to itself, the sweeping curve of its outside wall produced a gentle swelling beyond the plane of the rest of the garden façade of the house. The same elliptical curve carried upward, too, defined by a wrought-iron balustrade that enclosed a grand portico supported by sixteen-foot columns. The curved cornice at the roofline was crowned by another balustrade.

The Barrell house was a happy shock to Bostonians who, unlike Bulfinch, knew little of projecting elliptical interior spaces like those he had seen in London and in Mr. Jefferson's Paris. Until the Barrell house was built, the prevailing floor plan in the Massachusetts capital had remained uniformly foursquare: Take one center hall, the formula dictated, add chimneys on each side, then flank the stacks with rooms front and rear. The result? Four rooms per floor, a central stair, and a house neat and tidy as you like.

But Mr. Barrell's house? Those who got to visit Mr. Bulfinch's design found it a theatrical experience, its face seventy-four-feet wide, the footprint forty-two-feet deep. On arrival, the visitor entered the large house from a sheltering entrance porch framed by four twenty-foot tall columns (or "masts," as

Note in this circa 1792–93 elevation by Bulfinch the elliptical swelling of the oval room of
Mr. Barrell's mansion. *Boston Athenaeum*

Barrell referred to them in his correspondence, ever the merchant and
shipowner). The rectangular grand vestibule felt familiar enough, though
perhaps a bit generous for the time. But one's eye was quickly drawn to the
three arches that lined the wall opposite the entrance, drawing the visitor
forward. Passing though the central arch, Mr. Barrell's guests would find
themselves in a space dominated by an almost acrobatic stairway. Matching
runs of stairs rose from the extreme ends of the room to the right and left to
reach a central landing just overhead. Supported by a set of four fluted
columns, the thirty-two-foot-wide double staircase then diverged again, with
three shorter sets of stairs proceeding to the floor above. But the best was yet
to come upon passing from the stair hall through a flat-topped opening into
the salon.

The oval room or salon was a first for Boston and had been widely anticipated by those who had watched the house's rise on Lechmere Point, and it
fulfilled its promise. Its thirty-two-foot length extended along the line of the
house's rear wall. The sinuous curve of the large room (it was twenty-four feet
deep) traced an ever-changing curve around its perimeter, punctuated by two
symmetrically placed fireplaces. Above a tall cornice in the Adamesque style,
the first such in New England, a graceful cove rose to reach the domical ceiling; there wasn't a flat surface in sight. On the outside wall, three large windows framed a majestic view of Barrell's richly planted landscape. Barrell

Bulfinch's staircase at the Barrell house was sculpture of a bold, architectonic kind, with curving railings and boldly carved stair returns, a staccato of steps.
Historic New England

imported hundreds of trees—elm and poplar for shade, along with peach, pear, apricot, plum, and other fruiting varieties for his orchard. He bought dwarf and espaliered stock, as well as mulberries, walnut, and other nut trees, patronizing America's first successful commercial nursery, William Price and Son of New York. Beyond the trees and gardens, the property fell off gently to the riverside. The view was a panoramic vista of Boston, which seemed to have risen out of the sea.

Yet there was more: At either end of the oval room were doors that led to matching square rooms, one for dining and the other for withdrawing. The three large rooms formed a suite that lined the garden front. While similar plans had become familiar to sophisticated Parisians and to the clients of Robert Adam and John Soane in London, only one other building in the nation could boast the same design conceit with an elliptical room as its focal point. That was the President's House, designed by James Hoban, still far from complete, in the Federal City.

Bulfinch's design was a revelation, but Barrell added finishing touches. As a merchant, he shopped with care, wary of paying too much but wanting the best. The walls were of brick, the window caps, sills, and the belt-course of Scotch granite. The enormous wooden house frame, with some members sixteen inches square, was made of timbers shipped from Maine. Bricks were laid between layers of flooring to deaden sound. Barrell's house had a shower bath, damask curtains, Brussels carpets, the finest glass, English wallpaper, looking glasses that were fitted to overmantels and piers between openings, and carved marble chimneypieces. His elaborate landscape featured a two-hundred-foot-long greenhouse, warmed by stoves imported from England to assure the survival of the delicate oleander, olive, and lemon trees inside.

The Barrell house may have been Bulfinch's first design for a private residence, but both client and architect knew that it was a masterpiece. The home displayed his client's wealth, the skill of the carpenters who executed the staircase, and the genius of the designer. Even before its completion, the Barrell house was remarked upon as "infinitely the most elegant dwelling house ever yet built in New England." For years it would be the most talked of property in the region, the subject of diarists, journalists, and even poets, who would remark upon Mr. Barrell's uncommon taste and urbanity. The lines of Bulfinch's design, as well as its details and shapes, would be often imitated.

Many people admired the place, but one visitor in particular arrived not only to look but to measure and record its details on paper for his own later reference. Named Samuel McIntire, he was a blue-eyed man from Salem, Massachusetts, with a broken nose and the callused hands of a "mechanick."

III.
1795 . . . Essex Street . . . Salem, Massachusetts

BORN A BOSTON BRAHMIN, BULFINCH WAS A GENTLEMAN. Samuel McIntire was a tradesman, the son and grandson of humble housewrights, men who shaped ships as well as dwellings in their native town. McIntire, six years Bulfinch's senior, had already married and established himself as a builder well before Bulfinch returned from his Grand Tour. Despite their differences, the two men would travel parallel paths.

Great success in architecture is often a matter of timing. Just as Palladio had done, McIntire and Bulfinch entered the architectural scene at a moment of transition for their region. With Venice's trading monopoly with Asia coming to an end, Palladio's aristocratic clients had diversified, buying nearby agricultural lands on the terra firma of the Veneto. They hired Palladio to design unprecedented villas for them, elaborate farmhouses often with granaries in their attics and attached *barchesse* (barns). In the same fashion, McIntire and Bulfinch were at hand when profits from international trade swelled the coffers of the merchants of Salem and Boston, and they became the designers of choice in the ensuing building boom. Their names remain obligatory to students of the architectural past, their places "*Bulfinch's* Boston" and "*McIntire's* Salem."

By the 1790s, McIntire was on his way to becoming one of the finest artisans of his day as a housewright, wood-carver, sculptor, and furniture-maker, but not yet "the Architect of Salem," as one of his obituaries would have it at his death in 1811. His exposure to the work of Bulfinch made it possible for McIntire to take the extra step that elevated him above his peers, the countless other builders of his time and region who would be largely forgotten.

It was Dr. Kimball, of course, who first assembled the story of the convergence of Bulfinch and McIntire.

A book titled *The Wood-Carver of Salem* had been published by Little, Brown of Boston in 1916, the same year that *Thomas Jefferson, Architect* came off the presses. Always a man who kept abreast of the literature in his field, Kimball learned of the small volume of photographs and accompanying text, which had sold out its first and only printing of 930 copies within a week. But, as Kimball observed, the book "outraged the local authorities by its errors on almost every page," because the authors had assigned dates of construction and attributed buildings to McIntire on the basis of vague tradition. One result of the locals' dissatisfaction with the book was a letter to Kimball from the directors of the Essex Institute in Salem, Massachusetts. The Institute, a repository founded in 1815 in Essex County, Massachusetts, wished to publish an authoritative monograph. The directors wanted Kimball to do for Samuel McIntire what he had done for Jefferson.

The auspices were rather different: How could McIntire not pale next to the charismatic Jefferson, the aristocratic Virginian who had been one of the most visible and important figures of his time? McIntire had never traveled more than few miles from Salem, the seaport town of his birth where he lived in a plain house and kept his tools in a workshop behind it until his death at fifty-four years of age. While Jefferson had left tens of thousands of pages that recorded his thoughts about virtually everything, not a single signed letter of McIntire's survived. On the other hand, his tools did, many of them at the

Essex Institute, and much of McIntire's architectural handiwork lined the streets of Salem.

What clinched it for Kimball was the collection of original drawings relating to McIntire's work deposited at the Essex Institute. He knew from experience that they would harbor stories.

Though Kimball quickly agreed to write the book, other obligations prevented him from immersing himself in the project as he had done with *Thomas Jefferson, Architect*. After a brief visit to Salem in the spring of 1917 during his Sachs Fellowship, his work on the McIntire project would prove to be irregular. Over the next several years, he would complete his long overdue *A History of Architecture*, despite the heavy load of courses assigned him by Dean Lorch, his cranky superior at the University of Michigan. Later, when the Metropolitan Museum lectures came along, they, too, seemed more important, though, as it turned out, the work of adapting the talks into the manuscript for his book, *Domestic Architecture of the American Colonies and of the Early Republic*, caused Kimball to devote more than a few moments to researching McIntire and his houses. As McIntire emerged as a significant figure in the book, Kimball asked that McIntire's drawings be sent to him in Charlottesville. American Railway Express duly delivered them.

The Essex Institute's substantial collection included a miscellany of scrapbooks that had arrived in the second quarter of the nineteenth century, though no one knew exactly how or when because their entry into the collection predated the keeping of accession records. Two volumes were probably the "2 Books of Draughts," valued at one dollar, that appeared in the probate inventory of McIntire's estate prepared after his death. Another scrapbook contained engravings of English buildings that, Kimball concluded, McIntire had drawn upon for his ship carvings. Each of the books had been dismembered, leaving the drawings as loose sheets ready for shuffling.

A second lot of McIntire drawings had a clearer provenance, having been presented to the Institute just prior to the turn of the twentieth century. This large portfolio of drawings had descended in the family of the donor, Richard H. Derby of New York. The name Derby was well known to the directors of the Essex Institute as Salem's most prominent merchant family in the decades that followed the Revolutionary War. A good deal was known about them, thanks in part to a sea chest packed with bills, accounts, and other family papers. Purchased at Derby Wharf by an early Salem collector, the contents of the chest had later been acquired by the archive.

Kimball soon discovered that McIntire had often worked for the Derbys, building or remodeling at least a half-dozen homes. One in particular, despite having been demolished more than a century before, had assumed an almost mythical presence in Salem's past and seemed always to be referred to as the Derby *Mansion*. Despite the enduring interest in the place, its full history remained to be told.

ELIAS HASKET DERBY WAS AMERICA'S FIRST MILLIONAIRE. His estate at his death in 1799 would have been worth more than sixteen *billion* twenty-first-century dollars. He had owned a handful of ships when the Revolution began, but by the war's end he owned or co-owned eighty-five privateers that had captured almost a hundred and fifty British ships. His postwar shift to the China trade had only made him wealthier.

In 1780 he had employed the youthful McIntire to build a "hours Down by the worfe." Although the house was far from completed by 1783, construction was abandoned when Derby purchased an existing house several blocks away. Farther from the codfish odors of the waterfront, the location of the Pickman house seemed preferable in its more conspicuous neighborhood. But the structure itself wasn't quite to his liking, so Derby asked Samuel McIntire for a renovation plan. Two of McIntire's brothers executed the updating of the Pickman house—the house was refronted in a more fashionable mode—and, in 1786, the Derbys took up residence on Washington Street.

By the early 1790s, word of Mr. Bulfinch's new designs had reached Salem. Elizabeth Crowninshield Derby, a woman well known for her love of display, determined that she and her husband *must* have a grand house like Mr. Barrell's. Elias took more pride in his children than his possessions, but his wife was more ambitious. That he indulged her was confirmed by a visitor to Salem in 1797. A successful merchant from Baltimore, Robert Gilmor, noted in his diary, "Mr. Derby has just built a most superb house, more like a palace than the dwelling of an American merchant." Possessed of a modest talent for drawing, Gilmor sketched Salem harbor, placing Mr. Derby's new house at the center of his composition.

The elaborate house McIntire built for the Derbys wasn't destined to last: The Reverend Dr. William Bentley (1759–1819), the Salem chronicler whose collected diaries would be published many years later by the Essex Institute, recorded its demise in an entry dated November 20, 1815. "I took my last view of the mansion of the late eminent merchant E. H. Derby," he

Robert Gilmor's recording of the Derby Mansion, central to the Salem harborscape, on the occasion of his visit on August 17, 1797. *Boston Public Library*

wrote. "It was the best finished, most elegant, & best constructed House I ever saw. . . . The heirs could not agree to occupy it & the convenience of the spot for other buildings brought a sentence of destruction on it & before the world it was destroyed from its foundations. I saw the front demolished and left in ruins."

The house had gone up and it had come down, that much was clear; but to tell its whole story, Kimball had to dig deeper. He soon found that in 1793 the Derbys had set their sights on an empty manse with a distinguished pedigree. The house had been built more than a half-century before for Samuel Browne, a man remembered as the greatest Salem merchant of his day. The Derbys purchased the Browne property, then commissioned McIntire to devise a remodeling plan to make it au courant. Kimball identified a McIntire study for the job in the Essex Institute collection, which incorporated a Bulfinch-style elliptical stairway. But the McIntire sketch raised another question. While the Browne house on Essex Street had stood on the very spot of the Derby Mansion, why was there no resemblance whatever between it and the house Gilmor had sketched a few years later?

Dr. Bentley once more told the story. In a disapproving tone, he had recorded in his diary the events of May 9, 1795. "The taking down of the large house of Col. Brown by Mr. Derby is a strange event in this Town, it being the first sacrifice of a decent building ever made in the Town to convenience, or pleasure." In light of the demolition, Kimball took another look at "Mackentiers Plan." The configuration of the old house was such that the up-to-date elements Elizabeth Derby wanted—a *salon en suite* and a garden façade like those at the Barrell house—simply couldn't be incorporated into the existing house. Bentley again offered the answer. "It was at her instigation," he had noted in a diary entry a few years later, "[that] the Elegant Mansion house was built where colonel Browne's stood."

Kimball consulted the miscellany of drawings. Though some were signed, virtually none were dated and, as he had done with Jefferson's, Kimball conducted a minute examination of the paper on which they had been made, seeking watermarks and other distinguishing characteristics. He soon found that, unlike Jefferson, who purchased paper in large lots for shipment to his rural outpost in Charlottesville, Massachusetts men of McIntire's ilk had been able in the port town of Salem to purchase small amounts of paper from any of a dozen or more shops within walking distance. While his paper studies had helped Kimball establish a preliminary chronology for Jefferson's drawings, the sheer variety of those in the Essex Institute collection meant that the papers would be of little help in dating McIntire's drawings.

He shifted his focus to the content. The owners were named on a number of the drawings and the obvious correlation between particular elevations and surviving structures made some identifications easy. He worked his way through the hundred-odd drawings, assigning virtually all to specific projects. When he finished, he found that the largest single stack before him related to the Derby property.

He studied the handwriting on the subset of twenty-two drawings. McIntire's script was easily distinguished on many of them. His letters, especially the initial capitals, were florid and looping when he titled presentation drawings; when noting details, the writing grew tighter and more hurried. On several of the pages Kimball also recognized Elizabeth Crowninshield Derby's penmanship, usually in notes made on the verso. Her spelling was amusingly idiosyncratic; she had labeled the Browne house sketch, "Mackentiers Plan for repairing mi browns olde House." But it was one misspelling in particular that gave the game away. On the back of one of the floor plans, Mrs. Derby had written, "Mr. Bulfinsh's." It was the break Kimball needed.

He had firsthand knowledge of Bulfinch's drawings from earlier research at the Massachusetts Institute of Technology, where a cache of Bulfinch material, including drawings and books, had been deposited by a Bulfinch descendant. It was a simple matter to compare the Derby drawings ("Not McIntire!" Kimball had noted on the back of one) with the photostats of Bulfinch's drawings that he had on hand for the Bulfinch houses that would appear in *Domestic Architecture*. The conclusion was clear: "Every mannerism of Bulfinch's hand . . . proclaim the identity of authorship . . . above all the unmistakably individual writing of the abbreviation *ft.* with *f* and *t* crossed by a single rapid stroke." These drawings, Kimball was certain, were unmistakably Bulfinch's.

More than the handwriting set the drawings apart from the rest. The drawings illustrated a house whose precedents he recognized: It was elementary for Dr. Kimball to see the inspiration of Palladio, inherited and anglicized by Lord Burlington in a memorable London house (General Wade's), and later adapted for a Dublin house (the Provost's at Trinity College). Kimball was able to confirm that Charles Bulfinch had owned a print of the Provost's House. For Derby's house, the Bostonian had swathed the mass with the swags and delicate details of Robert Adam and his London followers.

One "Bulfinsh" drawing of this house stood out from the rest. Unlike the other drawings, this one was a faded photo print, the original apparently lost some years before. It portrayed the façade of the house but wasn't an elevation: It had been drawn as a perspective. Perspectives of any sort were extraordinarily rare in 1795, but Bulfinch had been intrigued by the principles of perspective drawing, and he had maintained an ongoing record of comparative methods of projecting a three-dimensional building in two dimensions. Kimball had read Bulfinch's notes in an informal treatise preserved at the MIT library. Intrigued by Bulfinch's unusual interest in what Kimball called "geometrical relations," he had even begun writing an article on Bulfinch's churches as exemplars of his spatial experimentation.

This particular drawing used an outmoded technique known as the Kirby method. A copy of a book by Joshua Kirby, *Dr. Brook Taylor's Method of Perspective Made Easy* (1754), had been at the Harvard Library during Bulfinch's student days. One of Bulfinch's entries in the treatise in his commonplace book demonstrated that he had studied it, since he had copied down passages verbatim from Kirby's *Perspective Made Easy*.

With the Kirby method, the front plane was drawn as an elevation, but the depth of the structure was represented, too. This involved *parallel* perspective, in which the vanishing point was placed well to one side. Having already published his earlier research into Benjamin Henry Latrobe, Kimball knew that the Englishman hadn't arrived until 1796, making Bulfinch among the very first in America to even attempt architectural perspectives. "In 1795, as long afterwards," Kimball concluded, "[Bulfinch] was the only man in New England capable of making a drawing such as the one in hand."

The three remaining Bulfinch drawings of the Derby Mansion were a floor plan, front elevation, and a study for the Palladian-style pavilions. In comparing the elevation, which lacked some of the elements that appeared in

The distortion of the parallel perspective technique is such that the drawing looks a bit
naïve today, but to the Derbys, Bulfinch's preliminary study must have seemed magical. The
house was completed in 1799, the same year that both Elias and Elizabeth died.
Peabody Essex Museum

Gilmor's sketch of the finished house, Kimball concluded the elevation had
come first, the perspective thereafter. He reached another conclusion, too:
Bulfinch had to have used the Derby Mansion perspective as a part of the design process itself as he developed his ideas. The elevation had hewed closely
to the Palladian-Burlington sources, while in the perspective Bulfinch had
added windows on the third floor, carrying the attic story openings from the
side around to the front. In Bulfinch's hands, Kimball decided, the perspective was a technical tool, a part of the process of design, as well as a selling
tool. The drawing caused Bulfinch to rethink elements of the scheme *and* it
provided a visual experience for the Derbys. It was another first for an American architect.

Not that Mrs. Derby was satisfied with Mr. Bulfinch's scheme. As dramatic as
his drawing was, Bulfinch had not given her all that she desired. She still
wanted the innovations found at Mr. Barrell's house. She yearned for an elliptical bow room that swelled from the rear of the house into the garden and a *salon en suite*—and Elizabeth Derby's dissatisfaction with the Bulfinch design, Dr.
Kimball determined, provided Samuel McIntire with the opportunity to step in.

As a social peer of the Barrells, Elias Hasket Derby obtained permission in 1795 for Samuel McIntire to visit Pleasant Hill (McIntire was certainly their social inferior, and he alone would not have presumed an inappropriate familiarity with Mr. Barrell and his lady). But Kimball demonstrated that not only did McIntire visit the much-commented-upon house but he examined it minutely with the practiced eye of a man who by then had himself built and designed numerous houses. Kimball confirmed McIntire's visit by identifying a surviving sheet—labeled in McIntire's script "Barrell House"—which recorded in precise, annotated sketches Adam-style details, including swags, bellflowers, and fluting and reeding. Kimball also identified two other sheets (one a floor plan, the other a sketchbook page covered with dozens of pilaster and baluster details) that survived from McIntire's survey of another advanced Bulfinch design in Charlestown.

Though he tried, Kimball was never able to confirm that the two men ever met; in the considerable collection of surviving Bulfinch papers, McIntire merited not one mention. Was it a one-day tour for McIntire of Mr. Bulfinch's Charlestown commissions? Kimball could not be sure, but he was certain that the plans demonstrated McIntire's firsthand knowledge of Bulfinch's new Boston style. McIntire would employ his insights into the new idiom for Elias Hasket Derby: It would be he and *not* Charles Bulfinch who drew the final floor plan of the fifteen-room house, incorporating the garden suite in a manner that McIntire had quite evidently adopted from the Bostonian's work.

The building of the Derby Mansion had been the occasion of a vitally important, though accidental, collaboration. In his preliminary design for the house, one man had advanced architectural drafting in America a full stride forward; the other partner in the collaboration had undergone a transformation in amending and executing the design, becoming in the process a significant architect in his own right.

Kimball described the end result. "Among the many fine houses in the style which Bulfinch created, the house as it left McIntire's hands . . . had in spite of its refined proportions and detail, a touch of the unsophistication which so often gives its charm to the work of the early American builders. As one traversed the interior from front to rear, one enjoyed one of the finest sequences of spatial effects to be found in an American house. Outside and in, there was on every hand a profusion of beautiful detail, much of it from the hand of our most gifted decorative carver. . . . We may well doubt if there existed in the early republic a finer example of the American house."

One can only hope the insatiable Mrs. Derby recognized how remarkable her house was. The evidence suggests that she probably did not, since Kimball found another of her inscriptions on the back of a working floor plan. "Not large a-nuf," she had written. Before she could experience the house in full, she would die in April of 1799, with her house not yet completed.

IV.
1928 and after . . . Gallery 289 . . . The Philadelphia Museum of Art

IN 1924, FISKE KIMBALL FOUND HIS DREAM JOB. Admittedly, he hadn't *known* that the directorship of a museum would be his true calling, but just one visit to Philadelphia that autumn persuaded him.

Kimball was a year into his tenure as Samuel F. B. Morse Professor at NYU when he got a visit from the president of the Philadelphia Museum, John D. McIlhenny. The directorship in Philadelphia seemed like the perfect next step after NYU. The job description could have been written with him in mind: *Museum director needed . . . architectural credentials required to supervise construction of building . . . proven administrative skills . . . knowledge of historic architecture to manage collection of historic houses . . . &c, &c.*

Kimball discovered he could not leave. When he confided his job hopes in Brown, the chancellor told him that departing barely a year into his directorship really wouldn't do. Kimball came away from his conversations with Brown feeling "bound in honor," and he withdrew from consideration for the Philadelphia job in order to remain on Washington Square Park. He remarked to Marie, "Well, Puss, opportunity has knocked, and you know they say she doesn't knock twice."

Sometimes, however, Fate does offer unexpected second chances, and in May 1925, McIlhenny rang again. This time Kimball obtained permission from his New York bosses to visit Philadelphia. His first evening there he dined at the McIlhennys' grand home in Germantown. McIlhenny's Irish immigrant father had invented the gas meter, leaving the family with immense wealth, and the house was filled with priceless art and antiques.

Kimball was seated by his hostess at dinner. He felt he had acquitted himself well until he heard his chair emit a loud, staccato *crack* as the company rose from the table after the meal. He looked down and, to his horror, he saw that the splat back on the chair, an authentic eighteenth-century antique from the workshop of the London master George Hepplewhite, had split in two. Kimball was abashed—*Did he appear to be a bull in a China shop merely impersonating a museum curator?* But the McIlhennys chose not to remark, then or ever, upon the incident. And on June 9, 1925, Kimball was formally offered the job as director of the Philadelphia Museum of Art.

He quickly signed on, but since his appointment did not take effect until September 25, he and Marie took their first trip to Europe together that summer. Fiske had not been abroad since winning the Sheldon Fellowship at Harvard in 1911, but his new salary at the PMA was a generous $13,500. The job also came with a house, Lemon Hill, a late eighteenth-century mansion that would be renovated under his guidance in Fairmount Park, less than a mile from the museum. He had been explicitly told that in his new role he needed to woo the rich and influential of Philadelphia. The museum needed their money as well as their art collections and, in order to be at one with them, Kimball knew he needed to be cosmopolitan, conversant with the talk of London and the Continent. Further, he was still a relative novice in the world of museums, so he wished to tour the great museums of Europe, among them the Louvre and the Victoria and Albert Museum in London.

His visit to the Kaiser-Friedrich Museum in Berlin proved particularly useful. There he saw architectural fragments incorporated into gallery settings. The approach was new to him, and he decided he could improve upon what had struck him as a very good idea. His notion was to use not just occasional architectural pieces but entire rooms to exhibit pictures and objects. While his friend R. T. H. Halsey had installed period rooms at the Metropolitan for the display of decorative arts, Kimball varied the approach. His rooms would be gallery spaces for the display of masterpieces of painting and sculpture as well as furniture and other decorative arts objects. Thus all the objects would be seen in situ, in order that the artists' works could be experienced in interiors of the appropriate period; the art, of course, hadn't been created for museums, there having been no such thing until the turn of the nineteenth century. Borrowing another notion from the Kaiser-Friedrich Museum, he planned to arrange the rooms chronologically. The composite cultural-historical effect would be, as Director Kimball publicly expressed it, "to enable the visitor to retrace the great historic pageant of the evolution of art."

Yet the museum he inherited was very far indeed from the one Kimball envisioned. Its existing collection consisted largely of American textiles, industrial arts, and ceramics. Founded as the Philadelphia Museum and School of Industrial Art, the museum resided in an outmoded exhibition building left over from the 1876 Centennial celebration. But Kimball, with his usual impeccable timing, inherited something else, too: In 1919 ground had been broken for a massive building atop Fairmount Hill, overlooking the city. Construction was already well advanced on the pavilions that would flank an immense Grecian temple at the center, meaning that for practical purposes Kimball inherited an incomplete and empty shell with an interior that consisted of a bare steel skeleton. As one Philadelphia artist had quipped, it looked like a "Greek garage." But Kimball's big ideas would prove more than ample to transform the place.

To grow and diversify the collections, he pursued important donors of Medieval, Renaissance, Oriental, and Modern art. His goal, as he put it, was to enable the museum to "emerge from a minor provincial position to become one of the leading museums of America, [one] not unworthy of comparison with those of Europe." He set out to "express the world's artistic culture in all mediums, merging architecture, painting, sculpture and the decorative arts." Barely a year after the museum opened to the public, the city's approval of what he was doing became clear: In May 1929, the museum's *Bulletin* reported that one million people had visited since the opening in March of the previous year, and the most popular exhibits were the period rooms in Kimball's "walk through time."

One of the stops on that historic saunter was a room featuring the work of his old friend, Samuel McIntire, the wood-carver of Salem.

THE MODEST PROPORTIONS OF GALLERY 289 of the Philadelphia Museum were small compared to several nearby galleries that contained immense eighteenth-century drawing rooms that had been dismantled in the north of England, shipped to Philadelphia (*Attention: Fiske Kimball*), and then lined with prideful gilt furniture and paintings by the likes of Thomas Gainsborough. In contrast, the Salem room was but a small rectangle, its dimensions roughly eighteen feet across by twenty-two feet wide, with a ceiling less than ten feet tall. Instead of dark English oak paneling, the walls in the Salem house were of mirror-smooth plaster, their planes broken only by a carved chair rail. The cornice was not a protruding box with heavy wooden moldings but only a few inches deep in profile, made of richly detailed stucco. With pale blue walls softened by the chaste white woodwork, the room came from an American Federal house—not an English Georgian one—and delicate carved swags topped the doorframes in the mode of Robert Adam.

The bones of the space, including the cornice, ceiling medallion, mantel, and other woodwork, came from the Ezekiel Hersey Derby House. Ezekiel was Elias Hasket Derby's third son and, like each of his siblings, he had been left a one-seventh share of his father's estate when his parents died within a few months of one another in 1799. Even a fractional share of the legacy amounted to a major fortune and, as Kimball explained, "Those of the [heirs] who had not received one of the fine existing houses as part of their inheritance began to build in feverish rivalry." Ezekiel Hersey Derby's house was begun in 1800 and completed in time for a well-remembered ball held in February 1804.

Once installed in Gallery 289, the pieces of Ezekiel Derby's house survived as a time-defying crossroads, a place of intersection where the paths of a number of important players met. Like his father, Ezekiel had hired the notable Mr. Bulfinch to design his house; the Bostonian's handwriting on no fewer than eight sketches revealed that he provided two designs, modifying his first proposal before young Derby proceeded to build the revised version. In keeping with family tradition, Ezekiel would hire the best local builder, meaning that Samuel McIntire's skilled carving would decorate the doorways, mantels, and the ornamented façade. Then, more than a century later, Dr. Kimball would purchase major pieces of the house in 1926 to install them in his museum.

Kimball would also tell the story. By 1908, the home had become stores and offices, with "the lower storey . . . defaced by ignoble shop windows." The upper floors had fallen into disuse, and some of the decorative elements inside were removed and sold. Just prior to his move to Philadelphia, Kimball himself had brokered the sale of at least one piece, a mantel, to an architectural client on Nantucket. When Kimball was conceiving his "walk though time," the Derby house quickly came to mind, and the shabby commercial building still housed enough good pieces in its upstairs hall and a front bedchamber to create a composite room.

For $1,521.97, Kimball bought the Derby architectural elements before more of the house could be dispersed to points unknown. A good deal more money was required to furnish the room with objects worthy of museum display, but Kimball found a Philadelphia angel, George Horace Lorimer, who was first vice president of the Curtis Publishing Company, the publisher of the *Saturday Evening Post, Ladies' Home Journal,* and other highly profitable magazines. Kimball persuaded Lorimer to underwrite the installation of the Derby room and its furnishings at an estimated cost of $50,000. Kimball scoured the

Ezekiel Hersey Derby's home was a townhouse of the sort Charles Bulfinch was perfecting in his Boston work. Three stories tall, with McIntire-carved pilasters and swags, it proffers an austere but distinguished face to the town. *Peabody Essex Museum*

antiques world, seeking out dealers, collectors, and other museum people to find suitable furnishings. Fiske and Marie lunched with Henry Francis du Pont in New York to talk about chairs and a sofa, though a loan from du Pont's museum home at Winterthur, Delaware, never materialized. Nevertheless, Kimball managed to furnish the room, for the most part with Salem objects. A carved mahogany sofa (it cost $5,518) and a pair of vase-back side chairs, each attributed to the hand of McIntire, were found. Two armchairs, one of them with an arm broken in two, arrived with an impeccable McIntire-Salem provenance. A tilt-top tea table was purchased from a Derby descendant, along with export China of the sort common in Salem, some of which bears the crest and monogram of Ezekiel Hersey Derby's father. According to Kimball's final tally, the total cost was $42,479.82.

The room became an architectural palimpsest, one whose history could be read like the layers on a recycled manuscript. The scholarly patina was Kimball's, but the geometry Bulfinch's, the surfaces McIntire's. Kimball lined walls with portraits. As if to add a personal grace note, Marie and Fiske contributed a piece of furniture themselves, a fine Boston card table attributed to the makers John and Thomas Seymour.

Kimball would recount his observations about the Derby room in the

Philadelphia Museum of Art Bulletin in 1930. But the work also prompted him to return to the labors of completing his McIntire book, which he had set aside for some years. Only in February 1934, seventeen years after agreeing to write it, was he able to write to his contact at the Essex Institute, "You will never believe it, but I have finally finished the manuscript of the McIntire book." Even then, a concatenation of events conspired to further postpone the book's publication.

Another of McIntire's projects would contribute to the delay. McIntire had designed a two-story confection for the Derbys' farm in a nearby town in 1793. The exquisitely detailed and elegantly proportioned little summerhouse, with a tea room on the upper level, was much admired in its time. Its appeal carried on through the years, too, as it was preserved and moved in 1901 to the property of a Derby descendant, the wealthy widow Mrs. William Crowninshield Endicott. Kimball, who had always maintained a small architectural practice outside his day jobs, working largely on historic buildings, had been asked in 1924 to copy the summerhouse for another Derby descendant, Martha Codman, Elias Derby's great-great-granddaughter. A replica of the original soon stood in the garden of her estate in Newport, Rhode Island.

Upon finally completing his manuscript, Kimball had sent it to the president of the Essex Institute, William C. Endicott Jr. A din of silence ensued. Though Kimball did not learn of the man's pique until after Endicott's death in 1936, Endicott had apparently been deeply unhappy with Kimball for copying McIntire's little folly after his cousin, Mrs. Codman, had shown it off to him when he had visited. Endicott was possessed by a strong sense of ownership—he himself had helped move McIntire's original summerhouse to his mother's Peabody farm—and it wasn't until well after Endicott's death that Kimball's McIntire manuscript reemerged from his files, its margins annotated with a bitter commentary from Endicott. The result was that the Essex Institute did not publish the book until 1940, when 695 copies of *Mr. Samuel McIntire, Carver* came off press.

V.
July 1817 . . . In the Company of President Monroe . . . Boston

THE PRESIDENT WAS COMING TO TOWN. John Adams and Thomas Jefferson had mended the rent in their friendship—the two great Founding

The Derby summerhouse seems a perfect summary of American Federal as practiced by
Mr. McIntire with its Palladian character and finely carved Adamesque details. This image
records the building's appearance in its second location on the Endicott property, circa 1939.

Fathers resumed writing to one another after many years of hostile silence—
and the newly dominant Republican party was trying to smooth over old differences with the remaining Federalists. James Monroe seized the moment
and embarked on a fifteen-week tour of the northern states, very much as
George Washington had done after his inauguration twenty-eight years before.

At noontime on July 2, 1817, Monroe arrived in South Boston. From one
belfry to the next, church bells carried the news of his approach. He made his
way north astride a white charger, leading a procession that grew to more
than two miles in length, with a military escort and a string of carriages trail-
ing him. The townspeople watched from doorways and rooftops, while four
thousand children waited to greet President Monroe on Boston Common.
All forty thousand of Boston's citizens seemed to have turned out to welcome
the Virginian.

Former President John Adams looked on as Monroe was formally received
before a large crowd at the seven-story Exchange Coffee House. The War of
1812 was over, trade was booming again, and manufacturing surged. Monroe,
who had won all but one electoral vote, had sought to diversify his cabinet by
naming a Southerner, John C. Calhoun, as secretary of war and Adams's son,
John Quincy Adams, as his secretary of state. It was a rare moment of national

unity. The chairman of the Board of Selectmen welcomed President Monroe on behalf of the people of Boston. He offered his hopes that "your administration may, with the blessing of Heaven . . . promote the advancement of our beloved Country, to the highest possible condition of Prosperity." A sense of national reconciliation was in the air, and a few days later a Boston newspaper, the *Columbian Centennial,* would describe the events as the beginning of an "era of good feelings."

During the six days he spent in Boston, Monroe got a thorough tour of the town. It had come to be regarded by many as the nation's handsomest city, with fine public buildings, including the majestic State House on Sentry Hill, the Suffolk County Court House, the new Almshouse, the State Prison at Charlestown, and University Hall at Harvard. The city boasted an elegant performance hall, the Boston Theatre. Houses of worship had arisen, too, including New North and New South Churches, the Gothic style Federal Street Church, and the Roman Catholic Holy Cross Church. Many grand new homes lined the city's finest streets, and the row houses in the Franklin Crescent and the Colonnade offered fresh notions of town planning. At the water's edge was the immense India Wharf, a half-mile-long string of warehouses, docks, and stores, a development project unrivaled in America. Not far away stood the old market and assembly room, Faneuil Hall, which itself had been tripled in size.

Touring the town, Monroe was amazed to learn that *all* of these structures and many more, too, were the work of Charles Bulfinch, the same reserved gentleman who had been his most constant companion since he arrived in Boston. Bulfinch walked with a limp, the result of a fall several years earlier on the ice-covered steps to Faneuil Hall. There he occupied a small office upstairs from which he administered the city as the chairman of the Board of Selectmen, the town's most important elective office (not until 1822 would Boston incorporate as a city and adopt a mayoral system of government). Monroe came to the realization that the slightly lame, soft-spoken Mr. Bulfinch had more than governed the town from his modest office; from his drawing board had come the city's architectural reinvention.

On July 8, Monroe would leave Boston, departing for Salem and bound for the northernmost stop on his goodwill journey, Portland, Maine. But during his days in Boston his visits to the town's buildings took him on an encapsulated tour of Charles Bulfinch's life story.

* * *

HIS FRIEND JOSEPH BARRELL HAD BEEN RESPONSIBLE for one of the high points in Charles Bulfinch's life in 1793; soon thereafter, Barrell facilitated one of the lowest moments.

Upon moving across the Charles River to his fine new mansion, Barrell vacated a property on Summer Street in Boston's most desirable neighborhood, the South End. Bulfinch's brother-in-law, Charles Vaughan, purchased the substantial tract of land in May 1793, but it was Bulfinch himself who conceived the scheme for its transformation. He persuaded Vaughan and another investor, apothecary William Scollay, to join him in carrying it out.

Bulfinch, just thirty, had matured since his Grand Tour. When abroad, the aristocratic young man had been given more to listening than to talking. In the Mather Brown portrait he commissioned in London, his beguiling face with its dark-eyed gaze had a directness; but below the almost feminine features on which a bold Roman nose was imposed, the expression of the full lips suggested a tentativeness. By 1793, however, that youthful uncertainty had been banished, and Bulfinch had established himself as his town's architectural avatar. He had built several churches as well as houses for Barrell and Joseph Coolidge, and had even begun a gracious one for himself. Construction was under way for the new Connecticut State House and Boston's first theater, both to his designs.

With his confidence running high, he had decided to try something different. In July 1793, Bulfinch announced his project. "The public are hereby informed that a plan is proposed for building a number of convenient and elegant Houses, in a central situation." The idea was not entirely new. Bath in the west of England had been transformed earlier in the eighteenth century by two men, both of whom bore the name John Wood. John Wood the Elder had been born in a city that, like the Boston of Bulfinch's youth, retained a distinctly medieval look. But thanks to Lord Burlington and others, Wood had been inspired to adopt Palladio's ideas and transformed Bath into a truly classical city. By the time Bulfinch visited England, Bath had become virtually its second capital, a highly fashionable resort for members of polite society, its look defined by the great rows of carved stone pilasters and columns and the heavy classical cornices that lined the fronts of its elegant buildings.

Unlike Palladio, the Woods had not specialized in building freestanding villas or palaces. Rather, they built sets of attached buildings. The most memorable of them, known as the Royal Crescent, consisted of a row of thirty dwellings, abutting one another along a great and gradual curve. Bulfinch returned from his travels and, with grand images of Bath near at hand in a fo-lio volume in his library, he conceived the notion of using what had formerly been Mr. Barrell's expansive garden to improve upon John Wood the Younger's idea. Instead of one crescent, he would construct two crescent-shaped rows of attached buildings facing each other across an elliptical "park space." He would call it Franklin Place after the beloved, Boston-born Found-ing Father. There would be sixteen houses in each row, eight on either side of a central arched structure. Taken together, the four-hundred-and-eighty-foot-long façades would have the look of urban palaces, brick structures painted gray to simulate stone, the wooden trim a creamy white like marble.

In August the first foundation stones were laid and the buildings rose quickly. They bore a schematic resemblance to the Woods' terraces in Bath, but instead of Palladian and Roman details, the three-story façades were dec-orated more simply with fanlights, swags in panels, and other details drawn from the school of Robert Adam, who himself had experimented with ter-race houses in London.

The plan was forward-looking, the detailing contemporary, and the con-veniences generous (each house had its own pump, cistern, stable, and wood house). Asher Benjamin, a younger designer-builder and follower of Bulfinch, called Franklin Place "the first impulse to good taste, and to archi-tecture, in this part of the country." Bulfinch's finishing touch was a memo-rial to Benjamin Franklin in the park space, an urn shaped from Bath stone, the same Oolitic limestone of which the grand buildings in that English city were built. The urn had been a souvenir of Bulfinch's Grand Tour.

Boston's first residence block won much admiration. But its business plan proved a terrible failure. Looking back years later, it was an indigestible mem-ory for Bulfinch. "With what remorse have I looked back on these events," he remembered, "when blindly gratifying a taste for my favorite pursuit."

Trade with Britain had been uncertain in the early 1790s and Bulfinch as-sumed greater financial responsibility for Franklin Place when Vaughan un-expectedly withdrew from the project. By then the plan had already been halved, with just one crescent under construction. "Still, I was so sanguine respecting the success of the project," Bulfinch recalled, "that I persevered in completing the whole range."

In finishing the sixteen houses on the crescent, Bulfinch found he was overcommitted. "I involved for life myself and wife with our children—my Fa-ther and Mother and Sisters, who all held the utmost confidence in my mea-sures and pride in my expected success." He went bankrupt in 1796, losing all his holdings, including a new house he had yet to inhabit. He moved his family into a small dwelling, for which a still-solvent brother-in-law paid the rent. Shortly after his bankruptcy, the ratification of the Jay Treaty resolved trade issues with England, and the houses in the crescent filled up rapidly. But the economic upturn had come too late to save the Bulfinches from financial disaster.

Family wealth accumulated over generations was suddenly gone, yet Bulfinch's reputation sustained little harm (perhaps because neither his creditors nor the workmen at the crescent sustained significant losses; only Bulfinch was ruined by Franklin Place). He had served as a selectman of the town a few years earlier, and his friends and neighbors soon reelected him to the board, this time as its chairman. It had traditionally been an unpaid post but, recognizing both Bulfinch's need and the advantages of being able to employ his unique abilities, a means was found of compensating him. "As no salary was connected to the office," Bulfinch himself reported, "they appointed me Superintendent of Police, with a salary of six hundred dollars." Only after assuming the job as chairman of the Selectmen was he able once again to afford the cost of housing his own family.

Bulfinch's selectman duties were varied. As the town's chief executive, he assumed responsibility for nothing less than the health, safety, and harmony of his fellow citizens. He became the town's school inspector, and oversaw the admission of children of both sexes to the public schools. His brief extended to tax collection, care of the town's poor, a system of street lighting, the inspection of wells, the establishment of fire and safety laws that dictated building materials (he would prohibit the erection of wooden buildings over ten feet wide), and even the enforcement of Boston's Sunday "blue laws," which prohibited nonemergency travel in and out of town from midnight Saturday until six o'clock Sunday.

By default, Bulfinch also assumed the role of the city's chief planner, designing city streets, walkways, sewers, and municipal buildings. He also became the man to whom most everyone who was anyone turned for building plans, whether the structure was to be public or private.

His bankruptcy forced him to relinquish his gentlemanly life of leisure. According to Bulfinch's wife, Hannah, "My husband . . . made Architecture his business, as it had been his pleasure." As Bulfinch himself remembered, "I found myself reduced to my personal exertions for support." No longer a gratuitous plan-giver, Charles Bulfinch, Architect, had been forced by his bankruptcy to become a fee-taker.

His amateur status was gone. In seeking payment for his designs—$40 here, $100 there—he became America's first native professional architect.

THE FRANKLIN PLACE FAILURE HAD BEEN PAINFUL FOR BULFINCH, but even as its sorry saga was unfolding, a happier tale took shape.

On July 4, 1795, Governor Samuel Adams, Masonic Grand Master Paul Revere, and other dignitaries watched as fifteen white horses, one to represent each of the states of the Union, hauled the cornerstone into place. Eight years after Bulfinch had submitted his "Rough Plan of the State House," construction had begun on the new home for the government of the Commonwealth of Massachusetts.

The setting for the new State House was by no means preordained. The townspeople of Plymouth, the Commonwealth's first town, and of Worcester each made claims to become the state's capital. The town of Boston itself had acquired a pasture in the South End a few years before for a new seat of government. But a reorientation of Boston's development had begun with Bulfinch's Memorial on Trimountain, and in early 1795, the town had decided the matter once and for all, acquiring "Hancock's Pasture" for the site of the new capitol.

Cattle still grazed on the Common directly in front of the building. The vicinity of Trimountain remained countrified, with a dotting of farmhouses on the open acres between the building site and the settled city grid. There was only one new house on the sloping hillside of Sentry Hill, now more often known as Beacon Hill, commissioned a few years earlier by John Joy, an old family friend of the Bulfinches. His wife had expressed "no little dismay at the prospect of living so far out," but the construction of the State House seemed to augur well for the neighborhood's fortunes. Real estate speculators were soon investing in properties on the western slope of Sentry Hill and the adjacent hilltop, Mount Vernon.

Charles Bulfinch marched in the formal procession on January 11, 1798, celebrating the move of the General Court to its new headquarters. The State House was not only the most ambitious building in New England; it was also the first building in America to rival the Jefferson-Clérisseau Capitol in Virginia for the most prominent public building in the land. The Capitol in the Federal City remained a single wing, its central rotunda and the south wing not yet begun. In comparison, Bulfinch's domed State House was, as Fiske Kimball observed, "the most conspicuous public building in the United States." Its broad façade extended 172 feet, its dome reached a height of 155 feet. Despite its tree-trunk columns, it was a building that possessed—to quote Kimball once again—"a monumentality and logic immeasurably superior to the naiveté of earlier [American] designs."

Like the Virginia Capitol, the State House derived from a recognizable source. Bulfinch himself had spoken in his original proposal years earlier of the design as being "in the style of a building celebrated all over Europe." He referred to Somerset House, a massive government building on the Strand in London, an edifice then still fresh in the young Grand Tourist's mind. Boston's State House bore an unmistakable resemblance to the central pavilion of Somerset House, home to the offices of the Royal Navy, with its stacking of ground-floor arcades beneath a second-floor balcony shaded by the pediment above. Bulfinch had reduced the scale of the wings, but both buildings had domes, the one on Boston's new building a fifty-three-foot wooden dome painted a lead color. Prior to Monroe's visit, it was sheathed (in 1802) by Paul Revere & Son, who clad its hemispherical surface with copper.

The image or even the mere mention of certain buildings brings to mind certain cities. One is immediately oriented upon hearing the names Leaning Tower, *La Tour Eiffel*, Big Ben, the Brandenburg Gate, the Empire State Building, or Palladio's San Giorgio Maggiore. In the same way, James Monroe, having been fêted there with a champagne reception on July 3, 1817, understood that the State House had become indisputably Boston's signature building.

ON MOST MORNINGS, HARRISON GRAY OTIS SLEPT LATE. His habit was to appear for breakfast after eight o'clock in a silk dressing gown. His Negro barber had standing instructions to tend to other customers first before arriving at Mr. Otis's home, but when he did appear, he would climb the service stair two flights to Mr. Otis's dressing room, a space that had become de rigueur in Bulfinch's luxurious houses. As usual, Mr. Otis had gone everyone else one better, adding a dressing room not only to his but to each of the three major bedchambers in the house.

This particular morning—it was Saturday, July 5, 1817—the agenda did not allow for a leisurely start to the day. As chairman of the arrangements

When Kimball was completing his work on McIntire and Bulfinch, the State House he knew
from visits to Boston looked as it did in this circa 1935 photograph.

committee for the presidential visit, Otis was off early, accompanying Monroe on an inspection tour of the Charlestown Navy Yard. That was to be followed by a "sumptuous and elegant *dejeuene*" at the commandant's residence.
Once again astride his white charger, the president would then proceed with
his entourage to Bunker Hill, where there was to be a ceremony and speechi-
fying at the site of the Revolutionary War battle. Next would be a cruise on
the twenty-seven-mile Middlesex Canal, followed by dinner at the governor's
mansion, and then a concert by the Handel and Haydn Society. Last but not
least, Mr. Otis's moment would arrive: He would host an elaborate party in
honor of the president back at 45 Beacon Street.

Had the president wished, he might already have known the comforts of
the mansion, as Harry Otis had earlier offered him the "accommodation and
felicitations of my house." But the nation's chief executive had demurred,
choosing to avoid the appearance of partisanship, and stayed instead at the
"superb apartments" at Boston's first hotel, the Exchange Coffee-House.
Capped with a dome, the immense seven-story bourse was the largest office
building and hotel in the country, intended to be the center of Boston's commercial life, with its showy ballroom and accommodations for strangers. It
happened to be one of the few major buildings in Boston not designed
by Bulfinch. But for his part, Mr. Otis felt no sense of rejection at Monroe's

decision to seek accommodations there. Otis himself was president of the corporation that had built it.

This evening's event was to be his opportunity to put himself, his house, and the taste of his town on display. It wasn't that he had anything to prove—he was wealthy, well-bred, and the previous fall the citizens of the Commonwealth had elected him to the United States Senate. But his Saturday-night fête would be an opportunity to demonstrate his goodwill in the face of a national prejudice against his state for its stance in opposition to the recent conflict with Britain. Otis also anticipated enjoying a share of borrowed light. As one accomplished young lawyer of his acquaintance expressed it, "There probably has never lived in Boston any individual with finer natural endowments than Mr. Otis. Possessing a noble presence, a beautifully modulated voice, great readiness and self-possession, and a cultivated intellect, he has rarely, if ever, been surpassed in the divine gift of eloquence."

Otis knew how to live in high style *and* whom to consult when he wanted a fine house. His four-story manse on Beacon Street was actually the third domicile that Bulfinch, his longtime friend and occasional business partner, had designed for him. Otis had for some years been Bulfinch's most essential patron, a partner in the commercial venture at India Wharf, and the leading force in the Mount Vernon Proprietors, the group determined to subdivide the acres atop Trimountain. This house and his previous one on nearby Mount Vernon Street were both show houses, intended to demonstrate to potential buyers what a fashionable residential district Beacon Hill was destined to become.

This address was the best yet. Beacon Street faced south, overlooking the Common, the forty-five acres of public land that Selectman Bulfinch had just managed to encircle with a tree-lined promenade. It had been transformed into a suitable place for the well-to-do to take their daily constitutionals, in order to see and be seen by their neighbors. To either side of Otis's house were carefully tended gardens and courtyards; to the rear were the stables with quarters above for the coachman, groom, and manservants. The house contained more than thirty rooms with fifteen fireplaces and eleven bedchambers. There was ample room for Otis's large family of nine children and a half-dozen maidservants. Not only was there a wine cellar in the basement but a ground-level storage room supplemented the supply of imported vintages.

The warm July evening proved perfect for the grand event. A queue of carriages, some scarlet, others yellow, some bearing coats of arms painted on their panels, lined Beacon Street; the day's events were finally bringing the celebration to Beacon Hill. The large windows of the Otis townhouse had been thrown open and the many guests upstairs (there would be three hundred) could be seen from the street as the late arrivals entered beneath a tall entrance porch supported by four Ionic columns. To the right of the ground-floor vestibule was Otis's office, to the left his library, but the new arrivals were ushered straight ahead to the large stair hall with its spiraling elliptical staircase that rose the full height of the house. Otis had tried to think of everything: Should any in his company grow thirsty on his or her ascent, a two-gallon punch bowl of fine English Lowestoft china was at hand on the stair landing to offer refreshment.

To enhance the sense of wealth and privilege, Bulfinch's design had placed the principal rooms on the second level, the *piano nobile*, in the European manner. There was a grand set of three public rooms that opened into one another at the front of the house. One was a "dining parlour," another a square "Saloon," and at the door of the third Mrs. Otis received her guests, welcoming them to the "oval room." Constructed as a twenty-by-twenty-eight-foot ellipse, the room had a great bow window opening onto the grounds, where some of the guests were taking a turn around the gardens.

When the time came for the entrance of the guest of honor, Mr. Otis announced in a booming voice to those assembled in the bow room, "Ladies and gentlemen, the President of the United States." His words cued the band on the balcony overlooking the garden to strike up a tune; fireworks shot skyward from the garden. The plain and unassuming Mr. Monroe entered and took a seat beside Mrs. Otis on the sofa. Introductions were begun to most of those present.

The guests milled about, admiring the house, its furnishings, and its paintings, which included a portrait of the master of the house by Gilbert Stuart. Many in the company took in the First Drawing Room, a square space at the front of the house. It offered the most dramatic views, overlooking the emerging city that seemed to have been laid out for Mr. Otis's personal approval. The triple-sash windows extended from the floor almost to the thirteen-and-a-half-foot ceiling, but only upon stepping out of one of them onto the flat roof of the entrance portico could one appreciate the panoramic view of the new Boston.

No longer did Sentry Hill overlook a bucolic landscape with the city docks in the distance. Instead, as Charles Bulfinch's mother had reported to her brother in England, "Almost every spot of land is cover'd with brick buildings, and the paved streets and hackney coaches make us very noisy." The Common was now surrounded by streets lined with houses. To the north along Park Street were numerous fine dwellings, including a set of four known as "Bulfinch Row." To the southeast stood the nineteen houses of the Colonnade, Bufinch's second assay in terrace housing; they fronted on Tremont Street, named for Trimountain, which had devolved to Trimount, thence to Tremont. There was even talk of turning the once-sacred pasturage and parade ground of the Common into a park.

When Charles Bulfinch had returned from his Grand Tour thirty years earlier, the triple peaks of Trimountain had dominated Boston, an earthen headland flanked by two hunched shoulders. But the shoulders were disappearing. Mount Vernon had been lowered starting in 1799, when a grid of streets was cut into the upland pastures once owned by John Singleton Copley, purchased by a syndicate headed by Harrison Gray Otis. A gravity railroad had carried loads of dirt westward, down to the bank of the Charles River. There the uncounted cubic yards of dirt and stone had produced more land along Charles Street, while reducing the height of the hill on which Mr. Otis's very house stood. Otis remarked that the earth moving "excited as much attention as Bonaparte's road over the Alps."

Great quantities of earth from the summit of Sentry Hill itself had been carted north to fill in Mill Pond, a reservoir that had been created from a marsh in the seventeenth century by damning North Cove. The "clean earth and gravel" carried down the slope in horse-drawn tipcarts was used to reclaim a triangle of fifty acres of land from the tidal waters.

From the balcony with its Chinese Chippendale iron railing, the next land reclamation project was visible to the southwest. Beyond the Common flowed the waters of the Back Bay, a broad expanse that extended to the Blue Hills beyond. But of late the earthworks of the Mill Dam had been abuilding, extending along the riverbank for almost a mile and a half. It would soon be completed, enclosing some six hundred acres of the Back Bay basin, destined to become another new neighborhood.

The ridge that was Trimountain was losing some sixty feet in altitude, and the "tight little island" that Bulfinch and Otis had known as boys was being transformed. Once promontories had projected like stubby fingers into the water around the town; now, like the feet of shorebirds, they were becoming

In this 1811 lithograph, Bulfinch's memorial column was in jeopardy; that November,
it would be demolished so that the earth beneath it could be carted off.
Bostonian Society/Old State House

webbed, with the town's land area rapidly increasing as the half-submerged
salt marshes and mudflats at its periphery were filled.

The steeples of Boston's churches spiked upward from the bands of low
buildings. The State House, once nestled into the brow of the hill, its back
shielded by the hill top, towered over the landscape, its portico pointing
upward to the tall dome that, in turn, was capped with a cupola. The
cityscape at Trimount, once a lesson in geology, had become an architectural essay.

As a first-time visitor, President James Monroe could hardly have imagined how much the topography of Boston had changed. Nor could he have
any memory of the edifice that had signaled the coming transformation, the
Sentry Hill Monument. It was gone: When the excavation had encroached
upon the six-rod precinct atop Sentry Hill in 1811, the Monument had been
dismantled.

President Monroe did grasp the magnitude of changes that Mr. Bulfinch—
albeit with the influence and funds of Mr. Otis and his friends—had wrought
upon Boston's built landscape. Monroe understood how central Bulfinch's vision and leadership had been to transforming an eighteenth-century town
into a nineteenth-century city. Bulfinch's was the sort of talent the federal
government needed, Monroe thought.

This likeness of Bulfinch was taken near the end of his life. When compared to the 1786 London portrait, the two make a before-and-after with the callow youth transformed by the rigors of his life into the Ancient Mariner. *Ellen Susan Bulfinch*

Just five months later Bulfinch would receive a letter from Washington from the desk of the Honorable Harrison Gray Otis, Senator of Massachusetts, informing him that the president had appointed him Architect of the Capitol.

CHAPTER 7

MONUMENTAL
CONTROVERSIES

"The author is altogether American in his views—his studies
having never been out of the United States and consequently had
very little advantage of and from a personal examination of the
celebrated works of antiquity."

—ROBERT MILLS,

THE ARCHITECTURAL WORKS OF ROBERT MILLS (CIRCA 1842)

I.
1800–1812 . . . Handshakes Through Time . . . Washington, D.C.

IF HE HAD NOT EXISTED, the temptation to invent him might have been irresistible. Though not yet twenty when he arrived on the scene, the young
man was quick to demonstrate that he was possessed of the ambition and per-
sistence to carry the story of the invention of American architecture into the
nineteenth century.

Robert Mills put himself at the nexus of the most important architectural
thinkers of his day; he would be the only man of the next generation who
would grasp the hand of all of the architectural founders of the Federal era,
the small group of individuals who set the architectural tone in the quarter-
century after the Revolution. And he would help advance architectural design toward its next great incarnation, the Grecian style.

The story of his handshakes goes like this.

Mills was a South Carolinian, born in 1781 in Charles Town, a city soon to
assume the less royal-sounding name of Charleston. His father was William

A tintype of Robert Mills, 1851. *South Carolina Historical Society*

Mills, an immigrant tailor from Scotland, his mother Ann Taylor, a descendant of an early governor of the colony. Being of the middling sort, Robert found himself at eighteen with no capital with which to launch himself, but he did possess a strong desire to become an architect. Likely he had received some lessons at his older brother's Charleston Academy, which offered instruction in "the principles of modern architecture, with drawing and designing."

Enter James Hoban, Mills's first mentor after his father dispatched the ambitious lad to the new Federal City in 1800. For two years Mills would work as Hoban's personal assistant in Washington in the office responsible for completing the President's House and superintending work on the Capitol. Mills learned architectural drafting, including the technique of using colored washes on his drawings to indicate various building materials. Hoban's office bore responsibility for buying bricks, nails, plaster, and other goods, so the business of purchasing came within Mills's purview, as did real estate dealings, since Mills was at hand as Hoban speculated in properties in the growing city. The experience of working for Hoban provided Mills with a sound and varied introduction to the practicalities of building.

Working in Washington and living in nearby Georgetown, from which he commuted each day, he encountered Dr. William Thornton, George Hadfield, and even Pierre L'Enfant, each of whom felt ill-used by the powers-that-be in the emerging capital and who were seen on its streets and regularly visited its building sites. But the next architectural notable to play a direct role in shaping Robert Mills's future would be Thomas Jefferson.

Much work remained to be done on the President's House even after

Jefferson's inauguration in 1801 and Hoban's young assistant—Mills turned twenty in December of that year—soon attracted the new chief executive's attention. Their conversations inevitably turned to books. "Pursuing my studies in the office of the architect of the President's house," Mills recalled, ". . . there were no architectural works to be had, [and] Mr. Jefferson kindly offered me the use of his library." That would be the opening gambit in a professional relationship that would prove of inestimable value to Mills.

He had begun looking beyond Hoban, whose designs seemed dated, and was intrigued by Jefferson's more eclectic approach to architecture. For his part, Jefferson admired Mills's drawing skills and asked him to execute a series of drawings of Monticello. The result was a series of long-forgotten drawings that surfaced in the Coolidge collection in Boston in 1914.

Kimball had easily attributed them to Mills upon spying the signature "R. Mills" on one drawing and "T. Jefferson, Arch't, R. Mills, Del[ineator] 1803" on another. "Beside a drawing which Mills made of Monticello as it then stood," Kimball would write in Thomas Jefferson, Architect, "he made a design of his own for a further remodelling. . . . The design was probably little more than a practice exercise, indulgently reviewed by Jefferson." It seems Jefferson assigned his protégé several exercises, among them a variation on the familiar Palladian theme, the Villa Rotonda, which Jefferson himself had earlier adapted for his anonymous entry into President's House competition. Mills drew the structure of the wooden dome according to the principles Jefferson had so admired at the Halle aux Bleds. In his sophisticated rendering, Mills inked in individual nailheads to illustrate the zigzag nailing pattern needed on the dome's laminated ribs.

In retrospect, the network of esteemed gentlemen seems to have knitted ever more neatly together, as Jefferson guided his Hoban-trained apprentice through an exercise in homage to Palladio. How much Jefferson taught him it is hard to say, as Mills already had drafting skills superior to Jefferson's after working for Hoban. But access to Jefferson's library, then the best architectural collection on the continent, proved valuable to Mills, and Jefferson's support bolstered the young man's confidence. As Mills would recall years later, "Mr. Jefferson was peculiarly partial to Architecture, and possessed a good taste in this branch of the fine Arts. He appeared highly pleased, that an American Youth had engaged in the Study of this Science, and gave [me] every encouragement to persevere." Jefferson also pointed the way to Mills's next handshake.

After the death of his father in April 1802, Mills came into a modest

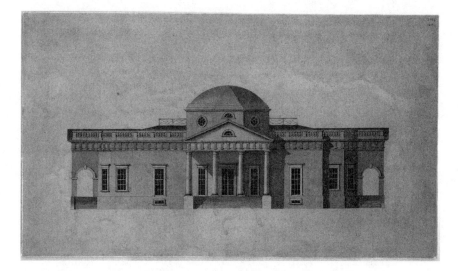

Mills's recording of Monticello, executed with Jefferson's guidance, would later mislead a variety of historians into believing that the South Carolinian had played a major role in designing Jefferson's house. It would be Kimball who got the story straight when he demonstrated that the house had already assumed its final shape before Mills's appearance on the scene. *Massachusetts Historical Society*

inheritance. With his newfound financial independence, he determined to embark on a "professional visit to all the principal cities and towns in the United States." When Mills departed on his journey in July, he carried with him letters of reference from Jefferson, one of which provided him valuable entrée in Boston.

"Sir,—The bearer hereof, Mr. Mills, a native of South Carolina, has passed some years at this place [Washington, D.C.] as a student in architecture," wrote Jefferson. "He is now setting out on a journey through the states to see what is worth seeing in that line in each state. He will visit Boston with the same view, and knowing your taste for the art, I take the liberty of recommending him to your notice." Addressed to Charles Bulfinch, the letter asked of its recipient that he act as a guide, a *cicerone*, very much as Jefferson himself had done for Bulfinch in Paris in 1786 and Clérisseau for Adam in Rome in the 1750s.

Mills duly took his Boston tour, and came away with clear recollections of the State House and the Sentry Hill Monument looming nearby. He continued north to New Hampshire and Maine. He made stops in Connecticut, New York, Pennsylvania, and Maryland, living up to his aim of seeing "all the principle buildings then erected in the major cities." Rather than the

Grand Tours that Latrobe, Bulfinch, and Jefferson had taken to visit European capitals, Mills's journey had taken him to the "Eastern States." He had seen Federal Hall, the mansions in Salem and Newport and Boston, and America's grandest city, Philadelphia. He knew Charleston and the emerging Washington. The closest he had come to the Old World was Mr. Jefferson's Virginia Capitol in Richmond: "The impression it made on my mind when first I came in view of it . . . gave me the effect of those Greek temples which are the admiration of the world."

He made drawings as he went, including one of St. Paul's Church in lower Manhattan, which he presented to Jefferson on his return to Washington. Then, in the summer of 1803, Jefferson would act the intermediary once more, as he recommended Mills to the man he had recently appointed Surveyor of the Public Buildings in Washington. Mills knew the work of Benjamin Henry Latrobe, having just made an ink-and-wash study of the Bank of Pennsylvania in Philadelphia, already a landmark building despite being barely two years finished. On his journey Mills had also seen and admired Latrobe's Philadelphia waterworks.

The placement of Mills in Labrobe's office would prove satisfactory to all parties. "The young Gentleman whom you did me the favor to recommend to me," Latrobe wrote to Jefferson on October 3, 1803, ". . . possesses that valuable substitute for Genius, laborious precision, in a very high degree and is therefore very useful to me, though his professional education has been hitherto much misdirected."

In Latrobe's office, Mills later told Jefferson, "I . . . imbibed the true and correct principles of Architecture." Those "principles," Mills felt, had a distinctly American flavor. With Jefferson, Hoban, Bulfinch, and Latrobe as his tutors, Mills could lay claim to "the honor of being the first native American who directed his studies to architecture as a profession."

MILLS WENT TO WORK FOR LATROBE in New Castle, Delaware, for $2 a day. Being in Latrobe's employ put him, quite simply, in the first professional architectural office in America. Unlike Hoban, who had been largely concerned with construction management, Latrobe was occupied with a range of design work, too. In addition to his new post as the nation's Surveyor, which involved completing the Capitol and remodeling the President's House to Jefferson's tastes, Latrobe was planning the Chesapeake and Delaware Canal, on which construction was about to begin. Mills would help conduct land surveys for the canal and, along with another gifted young apprentice with a bright future, William Strickland, he would complete a survey of New Castle. In the months to come Latrobe and his apprentice would begin work on drawings for the Baltimore Cathedral with its vast masonry vaults. In his years working for Latrobe, Mills would learn about hydraulic cement (which would harden under water), bridge building, and steam engines. He managed Latrobe's correspondence for far-flung projects. And in 1807 he would move to Philadelphia to become Latrobe's Clerk of the Works, supervising the construction at all of Latrobe's Philadelphia operations.

During his years working for Latrobe, Mills began to seek work on his own. He submitted a design for a circular church in Charleston, a kind of Protestant version of the Roman Pantheon based on his study of plates in two standard references, Palladio's *Four Books* and James Gibbs's *A Book of Architecture*. His design was adopted, but the finished building was a disappointment, since its exterior finish and interior proportions had been changed without Mills's approval. Even though Latrobe had not been involved in the Circular Church project, after the junior man confided his frustration, his mentor was able to turn it into a learning experience.

"In our country . . . the profession of an Architect is in a great measure new," Latrobe told Mills. That made it all the more important, Latrobe explained, for the architect to insist upon adherence to four principles in conducting business. First, he must be paid fairly: "The custom of all Europe has decided that 5 per Cent on the cost of a building, with all personal expenses incurred, shall be the pay of the Architect." Second, "the plan is [to be] *perfectly understood* . . . before the work begins." Third, the Architect must have direct control over workmen and all payments. Fourth, Latrobe concluded, the Architect must retain ownership of the plans. Although neither Latrobe nor Mills would be able to effect these standards in all their future dealings, Latrobe nevertheless established four cornerstones for their emerging profession.

Other commissions began to come Mills's way, including a gaol in Burlington County, New Jersey; a church in Augusta, Georgia; and houses and churches in Philadelphia. But it was a tragic fire in Richmond, Virginia, that established Mills's full independence.

During the performance of a Christmas pantomime on December 26, 1811, Richmond's theater caught fire and in the horrific blaze seventy-two people died, including the governor. The city fathers decided to commemorate the tragic events by interring the remains of the victims in a common grave on the site of the conflagration. A committee of local worthies contacted

Latrobe, inviting him to design both the tomb and a church on the same site. After some preliminaries, Latrobe concluded the available funds were insufficient to build both structures and submitted a design for the burial monument alone. Above a raised basement enclosing a vaulted crypt, a free-standing pyramid would rise steeply to a height of forty-eight feet. Believing his design all but approved, Latrobe began making inquiries into possible builders.

He was stunned to learn a few weeks later that his pyramid had not been approved. Far from it: His protégé had also been invited to submit a design, and the Virginians had taken a liking to the "Monumental Church" that Mills proposed for East Broad Street. His design made the church and tomb one, calling for "the erection of a temple for divine worship, making the entrance to it through a monumental hall." The entryway would be a stone portico in the Greek Doric order, a bold and boxy enclosure thirty-two feet square. Upon passing through the "monumental porch" where a commemorative funerary urn was to be displayed, the visitor would enter an octagonal sanctuary topped by a flattened dome with a monitor at its center to help illuminate the space. A tall steeple was to stand at the rear of the church.

Latrobe was invited to submit a competing design, but he declined. Not only was his artist's ego bruised but he felt betrayed by the man he called "my own professional child." He requested that the drawing he submitted be returned. Kimball later found it in the Latrobe family archive.

Mills and Latrobe would smooth over their rift after Mills explained he was unaware that he had been competing against his mentor. "As to permanent displeasure I am not capable of it," Latrobe wrote to Mills. "I shall always endeavor to serve you, & altho' my period of ability is passed for the present, it may again arrive." But their bond was broken.

From his apprenticeships with Hoban, Jefferson, and, in particular, Latrobe, Mills emerged a fully trained professional, one with a passion for permanent buildings, precise detailing, and a belief in the profession of architecture. He shied away from the atmospheric and vivid perspective drawings that were Latrobe's stock-in-trade; Mills's elevations, plans, and sections were exacting, but his draftsmanship lacked the drama of Latrobe's. He aimed to describe rather than delight. But whatever he lacked in artistic fire, he made up for with his discipline, ambition, and work ethic.

Following Latrobe's lead, he worked to break the hold that books had held on the American architectural imagination. Mills believed that "books are useful to the student but when he enters upon the practice of his profession,

Mills himself rarely made perspective drawings, but he was among the first architects to recognize the value of promoting his work by using printed images of his designs. His former co-worker in Latrobe's office, William Strickland, executed this drawing as a part of Mills's design proposal, which Mills then had engraved. He advertised it as "a handsome picture, capable of ornamenting any room." As Latrobe predicted, however, the construction budget at the Monumental Church would prove inadequate, so the steeple, as designed by Mills and drawn by Strickland, was never built. *Virginia Historical Society, Richmond, Virginia*

he should lay them aside and only consult them upon doubtful points, or in matters of detail or as mere studies, not to copy buildings from." He also adopted from his mentor a taste for Greek architecture. The vestibule at the Monumental Church, with its heavy Doric columns, broad piers, and shadowy interior, had the forthright simplicity of a Greek temple. It was a taste his countrymen would soon share.

Perhaps what truly distinguished Mills was his ability to design buildings that other Americans recognized as embodying the spirit of the Founding Fathers' generation. He wrote to Jefferson just as his days with Latrobe were ending, "Being the first American educated architect, I have flattered myself that with suitable recommendation . . . I may procure business from other parts of the Union. For the honor and benefit of my country I would desire to realize this." He was asking for Jefferson's endorsement, which undoubtedly helped him win subsequent commemorative commissions. But one that he did not win completes the little circle of handshakes that defined the first stage of his career.

In March 1825, Mills entered the competition for a monument in Charlestown, Massachusetts, in honor of the 1775 battle of Bunker Hill. He submitted two designs to the committee, a distinguished body whose membership included portraitist Gilbert Stuart, the rising politician Daniel Webster, and Harvard's George Ticknor. One plan was for a commemorative column, but Mills expressed his personal preference for the other design, a 220-foot-tall granite obelisk ("the obelisk form," explained Mills, "is peculiarly adapted to commemorate *great transactions*"). Mills never heard from the committee although, on May 19, the Bostonians resolved to construct an obelisk, a notion common to Mills's plan and at least one other submission. Boston builder Simon Willard was appointed to undertake construction and, according to tradition, was also its designer—though Willard himself, when Mills later sought to claim credit for the design of the monument, confided in Ticknor, "If you can give me any information where the design originated . . . it would oblige much."

What role—if any—Mills's proposal played remains a matter of conjecture, but certainly the matter was on his mind when he wrote to Jefferson the following winter. The two men had maintained a correspondence for many years, and in his letter of February 15, 1826, Mills referred in a postscript to his design for a Bunker Hill *"obelisk,"* emphasizing the word by underlining it. Jefferson wrote back a few days later, admitting that he was failing quickly—"My own health is quite broken down; For the last ten months I have been mostly confined to the house." Then he warmed, as he usually did, to talk of architecture. "Your idea of the obelisk monument is a very fine one," he concluded.

Jefferson dispatched his response to Mills but, in the privacy of his *cabinet*, he also made a note for posterity, one that he expected would survive him to be found by his heirs. In ink on a small, five-by-seven-inch sheet, he sketched his own tombstone. Given Jefferson's willing assistance to Mills early in the architect's career, there is a certain symmetry in his adoption of Mills's monument notion for himself, as the gravestone he sketched was in the shape of an obelisk.

Jefferson stowed the drawing carefully away. In the weeks after his death, when word of Jefferson's wishes reached the builders whom he had trained at his university, a group of them asked to be permitted to erect such a tombstone in Mr. Jefferson's honor. Soon they translated Jefferson's sketch into an eight-foot-tall, granite facsimile in the graveyard at Monticello.

II.
February 18, 1937 . . . 456 House Office Building . . . Washington, D.C.

THE INVITATION HAD COME DIRECTLY FROM THE PRESIDENT. That meant it was more like an induction than a request, but Kimball had been quick to recognize the opportunity when it crossed his path.

The timing was perfect. He was approaching his tenth anniversary as director at the Philadelphia Museum. During his years in the big building in Fairmount Park he had gained great confidence in his ability to manage the rich and powerful. At first, some of the museum's directors, the big donors, and the city pols in Philadelphia regarded him as an egghead on parole from academia, with his ever-present pince-nez, double-breasted jackets, and pinstriped pants. But after rubbing shoulders, swapping stories, and generally getting what he wanted, Kimball had earned their respect as tough, savvy, and very much their equal. His clever maneuvering had gotten substantial funds from the Works Progress Administration to complete unfinished galleries, and his museum had begun to garner national publicity.

The summons from Franklin Delano Roosevelt sounded to Kimball like the cue he had been waiting for. The national scene in Washington was just a larger stage, and he felt ready to make his entrance.

The 73rd Congress had passed Public Resolution No. 40 in 1934, establishing the Thomas Jefferson Memorial Commission and empowering the president to appoint a twelve-member board to make recommendations for a proposed memorial. Predictably, the commissioners included politicians, namely three senators and three congressmen. Chief among them was Chairman John J. Boylan, U.S. Representative from Manhattan's 15th Congressional District, and a man who, for more than a dozen years, had opened every session of Congress by introducing a resolution to build a memorial to his boyhood hero, Thomas Jefferson. There were also two well-connected attorneys (one each from New York and Washington); a former president of the Board of Education in New York City; and two Jefferson descendants, one a grandson of Jeff Randolph, the other, Thomas Jefferson Coolidge III, a great-grandson of Ellen Wayles Randolph Coolidge. Kimball was the twelfth member.

The idea of a monument to Jefferson wasn't new. In 1901 another commission, chaired by Michigan Senator James McMillan, had been formed to examine the city of Washington with an eye to updating L'Enfant's original plan for the twentieth century. Since L'Enfant's time the Federal City had become a dense cityscape, with its land area substantially increased by landfill operations along the banks of the Potomac. With a membership that included such notables as landscape architect Frederick Law Olmsted Jr., sculptor Augustus Saint-Gaudens, and architect Charles Follen McKim of the distinguished New York architectural firm McKim, Mead, and White, the McMillan Commission expanded upon L'Enfant's plat, enlarging the ceremonial greensward at its core by extending the two main axes to the west and south beyond the Washington Monument. The McMillan Commission had been succeeded by a permanent body, the Commission of Fine Arts, created to direct future urban improvements, and it had helped oversee design and construction of the Lincoln Memorial, dedicated in 1922. The Commission of Fine Arts had also considered a memorial to Jefferson, but the idea had lacked a powerful champion until Roosevelt prompted Congress to act in 1934.

To his surprise, Kimball found himself very much in charge at the first meeting of the Memorial Commission in April 1935. Boylan chaired the proceedings, but none of the other commissioners made any pretense of having architectural knowledge. The thoroughly prepared Kimball made his case to a receptive audience who brought to the table few notions of their own. He described his vision of a large, domed monument of marble, one that was a recognizable descendant of the Pantheon in Rome, for which Jefferson had repeatedly professed a great admiration and had even imitated in the Rotunda at his Academical Village. Kimball had further recommended the monument be set at the terminus of the city's longitudinal axis, due south of the White House, just as the Lincoln Memorial had been sited at the far western end, facing the Capitol.

The rest of the commissioners at the meeting offered no opposition, deferring to Kimball who was, everyone knew, *the* expert on Jefferson's architecture and himself an architect. Everyone wanted to honor Jefferson, it seemed, and the commissioners voted to approve the spectacular Tidal Basin site Kimball had recommended. When he proposed inviting a leading New York architect, John Russell Pope, to consult with them on the design, that idea, too, had been received with general approval. Kimball, the man in the room with the least political clout, found himself driving the bus.

The momentum had continued. The choice of Pope as architect for the Jefferson Memorial had seemed obvious enough. Though the two men had never met, Kimball regarded Pope as the preeminent classical architect in America. He had written in 1928 of Pope's Masonic temple in Washington in his book *American Architecture*. "John Russell Pope's Temple of the Scottish Rite at Washington [is] a superb restudy of the motive of the ancient Mausoleum. The square mass rising above the broad simple terraces of approach, the colonnade with its perfect uniformity every way, the centralizing pyramid above, unite in an effect of overwhelming simplicity and grandeur." Certainly that was an architectural mouthful, but the man's work remained uniformly excellent. He came with a strong political pedigree, too, as a protégé of McKim, the architect member of the original McMillan Commission. Kimball had also sensed "Jack" Pope could be counted on to make a strong impression on the other commissioners, which he did on appearing before them at their second meeting. Just as important to Kimball, Pope had been quick to adopt Kimball's notion of a domed design for the memorial.

Eighteen months was required to settle on a final design. Kimball had taken regular journeys to Pope's offices in New York and to Washington for meetings. On one occasion as he drove to Washington he realized he was running late for the 10:15 A.M. meeting with the president at the White House. Usually distracted but always adventuresome behind the wheel—Marie called him "my cowboy driver"—Fiske had picked up his pace, only to hear the rising shriek of a siren behind him. He pulled over but, refusing to be distracted from his errand that morning, he brusquely explained to the motorcycle cop *where* he was going. With his police escort, he made it to the meeting on time. In 1936, no senator, architect, or policeman would deflect Dr. Kimball from his mission.

Pope had presented four possible designs, but the Pantheon scheme had quickly reemerged as the favorite. Pope delivered preliminary drawings, along with a cost estimate for the circular temple in excess of $9 million. At a viewing in the Red Room at the White House, Roosevelt adjudged the cost too high, sending Pope reluctantly back to his drawing board. He returned with two less expensive alternatives, one of which was a scaled-down version of the Pantheon scheme. The other, suggested by Kimball, was a variation on Palladio's Villa Rotonda.

Kimball, Pope, and Chairman Boylan presented these plans to the president at the White House. Roosevelt examined them carefully, then requested that the plans be spread on the floor before him where, from his seated vantage, he could look down upon the large-scale architectural renderings. He studied them in silence for some minutes, then announced his preference for the circular design.

Now it was February 1937 and Kimball was awaiting what he hoped would be the last meeting of the Thomas Jefferson Memorial Commission. Less than two years had been required to carry the project to this juncture, and Kimball fully expected the committee would pass the decisive motion this day. When the meeting began, he remained silent, observing a short skirmish about the site that appeared to be largely posturing by politicians. A few minutes later, he bestirred himself to defend the monumental character of the project when one of the congressmen wondered about possible objections to its lack of utility. Kimball was forceful.

"I will say one thing," he began. "I have seen what we call memorials, memorial Y.M.C.A.'s, memorial hospitals, and a year or two later it is simply the hospital, the gymnasium, the Y.M.C.A. The idea of a memorial wears off and instead of a memorial project, in the end you have sold the memorial aspect of it 'down the river.' The only memorial that remains as a memorial to the person memorialized or the cause memorialized is something that is not utilitarian."

That ended the argument and, when Kimball proposed a resolution to approve the circular plan, it carried unanimously. Another resolution was offered to appoint John Russell Pope. All present were in favor. A final resolution was approved that effectively made the commission obsolete, designating the National Park Service to act as its "executive agent" in constructing the Thomas Jefferson Memorial.

Kimball had parsed the politics perfectly. The design was for a rotunda encircled with columns and capped by a dome. Inside would stand a statue of Jefferson. It was all enormous in scale and consisted entirely of elements drawn respectfully from Jefferson's works. The next day the finished design would be released to the press and the building specs sent out for bids.

He could almost hear the champagne corks popping. Fiske would go home to Marie and they would celebrate. For once his life, he didn't look over his shoulder at the past. Instead he went boldly forward. Which meant, of course, he was about to repeat a mistake that Robert Mills had made.

He had forgotten an undergraduate lesson learned as a student of Harvard philosopher George Santayana. "Santy," as Kimball remembered him, had spent many afternoons regaling Kimball, one of his favorite students (he once asked Kimball to be his assistant), with his sharp wit and gift for prophecy. What Kimball failed to recall was one particular aphorism, the very one that would remain Santayana's most enduring. "Those who cannot remember the past," he had observed, "are condemned to repeat it."

III.

March 1855 . . . New Jersey Avenue . . . Capitol Hill

THE STONE STRUCTURE DOMINATED THE WASHINGTON LANDSCAPE. Clad in its skin of white marble, it reached a height of 152 feet before abruptly terminating like an amputated limb. From his vantage on Capitol Hill, Robert Mills could not help but wonder whether his grandest architectural statement would remain forever unfinished. He feared that indeed it might and his imagined legacy, the Washington National Monument, would come to be regarded as no more than a folly.

When he looked back in time, he reviewed a life that had advanced in fits and starts since his decision, more than forty years earlier, to establish himself as an architect in his own right. After resigning his clerkship with Benjamin Henry Latrobe, Mills had continued working in Philadelphia. He had built churches, houses, and helped construct a bridge over the Schuylkill River. He met and married Eliza Smith, who would be the mother of their children and an enduring source of love and stability. Even as he gazed out the window that framed his view of the Federal City, she remained near at hand tending to him as he felt his life ebbing.

Another monument had lured him from Philadelphia when, in the autumn of 1813, he had submitted a series of drawings to a design competition in Baltimore. The object was to create the first major monument to George Washington, and Mills had accompanied his renderings with copious notes, among them one explaining that "the education I have received [has been] altogether American and unmixed with European habits." His wish to contrast himself with the two French émigrés in the competition had fallen on willing ears; the judges had been struck, too, by his plan for an immense column, with spiral stairs inside climbing to a platform at the top that would hold a sculpture of Washington. In the spring of 1814, Mills had won the $500 prize and, in 1815, he and his family had moved to Baltimore to supervise construction.

Mills learned a lesson there that, decades later in Washington, came to mind as he looked at the truncated obelisk standing to the west. Monumental works take time, he understood that; in Baltimore, where his Trajan-like column had eventually reached its planned 204-foot height, the task had taken some twenty years to complete, even in the absence of great controversy.

He had remained five years in Baltimore, supervising initial construction of the column and, in 1816, becoming president of the Baltimore Water Company. While the water system already existed, Mills was charged with building row houses on the company's properties. In 1820, when work on the Maryland monument was halted for lack of funds, he accepted an offer to return home to South Carolina. For the next decade he had wide responsibilities for designing courthouses, gaols, a psychiatric hospital, and other public works. His memorable County Records Building would prove a fine precedent for much of his later government work with its fireproof vaulting, which he had mastered while working for Latrobe.

He had returned to Washington, D.C., in March 1830 and, at first, business had been slow in coming. Eliza had had to take in boarders at their New York Avenue home, and she opened the Washington Female Academy, a school for young women. But Mills had come back to the Federal City for a reason: He had built his share of houses and private edifices, and even state buildings in South Carolina. Now he wanted to put his imprint on the nation's public architecture. In time, as he pursued every contact he could, the work had gradually come to him. First he was commissioned to design customs houses, then marine hospitals for sites around the country. Finally, in 1836, President Andrew Jackson had appointed him architect of the public buildings.

He remembered feeling deeply honored at becoming heir to both his mentor Latrobe and to Charles Bulfinch. His first major task had been to design a new Treasury Building, and the assignment had been to build not a traditional brick box with wood framing within but to use fireproof materials. Mills laid out groined arches on the inside and specified cut granite facings on the exterior. As the nation's chief architect, he also assumed responsibility for building the new Patent Office and then designing a new Post Office Building, both of which were begun in 1839. He had developed a strong personal style, one he thought of as truly American: Dignified, solid, usually fireproof, with the bold proportions of the Grecian style. But he soon found his job was subject to the tides of politics. When the presidency and the control of Congress changed hands in the election of 1840, he was forced to clear out his offices in the basement of the Treasury Building.

Architectural rules were shifting, too. He respected the younger architects, men who understood industrial materials like steel and iron. They were in the ascendant, he realized, and their new cast-iron building systems were becoming popular, threatening to supersede the fireproof masonry arches and vaulting that had become his trademark, a technology that had changed little since the Renaissance. Mills had seen his business drop off, though he continued to receive a few commissions for new buildings, and installed or updated hot-air heating systems, a speciality from his Baltimore days.

For a time, he continued to work as a draftsman at both the Treasury Department and Patent Office. He prepared plans for enlarging the Patent Office and the Capitol but, in 1851, he was summarily dismissed from both projects. It was the final changing of the guard for Mills, and he had no choice but to accept it.

He did have the satisfaction of completing one last major building, an addition to the rear of Mr. Jefferson's Rotunda at the University of Virginia in 1853. Called the Annex, the elongated building housed generous classroom space and an auditorium that accommodated twelve hundred, filling needs that Jefferson had not anticipated. He was proud to have contributed to Mr. Jefferson's Academical Village, but couldn't help but regret that the elaborate pedestal and statue of Jefferson he had proposed for the Academical Village remained unbuilt.

THE ONE GREAT CONSOLATION OF THESE LAST YEARS had been the Washington National Monument. As his other prospects diminished, his most cherished hope had become that he could complete the monument to celebrate the only president he hadn't known.

From boyhood, Mills could recall unanimous agreement on this one subject: A monument to George Washington would be a fitting tribute to the great general. Even prior to forming a new government, the Continental Congress on August 7, 1783 had resolved to construct "an equestrian statue . . . at the place where the residence of Congress shall be established in honor of George Washington." When Major L'Enfant laid out the new Federal City in 1792, he took pains to find a suitable site. Yet no move was made to create a Washington statue after construction had begun on the new capital's principal buildings.

At the great man's death at Mount Vernon in 1799, both houses of Congress approved a second resolution. Instead of a statue, proclaimed Congress, "a marble monument was to be erected by the United States at the City of Washington, and the family of General Washington . . . requested to permit his body to be deposited under it." While there was still unanimity in the land that a Washington monument was called for, the notion of a mausoleum dedicated to the old general in his namesake city was also destined to remain nothing more than inert political verbiage.

Only when Mills's own Baltimore monument approached completion had a measurable momentum begun to gather in the Federal City. In September 1833 a group of citizens founded the Washington Monument Society in the District of Columbia. Vowing to do what the government had not, the Society elected Chief Justice John Marshall as its first president and, when Marshall died in 1835, former president James Madison to succeed him. From the beginning, the Society made it clear they wanted something bigger and better than Baltimore's monument, announcing a fund-raising goal of *one million dollars*. In seeking a truly broad base of support, the Society asked that private citizens contribute no more than one dollar each per year. Fund-raising lagged and the Society's coffers contained only $30,000 after five years.

Mills's great moment had arrived in 1845 when the Society chose his design. There had been an earlier competition in 1836—he had entered that one, too—but no proposal had then been approved. This time Mills's new and immense design won the $100 premium. His vision was of a 500-foot-tall obelisk set atop a base consisting of a circular, colonnaded building with hundred-foot tall columns around its perimeter. This "National Pantheon" at the base would contain statues of other leaders of the Revolution, with the obelisk rising overhead from its center. The Washington National Monument, as the structure was called, would be the tallest structure in the world at 600 feet, exceeding the heights of the Cologne Cathedral (525 feet) and the pyramid of Cheops (480 feet).

To raise more money, the one-dollar limit had been abandoned. New strategies were employed, including the sale of lithographs of Mills's design and of the Gilbert Stuart portrait of Washington that hung in Faneuil Hall. By 1847, $87,000 dollars was on hand and the Society was emboldened to identify an appropriate location. Congress soon authorized the use of the very spot Pierre L'Enfant had designated for the equestrian statue of President Washington. Elevated twenty-six feet above the nearby Potomac at low tide, the site commanded a majestic view of the river. Mills was granted an annual supervisory fee of $500 and he set to work to find contractors to begin excavating an enormous foundation hole.

Even with his eyes closed in his bedchamber on Capitol Hill in 1855, Mills could envision the map of the city, with its two main axes. The north-south meridian centered on the President's House, while the east-west vector aligned with the center of the Capitol. It was at their crossing, the planned center of the American universe, that the 24,500-pound cornerstone had been laid on July 4, 1848. In his mind's eye, he could place himself in the long parade of fire companies, militia, Freemasons, and infantry men, all led by President Zachary Taylor and his escort of U.S. Dragoons and Horse Artillery. Mills had been alone in his carriage, riding to the accompaniment of the U.S. Marine Band playing "Yankee Doodle." He was charged with the care of the zinc case that contained a copy of the Society's constitution, along with books, memorabilia, and images of his design for the monument, including a lithograph, a medallion, and an electrotype. Set into a recess chiseled out of the cornerstone's marble mass, the time capsule had become a part of the eighty-by-eighty-foot-square foundation.

When he opened his eyes in 1855, what he saw was an unfinished obelisk, its top craggy and uneven, construction halted by politics, national and international. No move had been made to build the pantheon at the base—that could come later, the Society decided—but at first progress on the obelisk had been rapid, the foundations finished by September 1848. The monument had risen two feet at a time as the courses of marble blocks were laid. Annual rededications were held on Independence Day. As the building rose, derricks were positioned at the corners, powered by steam engines. Backed by rubble stone, the ashlar blocks of the face were carefully laid to a batter (receding upward slope) of one-quarter inch for each foot of elevation.

The exterior would be uniform, clad in pure white marble from the Beaver Dam quarry in Baltimore County, Maryland. The states, municipalities, and even other nations had been invited to contribute stones to line the interior walls. Many such four-foot by two-foot stones arrived, most of them bearing inscriptions. Every state in the union was represented. A block of white marble came from Greece, a relic from the ruins of the Parthenon. Stones from Turkey and China arrived, as did one from Italy.

As Mills looked back just a year, the Roman stone was the one that had shattered the public unanimity in support of the monument. Pope Pius IX had dispatched the block, which had been removed from the ruin of the Temple of Concord on the Roman Forum. Its ancient history had not mattered to the growing anti-Catholic "Know Nothing" party. Seventeen of its members had overpowered the night watchmen at the monument. Not only had they stolen the block, but they had then pitched it into an unmarked grave in the Potomac. The stone had not been recovered but, far worse, Know-Nothing Party members had seized control of the Society's board and progress at the monument had been halted.

From his deathbed, Mills could not help but focus on the half-risen spire in the near distance. On the day he died—March 3, 1855—a cold drizzle soaked the abandoned worksite, the rain dripping off the canvas tarps that covered workmen's sheds surrounded by untouched building materials. It was a worksite without workers, the very silence of the place a mute reproof. On that day no one could know whether, in the fullness of time, it would prove Mills's professional redemption or just the bitter failure of his highest hopes. No doubt he would have been pleased to learn that it would indeed be finished; equally, he would have been astonished that another twenty-nine years would be required to complete his Washington Monument.

IV.
1937–38 . . . Shack Mountain . . . Charlottesville, Virginia

KIMBALL REALLY SHOULD HAVE KNOWN BETTER. Controversy was inevitable with monuments in Washington, and he was quite familiar with Mills's cautionary tale.

Just a few years earlier, Kimball had written a brief biography of Mills for the *Dictionary of American Biography*. He had examined some of Mills's personal papers in Columbia, South Carolina, in 1917, and had made inquiries into others owned by Mills's descendants in New Orleans in 1919. Over a period of more than fifteen years he had encouraged Mrs. H. M. Pierce Gallagher in her research, sharing with her his own extensive files on Mills; he had also written an admiring introduction to Helen Gallagher's biography, *Robert Mills: Architect of the Washington Monument*.

The day after the Commission's approval of his Jefferson Memorial, he had returned to his office at the Philadelphia Museum. He worked as usual at his English partner's desk, an eighteenth-century antique, though its blurred provenance made it of practical use rather than of museum quality. The enormous desk suited him, as he had thickened with age and inclination, and his six-foot-one frame carried a portly two hundred and fifteen pounds. People remarked on his big, bald head; out of Dr. Kimball's earshot colleagues compared it to a cannon ball. In truth, his presence was at times ballistic as he wielded his immense energy, firing off the word "Bully!" as an enthusiastic affirmation for work well done. The expletive may have sounded anachronistic to some, but Kimball was a child of Roosevelt's time—not FDR's but TR's, since the earlier Roosevelt's presidency had coincided with Kimball's teenage years.

He drafted a letter to Jack Pope expressing that exact sentiment: "Bully for you," he enthused. "You have heard of our good day's work yesterday, and now we are hitting the papers and the public with your beautiful Jefferson Memorial. There will be squawks . . . but let them yell!"

The press releases went out, and many newspapers were quick to adopt a cheerleading tone. "The beautiful permanent memorial," reported one Washington paper, ". . . will be worthy of Jefferson's place in our history as the founder of American democracy and of stirring patriotic interest as long as the United States endures." But the murmurs of approval soon were lost in a cacophony of complaints.

For many, the site was the problem. The Daughters of the American Revolution and the Washington Board of Trade went on record as objecting to the removal of the cherry trees that rimmed the Tidal Basin. A gift of peace from the Japanese people in 1912, the ornamental trees were the focus of the annual Cherry Blossom Festival, and roughly half of them would have to go in the planned redesign of the landscape at the proposed site of the Memorial.

Others objected to the price: three million dollars was the estimated cost, and some critics argued that in a time of economic depression and high unemployment, federal monies could be better spent elsewhere. Still other experts asserted that, given soil conditions at the site, the budget would be woefully inadequate. Some critics suggested redesigning the building to be of utilitarian use, one recommending it become an auditorium for ceremonies like the Inauguration in the event of inclement weather. Others worried about traffic at the site. And Frederick Law Olmsted Jr. called the project "a leap in the dark with failure more likely than success." In particular, he was concerned that the large monument, when built on its proposed site at the southern terminus of the city's main north-south axis, would close off one of the last remaining vistas.

Most everybody, it seemed, had an objection, but the most virulent opposition came from the Modernists, the architects and artists who proclaimed that Classicism was dead. They complained that a design so clearly based on classical Roman precedents lacked vitality and imagination. The staff of the

School of Architecture at Columbia signed a letter that collectively damned the project, seeing it as an insult to the entire profession. The architects were angry, too, at having been excluded. "This great monument," they wrote, "to be built with national funds for a national hero, was chosen without a nation-wide competition or series of competitions."

Architect William Lescaze, Harvard's Dean of the Graduate School of Design Joseph Hudnut, and others wrote impassioned condemnations. That spring the pages of the *Magazine of Art* were ablaze with overheated polemics. Frank Lloyd Wright chimed in, too, writing directly to President Roosevelt. "This proposed design is one more world-famous miscarriage of grace."

The furor was such that Commission Chairman Boylan felt he had no choice but to open the matter up for public discussion, and he scheduled congressional hearings. Museum of Modern Art director Alfred H. Barr Jr., architect Henry Churchill, and historian Talbot Hamlin all opposed the Pope-Kimball design. Kimball was called to defend the project, along with the two Jefferson descendants on the Commission.

Later the politicians took their turn, too, on the floor of Congress. Typical of the debate was an exchange initiated by Congressman Jed Johnson from Oklahoma. "The committee proposes to start this so-called 'emergency memorial' by spending $500,000, which must be borrowed and for which bonds must be voted, when there are 10,000,000 to 12,000,000 men out of work. . . ." Francis D. Culkin of New York, a member of the Thomas Jefferson Memorial Commission, quickly rose to refute his brother member. "I say it unqualifiedly that instead of . . . pouring money down political rat holes— and I say this as a matter of challenge to those on this side of the aisle—you cannot do better service to the cause of democracy than to rear this exquisite, beautiful memorial to the memory of this great man to encourage the youth of the country to learn what this country stands for and what popular government really means."

Other voices spoke in favor, but John Russell Pope's was not among them. He made no pretense of being a theorist and, with the Classical and Modernist camps trading salvos, he elected to stay out of the crossfire, preferring to let his design speak for him. He was also sick and in pain, having been diagnosed with metastatic abdominal cancer.

Late that summer, the appropriation for the Jefferson Memorial disappeared in committee, deleted from the budget. And four days after his firm was instructed to stop work on the project, Jack Pope died on August 27, 1937.

Perhaps, thought Kimball, the Monument was dead in the water, too, becalmed by politics and changing tastes.

WHILE THE VOICES OF MODERNISM seemed to be shouting down Classicism in Washington, Fiske and Marie Kimball kept listening to their own tastes.

Kimball's professional commitments had drawn them back repeatedly to the Old Dominion. In 1928, he had joined the architectural advisory board at Mr. Rockefeller's experiment in time travel, Colonial Williamsburg. Tight budgets and layoffs at the Philadelphia Museum in the early thirties had led him to accept consulting work at Stratford Hall, Robert E. Lee's birthplace. And his and Marie's association with Monticello, begun in 1924, had begun to require more and more of their energies. Fiske and Marie both had a great affection for Charlottesville, and they decided it should be the site of their vacation home to which, some years hence, they might retire.

They looked at various properties in Albemarle County. Their first choice had been to buy a historic house, but the right one hadn't come along. They had taken a long look at Edgemont, a property south of Charlottesville with an elegant dwelling at its center. They were tempted: Despite needing a complete restoration, the house had a personal appeal to them, since Kimball believed it had been built to a plan he had found in the Coolidge collection, which Jefferson had sketched for a friend and neighbor. Finally, though, Marie and Fiske decided they wanted to be closer to the university.

By 1935, they shifted their search from houses to property, deciding to build their own home (Kimball told one realtor, "I am pretty good at faking an old house myself "). Soon they found a 113-acre hilltop four miles north and west of the Academical Village. Much of the acreage was wooded, but it also contained a dramatic house site overlooking an open field with a backdrop of the Blue Ridge Mountains. In return for $4,234.76, the Kimballs owned it.

Next, Kimball put pencil to paper, setting out to design "a house of Jeffersonian character." As with Monticello itself, Dr. Kimball's design didn't leap full-blown from its creator's imagination. An early draft looked as if it owed more to Bulfinch than Jefferson, with a projecting drawing room and oval staircase. Over the next two years, Kimball devised a series of plans that, as the cost estimates came in, diminished in size from one version to the next. Two stories became one; double pile became single. Perhaps by coincidence, perhaps not, the design that emerged closely resembled a scaled-down version

The final version of Shack Mountain had a remarkable grandeur for a house that is, essentially, two public rooms with very modest service spaces to the rear. Kimball also added a distinctly Jeffersonian touch, making both ends semi-octagonal. *Roger Straus III*

of the Kimballs' favorite accommodation on their visits to Charlottesville. That was Jefferson's Farmington, a house he designed for a friend in 1802 that much later had become the clubhouse for the Farmington Golf Club.

The main section of the Kimballs' house, like that of Farmington, would be an elongated octagon that contained the parlor and dining room, with service rooms and bedrooms to the rear of the T-shaped plan. But Kimball borrowed more than the overall geometry from Jefferson, noting in his specifications, "mortar joints to match Farmington; wood moldings, doors, and windows to match the University." He also specified that the Tuscan order on its columns and tall cornice was to be borrowed directly from the colonnades at the University.

The house was constructed in 1937 and 1938, during the same sixteen-month span when the Jefferson Memorial controversy was at its height. As the brick walls rose, as the standing seam roof was applied and the plasterers began their work, Kimball was distracted from the very public brouhaha in Washington by a string of letters and phone calls to his builder, Robert E. Lee of Charlottesville. Kimball called the place "Tusculum," but Lee and other Charlottesvillians never quite got out the habit of referring to it as Shack Mountain, after the Shackelford family who had long owned the property.

In September of 1938, the Kimballs' new house was complete. Shack Mountain had cost $19,375.00, and the end result was impressive. In making his succession of five designs, Kimball had honed the grandiose into the grand. He had created a persuasive imitation, that is, an imitation in the classical sense of taking general hints from the original but not slavishly copying. Despite its numerous nods to Jefferson, the house didn't feel like a copy. Kimball had managed to capture some of the same Jeffersonian playfulness that Monticello conveys to its visitors—the house is light, detailed but not fussy, and possessed of an elegance out of all proportion to its size at some 2,400 square feet.

At least half-consciously, Kimball had also created an architectural rebuttal to all those who said that the classical was dead and irrelevant. In his undergraduate days, Kimball had found himself uncomfortable with modernist dogma, as espoused by Louis Sullivan (and later co-opted by others), that "form follows function." From boyhood he had been "very skeptical of the vocal claims of the modern functionalists working with newer materials." His comfort with Classicism would never change, as he held to the old verities of balance, harmony, and unity.

He succeeded in Charlottesville in making a personal classical statement. But he also understood from his Washington experience that he, along with his fellow practitioners of Classicism, were very much in the minority.

BY SEPTEMBER 1937, KIMBALL HAD CONCEIVED A NEW STRATEGY. He was determined to see the Jefferson Memorial through to completion. He found a new inspiration in the late Jack Pope, who had become a friend during their three-year collaboration.

Some critics dismissed Pope as the ultimate society architect, a mannered and gracious gentleman with embarrassingly large homes in Manhattan and Newport. His client list was studded with the names of the richest and best-connected families in America. He had become one of them, dining at their tables and joining their clubs. The commissions he received from them were for grand and refined classical buildings, which his detractors described as outdated and irrelevant. Kimball chose to see something more profound. "In John Russell Pope," he wrote in the days after Pope's funeral, "American architecture has lost an artist of authentic gifts, who enriched it with works of abiding value."

Kimball saw Pope as a kindred spirit. Both men came from families of modest means. Kimball's father had been a teacher and headmaster, Pope's a portrait painter, his mother a piano teacher. Kimball's father had exhorted him on the occasion of his twentieth birthday "to become a leader in America's renaissance, not only in art but in all civic improvement." In Pope's life, Kimball recognized a similar idealism. "His work was far removed from that of the plan-factory in which classical motives served chiefly as handy formulae, ready to be served up in varying banal combinations with a minimum of time and study." Pope was an original, Kimball believed, admittedly one working in a traditional mode.

Thus Pope was also a victim—as he himself was, Kimball realized—of circumstances. Kimball and Pope had enjoyed "a moment of dominance for the classical influence in America [when] . . . the only voices raised against this dominance were those, powerful to be sure, of two isolated artists of genius, [Louis] Sullivan and [Frank Lloyd] Wright, then crying in the wilderness." The early decades of the twentieth century had seen a grand classical revival, but "Pope's death comes at a different moment, when the value of any neoclassic work is called into question, not only by Wright, but by a host of secondary men, themselves mostly imitators."

Kimball was onto something and he knew it as he put his thoughts on paper. Much of the drama during the summer of 1937 had been played out in the pages of the newspapers and magazines, in particular in the *Magazine of Art* where the dissenting voices of Modernism had been heard in full cry. Now he would rebut them, though not as he had done before from a defensive posture. He would take the opportunity offered by Pope's death, sad though it was. He would point out that Pope's work hadn't changed; the rules had. He would not merely bury Caesar, but he would take advantage of the occasion to change the terms of the debate.

"True, at any given time in the history of art," wrote Kimball, "one trend is always waning, another waxing. It is human for youth to identify value only with the newer, to regard the older as worthless obstruction; just as it is human for age to identify value only with the older trend, to view the newer as subversive nonsense.

"True, also, that in a new generation the greater creative opportunity is with the newer trend, in line with obscure but powerful forces of the new time; but it is just as true that the creative spirit of the past generation will have expressed itself in quite other ways. We need not expect the creative artist himself to admit these axioms; the great artist in his work must be a bigot, even a fanatic, and is apt to be so in his thought." Kimball was in museum-director mode, explaining, shaping, preparing his reader.

"The possibility of artistic creation with traditional elements has indeed been often questioned, even as to the masters of the Renaissance, yet only the fanatic can deny that they achieved it. To the neo-classic artists, still in-volved in the passions of contemporary struggle, it is harder to render justice. They cannot hope, of course, for the veneration reserved only for the men who inaugurated vast movements of fundamentally original character, like Michelangelo . . . but we can still judge them on the success of their efforts to fuse the derivative elements in new wholes, and thus in works of art wor-thy of the name."

Kimball hoped his argument would appeal to those politicians and mem-bers of the public who, uncertain about the new Modernsim, weren't quite ready to reject all that came before.

"Jack Pope is gone. We could have spared the modernist pretenders who cling to skirts of the few giants of our day, as we could have spared the multi-tude of classical hacks of yesterday, rather than have lost the sensitive master of form who was John Russell Pope."

Kimball crafted his obituary (nay, essay) with a full heart—but with all the stealth of a man with a gift for political infighting. His appreciation of his friend Jack Pope emerged in an outpouring, as few scratchouts marred the flow of his handwriting in the original manuscript, and Kimball, uncharac-teristically, made even fewer edits when reviewing the typescript and proofs. In a mere thousand words, Kimball managed to equate Frank Lloyd Wright, John Russell Pope, and Michelangelo. *It's not a matter of style*, argued Kim-ball. *It's a matter of artistry. And the great artists*, he concluded, *whatever their time or school, stand taller than the rest.*

He gave the piece a tombstone title, "John Russell Pope: 1874–1937," and sent the typescript to a friend at the magazine *American Architect*. When it appeared, his article redefined the debate, just as he had hoped.

The battle was rejoined. When word reached them that the opposition had employed a public relations firm to conduct a negative campaign, Kim-ball, Boylan, and the partner in charge at Pope's firm hired its own firm, H. H. Bruno, "to conduct a campaign to help flatten the work already done by the [opposition.]" It was the message of Kimball's piece on Pope that would underlie the public relations strategy, which over the next few months regained the political momentum. The debate was waged in Congress and in the papers, and the Commission seemed poised to prevail when a behind-the-scenes exchange settled the matter once and for all.

The architect's widow, Sadie Pope, wrote directly to Franklin Delano Roo-sevelt, a cousin by marriage. She was angry and hurt, insistent that the Memo-rial be built as her husband had designed it. The president and virtually everyone else in Washington had tired of the argument, and he saw to getting it done. Kimball, waiting at Shack Mountain, got a telegram on June 15, 1938.

APPROPRIATION FOR MEMORIAL PASSED SENATE THIS COMPLETES LEGISLATIVE ACTION STOP CONGRATULATIONS

JOHN J BOYLAN MC

V.
April 13, 1943 . . . The Tidal Basin . . . Washington, D.C.

THE ENGRAVED INVITATIONS HAD GONE OUT bearing the presidential seal. The time of the ceremony had been changed to accommodate the president, moving the dedication up to noon. Promptly at 11:30 A.M. the Marine Band would begin to play and at the twelve o'clock hour President Franklin Delano Roosevelt would arrive at the viewing stand. After the invocation, FDR would deliver an address. The time had come to dedicate the completed Jefferson Memorial.

Kimball had helped manage every aspect. He had worked with Olmsted Brothers of Brookline, Massachusetts, in reshaping the shore of the Tidal Basin. In collaboration with Park Service administrators and the architects at Pope's firm who took over the project, Daniel P. Higgins and Otto R. Eggers, he supervised construction, which had been completed the previous year. He chaired the Committee on Sculpture, which conducted a competition to find a sculptor to create a likeness of Jefferson, then worked with the sculptor, Rudolph Evans, to address various concerns by Roosevelt, whose interest in the project continued. A temporary plaster version of the nineteen-foot-tall statue was in place, but the plan was to cast one in bronze after the wartime restrictions on the use of metals were lifted. He even arranged for a soprano from the Metropolitan Opera to sing the national anthem.

The job had drawn upon virtually all of Kimball's remarkable range of talents: his vision as designer, his pragmatism as a construction manager, his instinct for public relations, his toughness as a political infighter, his artistic sensitivity. In spite of withering criticism, political pitfalls, and the war in Europe, he had gotten the job done.

* * *

The Jefferson Memorial in a press photo from the time of its dedication.
The University of Virginia

ANYONE TIRING OF THE SPEECHES at the Jefferson Memorial that afternoon could, merely by gazing north across the Tidal Basin, survey the Federal
City. The dominant element in the panorama that day—or any day—would
have been Robert Mills's Washington National Monument.

After Mills's death, the monument had remained a picturesque ruin for
two decades. Only with the Centennial celebration was a new momentum
found. Even then a philosophical debate had ensued, pitting art against
mathematics. For those in the camp of art, their platform was the Victorian
aesthetic in which artful meant ornamented and exotic. That translated into
proposals to remake the plain-faced obelisk to resemble a "Hindu pagoda" or
a northern Italian Gothic campanile. But science and mathematics had
eventually prevailed, and an army colonel, Thomas Lincoln Casey of the
Corps of Engineers, had been put in charge.

Because some uneven settlement was evident, Casey enlarged and
strengthened the foundations. Then in 1880 the obelisk had, once again, begun its rise. Archaeological findings had established that the Egyptian ratio
was ten-to-one for an obelisk's height-to-base, so the shaft was topped out at

a height of five hundred feet. Mills's design had called for an essentially flat
cap, but Casey's men constructed a pyramid atop the immense structure,
which rose steeply another fifty-five feet. Completing it was a 9½-inch apex
of a new and rare material called aluminum. When installed in 1884, the six-
pound "cap-stone" was the largest piece of aluminum ever cast. In another of
the eerie parallels between the two presidential memorials, just as the Jefferson's represented the last gasp of a style suddenly gone stale, the Washington
Monument, completed in a new age of iron and steel buildings, became the
tallest masonry structure in the world.

Viewed across the Tidal Basin, the Washington National Monument
added a powerful but plain dignity to the Federal City. Just as George Washington's presence alone had commanded respect, so did the stark, skyward
tower of unadorned stone. And in the eyes of more than one beholder that
dedication day at the Jefferson Memorial, it looked prescient indeed, so sleek
and modernist despite its ancient shape.

KIMBALL HAD WON THE BATTLE OVER THE JEFFERSON MEMORIAL, but
the war for classicism was lost. Harvard architecture dean Joseph Hudnut had
been deriding Pope when, once again in the *Magazine of Art*, he dismissed
him as "the last of the Romans" in 1940. But the brickbat had been intended
for Kimball, too.

Kimball could content himself that, within his personal universe, he inhabited two buildings that stood as important examples of the American renaissance in architecture. One was Shack Mountain, the modest house that
would prompt art historian Kenneth Clark to exclaim on first viewing, "It's a
temple in the woods." The other was the great "Greek Garage," now finished
and chockablock with art in Philadelphia.

Kimball had come of age at a time when the classical had ruled. Early in the
century, the works of McKim, Mead and White, John Russell Pope, and others
had been built to what seemed to be automatic admiration. But by the thirties,
architecture with an historical consciousness became outré, old-fashioned—in
short, un-modern. The classical went into eclipse, and decades would elapse before the Bicentennial would make Postmodernism and the preservation movement possible. Kimball's public career in architecture collapsed, too. If his work
on the Jefferson monument had not been tainted by controversy, he almost certainly would have been tapped by FDR for bigger things. How high he might

Kimball's house: Like the man, Shack Mountain puts itself forward, bold, imposing, carrying the weight of history. *Philadelphia Museum of Art Archives/Fiske Kimball Papers*

have risen is a matter of conjecture, but what is clear is that the national spot-light fell upon Fiske Kimball for a few moments—there he was, Jefferson expert, taste maker, man of ambition—then all too quickly flickered and went out. He had proved a better judge of architecture's past than predictor of its future.

Travels in Time

FISKE KIMBALL WOULD LIVE OUT HIS LIFE IN PHILADELPHIA. With him as director from 1925 to 1955, the Philadelphia Museum emerged as one of the finest art museums in the country. He persuaded Thomas Eakins's widow to give the museum more than seventy-five of her husband's paintings. Canvases by Rubens, Poussin, and Cezanne came to the museum on his watch, as did the Foulc Collection of Renaissance objects. His courting of Louise and Walter Arensberg led them to leave the museum their collection, which ranged from pre-Columbian art to a variety of twentieth-century masters, in particular numerous works by their friend Marcel Duchamp. Beyond the walls of the immense museum building, Kimball also supervised the restoration of what he called the "Colonial Chain," a group of nine historic mansions in Fairmount Park that the city placed under the museum's aegis. He restored the freestanding houses, all in their original settings, then furnished them with objects from the museum's collections.

Kimball proved to be the consummate museum director, a showman who brought in the multitudes, a diplomat who charmed donors of art and money, a visionary who saw museums in evolutionary terms (he commissioned a pioneering study of "museum fatigue"), and a financial manager who, during the Great Depression when his salary was cut and many of his employees laid off, found ways to get things done despite deficits.

He drifted away from American architectural subjects during his museum years. "I was beginning to get tired of it," he said. "The soil was too fallow, and any reputation gained was too parochial. I remember thinking it would be no harder to work on Michelangelo than on McIntire." After the near-fiasco on the Jefferson Memorial Commission, Kimball redirected his research energies and published *The Creation of the Rococo* in 1943. An influential treatise that helped initiate serious scholarship into a rarely examined period, the book was also a return for Kimball to what had been an early academic passion (he had noted in his diary in 1912, "I want . . . specially to write about the French eighteenth century, which I had fallen in love with in Paris"). He admitted to an old friend at the time *The Creation of the Rococo* was published, "I am wholly seduced by the study of French interiors."

Still, he never altogether abandoned the discipline of American architectural history. As he wrote to another friend in 1942, "I have indeed had a great deal of fun with Americana . . . although I had to get this fun in the old days by getting up at five o'clock in the morning, when I still had that much energy, and in recent years by making it my Sunday-morning golf." Physically clumsy and uninterested in sports, he never played golf; but his rooting interest in "Americana" continually led him to make his expertise available to a variety of organizations.

In 1927, the year before the Williamsburg Holding Corporation was formed to acquire properties in that sleepy Tidewater town, Kimball had been consulted regarding the preliminary plans for the restoration. He immediately expressed his approval and then, quite unprompted, promulgated what he called "the best principles of restoration." These were, in short, to preserve what survives where it is; to use evidence of what no longer exists to establish what the old was actually like; and, in the absence of any such evidence, "to work scrupulously in the style of the very time and place, yet with artistic sensitiveness." Often restated and elaborated upon, this philosophy has been the essence of sound preservation practice ever since. At Williamsburg, Kimball would regularly be on hand to watch what he called "the resurrection of Colonial Williamsburg" as a member of the Architects Advisory Committee. Starting in 1928, his "Prussian attitude" and "foghorn voice" were known to dominate meetings for the next twenty years.

His restoration work would help put Monticello on the nickel. He was also chairman of the American Institute of Architects' Committee on Historic Monuments and Scenic Beauties. He was on the Park Service advisory board, which was then just beginning to assemble its collection of museum houses. But Kimball, despite his instinct for preservation, was not perfect.

Some recent critics condescend to recall as him a "motif-monger," complaining that his understanding of eighteenth-century design relied too much on books and too little on an anthropological appreciation of the cultural landscape. His habit was to conclude that a resemblance between a printed plate and, say, a historic mantelpiece meant the craftsmen had

Director Fiske Kimball at his desk at the Philadelphia Museum circa 1937, looking preoccupied and, as always, determined. *Philadelphia Museum of Art Archives/Fiske Kimball Papers*

known the same source. Scholars today are inclined to ask more questions about craft traditions, material culture, and even the personal narratives of the builders. As a result, more recent architectural historians have been second-guessing a variety of his conclusions at several historic sites, including Monticello, Gunston Hall, and Stratford Hall.

His work at Stratford Hall, in particular, has led to dismissive remarks about "Kimballization." He guided the initial restoration of the eighteenth-century house after the Robert E. Lee Memorial Association acquired the home to restore it as a shrine to the Confederate general. In doing so, he made certain suppositions, relying to an exaggerated degree upon his own architectural taste (which, as usual, was classical). The fan-shaped, parapetted brick staircases he installed at Stratford seem to have been based upon Burlington's Chiswick rather than the archaeology at Stratford. But that was an unusual lapse; more often, his restoration work hewed closer to the progressive principles he had articulated for Colonial Williamsburg. As early as 1916, he had bemoaned "destructive remodeling" and "the absence of careful archaeological examinations." As he himself put it to a fellow museum director in 1932, the restoration architect had to acknowledge that "preserving and restoring an old house is quite a different thing from designing a new one, and takes quite different qualities in an architect—not imagination, but historical knowledge, not originality, but self-abnegation."

The mistakes seem less important when contrasted to the fundamental philosophical changes he fostered. When Kimball burst onto the scene, he was a realist among romantics. Homer Eaton Keyes, founder and editor of *Antiques Magazine*, characterized the tone of the time as "in quest of the quaint." The orientation of most people concerned with artifacts of the American past was not to embark upon an intellectual quest to find documentary resources to support conclusions. Most satisfied themselves with a soft, emotional sense of wonderment at the charm or naïveté of an object or a place. Newer generations of architectural scholars have put added emphasis on physical evidence, on close examination of the object itself. Paul Buchanan, an influential architectural historian of the next generation, would spend three decades at Williamsburg. He regarded Kimball as a friend and mentor but later came to know both Gunston and Stratford Halls more intimately than Kimball ever did. Buchanan's methodology involved getting down on his hands and knees and crawling behind the paneling (it was he who found Buckland's tiny drawings at Gunston Hall). Physical investigation was Buchanan's forte, and it has become an essential partner to documentary research. Not that Kimball didn't investigate the artifacts; certainly he did, as his research notes and writings contain comparative analyses of bricks, glass sizes, and other physical elements, and his notes are accompanied with architectural renderings (Kimball drew easily and well). In truth, though, he was most comfortable with inventories, deeds, documentary evidence, and, in particular, with architectural drawings.

Kimball transformed himself into America's first true restoration architect and his research initiated a new academic discipline. The formal study of architectural history didn't exist in the United States until he came along and began to shape it. Early in his career, he attempted in an essay to define the language of his nascent discipline, which lacked any formal nomenclature. Kimball developed a methodology for the study of architectural history: He believed in an archaeological investigation of artifacts and a reliance on primary documents. He moved the field away from the moral musings of English art historian John Ruskin and his Victorian followers. In 1941 he helped found the field's major publication, the *Journal of the American Society of Architectural Historians*, and contributed an article to its first issue, "The Preservation Movement in America." He was uniquely positioned to write such an article, as perhaps the most essential member of the first generation of old-house fanciers who not only venerated antique buildings but respected them, studied them, compared them to surviving documentary materials, and gave them a historic context. As one reviewer had said of Kimball's *A History of Architecture* in 1928, "The subject is discussed with scientific precision and freedom from emotional bias." Kimball could not have said it better himself.

IN HIS LAST YEARS, KIMBALL KNEW HE WAS AT THE CLOSE OF A GRAND career. His temper sometimes got the better of him. He couldn't help it. His best work was behind him and he wasn't as tough or as disciplined as he once had been. "Alas, the iron hand in the velvet glove is getting rusty," he admitted to a friend after giving in to the ladies of Gunston Hall on a restoration question. He was worried about the future not only for himself as his powers deteriorated, but for his beloved wife, helpmate, and collaborator. Marie had been frequently hospitalized with a weak heart since the mid-1930s. An elevator had been installed at Lemon Hill, their historic home in Fairmount Park, to save her the exertion of climbing stairs. Her flagging energies had meant the final two books of her proposed five-volume biography of Jefferson were on hold.

Kimball had become his field's elder statesman. One young graduate student found that every turn seemed to put him on Kimball Street, and he admitted as much to the man himself when he screwed up his courage and wrote to architectural history's éminence grise in May 1952. "Every subject I have thought of writing on has already been done by you," read Thomas J. McCormick's plaintive postscript.

The main text of his letter wasn't so self-pitying. He thought that maybe, just maybe, enough remained to be learned about a certain eighteenth-century French antiquarian to satisfy his professors at Princeton; he got a response by return mail. "Clérisseau would be a fine subject," Kimball wrote, "one which I have considered since 1914."

Kimball wasn't exaggerating. In the years since his own dissertation, a sturdy and unmistakable thread stitched dozens of his publications together. Jefferson held pride of place, of course, central to a body of work that included eight books and many hundreds of articles in periodicals as varied as *The Magazine Antiques*, *Architectural Record*, *Gazette des Beaux-Arts*, and the *New York Times Magazine*. The lives and works of the men with whom Jefferson had worked constantly appeared and reappeared in Kimball's work.

Kimball and McCormick exchanged letters. McCormick would update Kimball on his research progress; in turn, Kimball offered encouragement. He extended an invitation, too. "I would love to meet you some time you are

Fiske Kimball at Mr. Jefferson's grave. *Philadelphia Museum of Art Archives/Fiske Kimball Papers*

down this way," he wrote McCormick from Philadelphia in late 1952.

Kimball's curiosity extended to many subjects and he often encouraged other scholars, especially younger ones, but the neoclassical tradition to which Clérisseau belonged was central to Kimball's passion. His detective work had not only reawakened the world to Thomas Jefferson, Architect, but in 1927 Kimball had done the same for Richard Boyle, third Earl of Burlington. His two-part article "Burlington Arcitectus" in the *Journal of the Royal Institute of British Architects* pointed to "many elaborately rendered drawings"—as usual, Kimball had gone straight to the drawings—that demonstrated the so-called Architect Earl had been more than an amateur. At first the articles provoked a dismissive outcry in England, but from his 1950s vantage, McCormick could see how Kimball's thesis had prevailed. It had become a commonplace that Burlington was not merely a patron but an important architect, too. And Kimball had been made an honorary member of the Royal Institute of British Architects.

Kimball liked nothing better than the unanswered question, except perhaps the unopened treasure chest filled with drawings that scholars less assiduous than he had failed to find. When young Tom McCormick came to visit in March of 1953, Kimball was thrilled to see his "wonderful collection of every document concerning Clérisseau."

The two made an amusing sight. McCormick was slight, of moderate height, a man inclined to dry humor and thoughtful pauses. The extroverted Kimball was intimidating and loud, a big man with a manner to match. "He came on very strong," thought McCormick. But they had lots to talk about as the younger man presented his researches.

McCormick, Kimball found, had ferreted out Clérisseau collections in various English museums, as well as those in private hands. He knew more than Kimball did of the Russian drawings bought by Catherine the Great, which remained locked behind the Iron Curtain in Stalinist Russia. McCormick's work so impressed Kimball that the very next day he penned a brief article for *Architectural Review* about McCormick and, not incidentally, how McCormick's findings corroborated his own theories of the Adam style. (Whatever his indebtedness to his old teacher Clérisseau, asserted Kimball, "It was Adam, not Piranesi or Clérisseau who invented the Adam style." Clérisseau, once more, got little credit.)

As they talked that day in the director's office, McCormick sensed the intense energy that Kimball exuded. But there was more, too, since during their talk McCormick noticed the smell of smoke. Not just their cigarettes, he realized, but something else was burning. Kimball seemed oblivious. After a time, McCormick saw flames licking over the mouth of the wastebasket where Kimball had carelessly emptied his ashtray, a butt or two still smoldering. Apparently this sort of thing happened regularly. Before McCormick could say a word, Kimball's secretary bustled in and efficiently doused the small blaze.

McCormick felt a bit stunned as the sour smell of the dampened fire settled over them, but the middle-aged Mrs. Kane seemed entirely unfazed as she returned to her own desk. And so did Kimball, who had never broken stride as his scholarly monologue continued across the landscape of eighteenth-century Europe.

THE AGING KIMBALL IS REMEMBERED AS GETTING GREAT JOY from facing down the young people at the Philadelphia Museum of Art. He still had his gruffness, though he tempered it with his enthusiasm for the chase. He would catch the twenty-somethings in the lunchroom, where he would settle his bulk into a chair at a table filled with young staff members. He would quiz them about their research. *What are you working on?* he would ask. *Where will it take you? What are your sources?* He would inquire about a new book or article and, if the aspiring young person did not know it, he would take him or her to the research library and find it. Once there, he did not bother to whisper, but squatted in the stacks, talking and teaching and questioning.

This recollection of Kimball as mentor to the young represents one aspect of his endgame. The story has been repeated over the years and, in the retelling, the vignette has developed the patina of age. While its truth is undoubted, the story actually reveals as much about the teller's point of view as it does about Kimball.

A more realistic take on his last months offers a grimmer portrait, since it is also an accepted fact among those who knew him that Kimball died "mad." Mad, that is, in the old sense of suffering from a mental disease.

Over the years, Kimball had become a man for whom people made allowances. He was known to tell jokes in appalling taste at inappropriate times, and he relished being called the "bad boy." He could be brusque, crude, insensitive, impolitic, arrogant, and insulting. But his commitment to art, architecture, and his institution was so absolute that he had maintained the loyalty of his staff and the respect of his fellow Philadelphians.

When Kimball had turned 65 in 1953, he was no grandfather figure. He still brought the same high standards and intensity to his work that he always had, but his behavior was beginning to show signs of veering from the eccentric to the antisocial. He had long since habituated to the essential notion that one must lavish unto one's donors the kindnesses that one would have them return as gifts of *objets*, but Kimball began forgetting the museum man's Golden Rule. His moods seemed to elevate to new heights only to crash. Depending upon their temperaments, his coworkers at the museum either took to avoiding him or to protecting him when he behaved peculiarly. More than once the suggestion was made that he seek a psychiatric consultation, but he wouldn't hear of it.

Two events would precipitate Kimball's end. One was his forced resignation from the museum when his public outbursts made his continued employment as Director untenable. That came in January of 1955. Failing health and the wish to devote more time to his research were the reasons cited, and the Museum's board accompanied the announcement with a resolution listing his accomplishments.

Then, on March 2, Marie suffered a severe heart attack. A stroke followed and, in a matter of hours, she was dead.

Through the nearly forty-one years of their marriage, Kimball's letters to Marie when they were apart had opened with "Dear Sweetheart" or "My Dearest Sweetheart." When they were together, his favorite endearment was "Mia." Theirs had been a love match and, despite her long illness and Kimball's appetite for life, there was no suggestion that he ever sought the companionship of another woman. Marie had helped him with his work; just as

Fiske found among Marie's papers a farewell note that she wanted read at her funeral. In it she spoke warmly of her father, then moved on to Kimball. "I want to pay as great a tribute to my dearly beloved husband, the best and truest man who ever lived. Not only did he devote his life to gratifying my every wish and desire—and I am ashamed how many there were—but he introduced me to the treasures of Europe and of art, without which my life would indeed have been arid." Just as she had hoped, he showed her the world beyond Champaign-Urbana. This studio portrait dates from circa 1938.
Philadelphia Museum of Art Archives/Fiske Kimball Papers

important, perhaps, she had worshiped him, admired him, and provided him with the kind of emotional sustenance that nurtures a marriage of equals. With his wife dead, life for Kimball was almost unfathomable. He would live another five and a half months, first in Philadelphia and Charlottesville, then abroad after April 15. He found moments of peace in Amsterdam, Florence, and Germany, but he still rode the roller coaster of high sprits and low. After a series of strokes, he died on August 14, 1955, in a clinic in Munich.

Even a half-century after his death, the handful of survivors who knew him speak reluctantly or not at all about Kimball's last years. Like mute pallbearers, they wish to carry the more difficult memories of the deceased and bury those, too. But that seems a paradoxical kindness.

Today, living as we do in the age of Alzheimer's, the wish to suppress discussion of Kimball's deterioration seems misplaced. His accomplishments were too numerous, varied, and important to be diminished by a recognition that, during the last years of his life, he suffered from "an increasingly severe manic affliction," as one unusually forthright coworker described his condition. It is impossible to know what Kimball would have said of a well-intentioned conspiracy to suppress the facts of his end, but he did devote his life to looking frankly into the mists of time. That he would have approved of adding a scrim that left his image illuminated by some faux chiaroscuro seems improbable.

One might choose to freeze-frame Kimball at any one of many moments in his career. Vignettes come to mind: Kimball at the White House with Roosevelt; in Ferdie Latrobe's study; courting Marie in Champaign-Urbana. One could imagine a dissolve, too, capturing one of the times where his mental equilibrium deserted him.

I prefer hearkening back to the Jefferson project, which set the course for Kimball's life. My choice, then, is to see him seated in the second-floor reading room of the Massachusetts Historical Society on April 6, 1914. Surrounding him is the great cache of Jefferson drawings, which to the young and eager Kimball must have seemed like leprechauns' gold. He would use them to pull the Virginian's architectural work back from the brink of permanent obscurity; he would go on to identify many important designer-builders, giving Latrobe, Thornton, and others new status as the Founding Fathers of American building. He would subsequently restore dozens of buildings and tell countless important stories. And that is without reference to the other half of his life, the three remarkable decades spent creating the Philadelphia Museum of Art.

AS I WAS COMPLETING THE MANUSCRIPT FOR THIS BOOK, I went to Boston for a closer look at Jefferson's drawings of the Virginia Capitol. Facsimiles of them could be seen both in the pages of Dr. Kimball's book, *Thomas Jefferson, Architect*, and in high-resolution scans that were a few mouse clicks away on the Web. But I begged and pleaded my way into viewing the original drawings that, as fragile and priceless artifacts, are zealously safeguarded by their caretakers.

My hope was that I might infer something new about the Jefferson-Clérisseau collaboration, but no such insight offered itself in looking at the renderings. On the other hand, I was reminded of something else, particularly in examining the workmanlike floor plans on which Jefferson's faded pencil markings are but dimly visible through the orangey grid of the coördinate paper he had bought in Paris at the shop named Chez Crépy.

Thomas Jefferson, Draftsman, circa 1785, was a rank amateur. His skills as a delineator would improve over the next thirty years, but even his later drawings would be amateurish, particularly in comparison with the work of Latrobe and Mills. I wondered to myself in looking at the drawings, forgotten all those years in a Charlottesville attic, might not that actually be the essential point? Jefferson was largely responsible for a fundamental change, but it was not as a result of his draftsmanship or because he possessed a particular genius for unprecedented designs (his friend Benjamin Henry Latrobe once offered the rather backhanded compliment that Jefferson was an "excellent architect out of books"). Wasn't the heart of the matter his aspiration to open the field to those who had greater skills and talent?

In architecture, as in politics, Jefferson's genius was philosophical. He envisioned his country, a place characterized in his youth by "rude, mis-shapen piles," becoming one in which buildings would be well built and possess genuine artistic merit. At the Virginia Capitol and his Academical Village, he created models that he hoped would be studied and imitated. Throughout his public and private life, he cajoled, pontificated, encouraged, lobbied, and otherwise exhorted his countrymen to improve the architecture of their country.

And he succeeded. Not single-handedly, of course; he had other great men to help him. And not all of them spoke with one voice. Jefferson had his enthusiasms ("Mr. Jefferson was altogether Roman in his taste for architecture," observed Robert Mills), and Latrobe had his (he described himself as a "bigoted Greek"). Straddling the Roman and the Greek revivals was the other great architectural tastemaker of the Federal era, Charles Bulfinch, who favored the English, the Adamesque.

The work of these three men and their followers has been loosely characterized as being in the "Federal style." The rubric is aesthetically vague, with its rhetorical implications about the way the patriots had thrown off the Georgian style, just as they had their English rulers. Yet it was the *Federal* City, thanks to Washington and Jefferson, that proved to be the essential agency for change in transforming American building. The designations "American Neoclassical," "Early Classical Revival," "Adamesque," and "Jeffersonian" are useful as individual typologies but collectively these men created the Federal Style.

Let's return to the drawings.

In recalling his brief clerkship for Jefferson, Robert Mills noted the reaction of the craftsmen at Monticello upon seeing the paper plans. "The details were all drawn and proportioned by Mr. Jefferson and with an accuracy which astonished the workmen engaged in carrying them into execution." It wasn't the quality of the drawings that impressed the joiners and the masons (with the passage of just a few years, Jefferson's drawings would appear crude to a new generation of builders grown accustomed to working from architectural plans). But in 1802, the salient fact was that detailed drawings of Monticello *existed at all.*

Drawings became the lingua franca of building. Mere words or common guild practices were no longer sufficient. More sophisticated drawings made possible more visually and structurally complex buildings. The architect distinguished himself from the carpenter-builder by his ability to express his vision in elevations, floor plans, and details.

The ability to execute architectural drawings also amounted to a new kind of authority, a new supervisory layer of management. Gentlemen amateurs with the leisure to sketch their dreams from the pages of books were replaced by merchants with businesses to run who wished to know what they were buying. It was the perspective drawing that enabled the architect to persuade the client to do things that a builder might not even have dreamed of doing.

As the craft of building was joined by the discipline of architecture, the vision could became more plastic. Latrobe expressed himself best in shaping spaces, while Bulfinch's tastes ran to elegantly decorated surfaces, as did Jefferson's, with their tendency studiously to re-create classical motifs (as Kimball observed, "Jefferson's art was the art of retrospection and of science"). But Latrobe (and Robert Mills) were the advance guard: They thought of buildings in three dimensions. An architectural problem—whether it was a church, a government building, or a domicile—was conceived of in geometrical terms, from the inside out. Its volumes were to be imagined from within, its masses then sculpted into one composition. Perspective drawings enhanced this process, portraying buildings as forms alive in the landscape, related to their setting, conveying the illusion that the viewer could enter the drawing and experience the place. Latrobe's drawings were so good that even Charles Bulfinch would admit that "at first view of [his] drawings, my courage almost failed me."

Jefferson was a dreamer: He learned from books, from enlightened and open-minded observation, and from making buildings. Latrobe was a professional, trained by English professionals, who had worked in the context of architectural and engineering practice. Bulfinch's personal crucible was neither avocational nor professional, but born of economic necessity. He brought a gentleman's taste to the harsh demands of feeding his family, and designed buildings and streetscapes for his rapidly growing city.

They abandoned the box. Jefferson's hallmark was the octagon, whether halved, elongated, or pure. Bulfinch's was the bow, usually elliptical, its protrusion adding a third dimension to an exterior elevation. And Latrobe? His imagination shaped soaring spaces. The geometry of architecture in their time grew more complex as a sophisticated aesthetic took over from the folk tradition; the artisan was succeeded by the architect. As building, once largely the province of builders, gained a new management layer, so the buildings themselves became more complex, the shapes more varied. The work of these three men was distinctly different, yet, taken together, their buildings form the basis of the first generation of distinctly American architecture.

When I set out to write about Kimball, I imagined he could guide us through time. In a sense, he has done so, since his work offers lessons about history's many lapses, about how the forgotten can be recovered, how the blurring can be corrected. Kimball has helped me understand that trustworthy history isn't about random, unfiltered recollections; it's about collective memory, shaped as objectively as possible. Without Kimball, the stories in this book might have been told quite differently. After all, to visit the past one needs a map, and Kimball left us an indelible topography.

ACKNOWLEDGMENTS

IN RESEARCHING THIS BOOK, I attempted to find every source, published and unpublished, primary and secondary, pertaining to the characters who carry its story. My goal from the beginning was to identify moments in the past when one or more of these men advanced the cause of American architecture. In particular, I sought episodes when they collaborated, places where their paths crossed, and evidence that had been uncovered by Dr. Kimball as he investigated their lives.

Every detail in this book, then, comes from a historic source. I have drawn upon letters, wills, contracts, sketches, journals, notebooks, newspaper articles, and other documentary and physical evidence. Every quotation is from a letter, diary, memoir, draft manuscript, book, or published article.

I have in some instances drawn upon the educated suppositions of other historians. For example, I accepted the notion of the late Paul Buchanan that Buckland executed the pencil sketches he found in the walls at Gunston Hall. I accepted the prevailing assumption among bibliographers that Buckland arrived with architectural books bought in London. While no documents survive to affirm that Mathias Hammond was jilted by a Philadelphia fiancée, the story, repeated so often and for so many years, had the aura of truth about it so I employed it in the narrative, though with a qualification.

Another educated conjecture put Jefferson and Clérisseau together, leaning over a copy of the latter's *Antiquités de la France*. While the precise circumstances of their first meeting are unknown, we do know for certain that they met and discussed the design of the Virginia Capitol on several occasions; that they exchanged drawings and developed an enduring rapport; and that Jefferson purchased a copy of the Frenchman's book from him for seventy-two francs. Whether their initial meeting unfolded in August of 1785 in the Frenchman's atelier in the Louvre is uncertain—but probable.

In sum, then, while my standards of proof are high, there are interpolative conjectures in these pages, most of them already advanced by scholars and re-searchers. All are consonant with the known facts, and the buildings, the people, and the relationships all existed. I believe that in all likelihood the events tran-spired very much as recounted here.

I HAVE MANY PEOPLE TO THANK. This book began in Virginia a good many years ago, so I must thank the men who first dispatched me in that direction. John I Mesick's restoration labors at the Academical Village prompted my first visit there in 1989 when I was at work on my book *The Preservationist's Progress* (1991). The experience opened a window for me on a wall where I hadn't known there was one. When it came to experiencing a number of the places in this book, I owe a debt of gratitude to Bob Vila, who, by hiring me as the writer, re-searcher, and scout for his A&E Networks specials "Bob Vila's Guide to Historic Homes," launched me on an unexpected personal odyssey that led by indirect means to a series of books, including this one.

Next comes Roger Straus III. With his panoramic cameras and an endless sup-ply of 120 Fuji film on hand, he joined me on trips to Jefferson's house, as well as Gunston Hall, Stratford Hall, and perhaps a hundred other sites as we collabo-rated on several visual book projects, including our own version of Kimball's *Thomas Jefferson, Architect*.

As the notion of a Kimball biography began to take shape in my mind, my friend and agent, Gail Hochman, helped transform them into a proposal for a recognizable book; later, she brought her enthusiasm and encouragement to the project at just the right moments. Gillian Blake, my editor at Bloomsbury, saw the future of the book at an early stage and brought a disciplined eye and flashes of invaluable insight to the editing process. My appreciation, as well, to Greg Villepique, Bloomsbury's managing editor, for seeing the book through to press; to Peter Miller for his excel-lent efforts to alert the world to this book's existence; to Benjamin Adams for his at-tention to a multitude of details; and to Jiyeon Dew for her clean and unified design. And to my dear friend and sometime colleague, Jean Atcheson, whose careful edit-ing steered me around a goodly number of verbal potholes. There were also profes-sional readers along the way, in particular architectural historians Travis Macdonald, Tom McCormick, and Brian Pfeiffer, each of whom reviewed portions of the manuscript and offered corrections and useful commentary.

For research assistance, I must first thank Susan K. Anderson, archivist, at the Philadelphia Museum of Art for her patience and good company on my numerous encampments in her office to read and study Kimball's papers; and Katherine Stefko, who reorganized Kimball's papers and prepared the finding aids that made my forays into his forest of paper very much easier than it might have been. My thanks, too, to Amanda Bowen for making me welcome at the Harvard University Fine Arts Library, where many of Kimball's architectural papers are deposited. For providing access to still more Kimball papers, my appreciation to Susan Borchardt, then assistant director, and Kevin Shupe, archivist, at Gunston Hall; Judith S. Hynson at Stratford Hall Plantation; and Irene V. Axelrod at the Peabody Essex Museum. For teaching me about Peale's Buckland portrait, I thank Helen Cooper and, in particular, Graham C. Boettcher at the Yale University Art Gallery; for lessons in Buckland's Hammond-Harwood House, my appreciation to Carter Lively and Lisa Mason-Chaney. I had fruitful exchanges as well with Joseph J. Rishel, Alexandra A. Kitley, and Melissa Kerr regarding various objects in the collections at the Philadelphia Museum.

Other libraries provided more general materials and reference guidance, among them the Sterling and Francine Clark Art Institute Library; the Sawyer Library at Williams College; and the New York Public Library. My thanks, too, to Peter Drummey and Kim Nusco at the Massachusetts Historical Society; Bruce Kirby at the Library of Congress; Jan Hilley, Kristine Paulus, and Jenny Gotwals at the New-York Historical Society; and the staff at the Chatham Library in Chatham, New York. A grant from the Graham Foundation for Advanced Studies in the Fine Arts made it possible for me to extend my research time, adding to the richness of historic detail. For the privilege of learning more, I am grateful.

Mrs. Jane Moore, owner and for almost half a century occupant of Dr. Kimball's Shack Mountain, has been a source of stories and inspiration. She has made Shack Mountain very much her own, yet visiting there gave me a certain angular access to Kimball. In the special thanks category, I must also single out Thomas J. McCormick, who told me of his meetings with Kimball in the 1950s, and opened to me his correspondence files.

In more general ways, the following generous people guided, provoked, or stimulated my thinking in conversations and correspondence: Sylvan Barnet, William Beiswanger, Bennie Brown Jr., Donald Carpentier Jr., Edward Chappell, Willie Graham, Bryan Clark Green, Joseph Dye Lahendro, Carl R. Lounsbury, W. Barksdale Maynard, Ronald W. Miller, Wayne Mogielnicki, David Pinnegar, Robert Self, Thomas Gordon Smith, Susan Stein, Duncan Stroik, Mark R. Wenger, Richard Guy Wilson, and James Wootton.

Finally, I have the women in my life to thank for never objecting to Dr. Kimball's presence in our lives—at the dinner table, on trips, and preoccupying my mind. My love and thanks to Betsy, Sarah, and Elizabeth.

APPENDIX I

BIOGRAPHICAL NOTES

DR. KIMBALL'S STORY HAS SUPPLIED THE MATRIX, providing the freedom to travel in the preceding pages to and from the past. However, the event-by-event narrative of this book has left unfinished the stories of those who helped invent American architecture.

Jefferson's Parisian collaborator, CHARLES-LOUIS CLÉRISSEAU, lived for many years after Jefferson returned to America, though he never traveled across the Atlantic to see the Capitol he had helped design for the Commonwealth of Virginia. For the last twenty-five years of his life, he seems to have designed and painted but little, though more than a few public acknowledgments of his skills finally came his way. In 1804, Napoleon granted him a pension; among his other honors was membership in the Légion d'Honneur.

After his death at age ninety-nine in 1820, his library, thought by some to be the finest owned by any architect of his time, was sold at auction. His story had been told only in piecemeal fashion by Kimball and others until *Charles-Louis Clérisseau and the Genesis of Neo-Classicism* appeared in 1990. Its author was Thomas J. McCormick, the young man Kimball had counseled in the early 1950s.

MARIA COSWAY, the woman who reawakened the passionate nature of widower Jefferson, corresponded sporadically with him after he returned home. Having lost her daughter and lived through the Terror in the 1790s, she withdrew from society to become superintendent of a girls' convent school in England. Later she retired to the Continent, first to Lyon, then to Italy, where she founded a school for young Italian girls of good family. She died in a convent, the Instituto Maria SS Bambina, in Lodi in 1838. Among her possessions was the miniature oil of Jefferson that John Trumbull painted at her insistence in 1788 from the working canvas for his "Declaration of Independence." The little portrait on board (it's only slightly larger than a playing card) remained at the Suore di Maria SS Bambina until 1976, when the Italian government, in honor of Jefferson and the Bicentennial, gifted it to the U. S. government. Trumbull's little memory piece now hangs in the White House.

After his dismissal as architect of the Capitol, GEORGE HADFIELD, Maria Cosway's brother, went on to design Washington's City Hall, a prison, and the Custis Mansion, a highly visible home for George Washington's grandson, which today overlooks Arlington Cemetery from its perch across the Potomac from Washington, D.C. Despite these accomplishments, he ended his life reduced to ghostwriting, penning a chapter in the city's first guidebook.

Among those buried in Arlington (his remains were moved there in 1909) was MAJOR PIERRE CHARLES L'ENFANT. His once-brilliant future rapidly dimmed after President Washington was forced to dismiss him (at the time, he walked off with his and Clérisseau's Capitol plans, none of which have ever been found). L'Enfant had been so confident of his standing with the president that he had done his work without benefit of title, salary, or other funds. He was known to appear at the Capitol during its prolonged construction wearing a worn blue military coat and napless beaver hat. In one hand he carried a hickory cane; in the other, he always seemed to be have legal papers in support of his case against the government for compensation. He ended his life as an aging and embittered retainer to a wealthy Maryland family, living in an outbuilding on their country estate. When he died, his worldly goods consisted of his personal effects, a few books and maps, and his surveying instruments. Taken together, they were valued at $45.00. His Federal Hall had been demolished in 1812.

The vain, contentious, handsome, and variously talented DR. WILLIAM THORNTON fared only slightly better. He could draw a lifelike portrait as Latrobe never could; but as an architect, he was content to remain a dilettante. After instinctively tossing off the Capitol design that Jefferson and Washington embraced, he succeeded in the years to come in undermining the work of the professionals, among them George Hadfield and Benjamin Latrobe. His insults became too much for Latrobe, who finally sued him for libel. After years in the courts, the case was resolved in favor of Latrobe, but the judge awarded him *one cent* in damages.

Thornton's wife wrote of him in 1828, the year he died, "Wou'd to God he had remained [in Philadelphia], where he might have become an eminent physician and professor, and not been a seeker of office from *illiberal and selfish* politicians!" Yet his contributions not only as the designer of the Capitol but as a volunteer American are incontrovertible. He had repaid the trust put in him as

Superintendent of the Patent Office when, during the British sacking of Washington, he had saved it from almost certain destruction. Arriving just as an English officer ordered a gun turned on the building, Thornton leaped off his horse and demanded, "Are you Englishmen, or Goths and Vandals?" Everything stopped. "This is the Patent Office!" Thornton had exhorted. "The depository of the inventive genius of America, with which the whole civilized world is concerned. Would you destroy it? If so, fire away, and let the charge pass through my body."

JAMES HOBAN managed to be both a designer (of the State Department and War Department buildings, as well as the President's House) and one of Washington's best builders (he managed construction at the Capitol for many years and built the President's House twice, first in executing his original design, then rebuilding it after the British burned it during the War of 1812). He invested successfully in Washington real estate and built one of the city's first hotels, Blodgett's. He served on the city council for many years and, when he died in 1831, left a substantial estate of some $60,000.

The best and most influential architect in America in his time, BENJAMIN HENRY LATROBE, was perhaps the least lucky of a rather unlucky crew. He did two tours of duty at the Capitol, leaving his unmistakable imprint there, not least with the "American Order" in which he used native corn as a decorative motif. He built the Baltimore Cathedral with its immense coffered dome. As large as his talent was, it didn't extend to money management. Twice he found himself virtually destitute, and his career proved peripatetic, as he was obliged to travel to find employment. As a result, he did important work not only in Washington, Philadelphia, and Baltimore but in Virginia, Kentucky, Ohio, and Louisiana. In 1820 he contracted "Yellow Jack" in Louisiana, dying at just fifty-six years of age.

He wrote to a childhood friend back in England near the end of his life, "[I am] the father of Architecture on this side of the atlantic." It was no exaggeration, as he had led American architecture to a new independence of English and European models. He helped break the book cycle, too, refusing to rely on books as his predecessors had done (the personal library he left behind filled only "two small shelves").

Talbot Hamlin, Columbia University professor of architecture, librarian, and author of the basic book on the Greek Revival (*Greek Revival Architecture in America*, 1944), would win Ferdinand Latrobe's cooperation in writing the definitive biography of Ferdie's great-grandfather. Hamlin's description of the Bank of Pennsylvania says a great deal about the breadth of Latrobe's genius: "In the new country it was the first building to be erected in which the structural concept, the plan conceived as a functional agent, and the effect both inside and out were completely integrated, completely harmonious." Hamlin termed Latrobe a "genius," "an artist of the greatest creative talent," and "a revolutionary . . . trying to establish architecture as a high and respected profession in a country which still thought of building largely in terms of the contractor-designers." Hamlin's masterful *Benjamin Henry Latrobe*, a book Kimball had often imagined he would write, was published in 1955, the year of Kimball's death.

In 1811, at the age of 54, SAMUEL MCINTIRE died unexpectedly of pneumonia after saving a child from drowning. His son, Samuel Field McIntire, also a gifted carver, survived him but McIntire's true legacy is Salem. His buildings, along with those of others influenced by him, line its streets, giving Salem its unique place in the history of American Federal architecture. In particular McIntire's presence is to be observed in his three-story dwellings, with their subtle and sophisticated exteriors and ravishing interiors with richly carved woodwork. As the Reverend Bentley, Salem's trustworthy chronicler, noted in his diary, "This day Salem was deprived of one of the most ingenious men it had in it . . . [U]pon the death of Mr. McIntire no man is left [in Salem] to be consulted upon a new plan of execution beyond his bare practice."

CHARLES BULFINCH, invited by President Monroe in 1817 to be architect of the Capitol, remained in Washington until 1830, where he also designed a penitentiary and church, and consulted on other government buildings. He remembered the period warmly, describing the time as "the happiest years of my life [spent] in pursuits congenial to my taste, and where my labors were well received." At $2,500 a year his compensation was adequate to live on, so he faced no financial woes.

In his work at the Capitol, he respected the designs of Thornton and Latrobe for the most part, though he chose to top the main block with a low wooden dome of his own design. His work brought to a close more than thirty-five years of sporadic construction under the aegis of Hallet, Hadfield, Thornton, Hoban, and Latrobe. It is only fitting that the man who finished the United States Capitol was the only American on the list.

Although his last commission, the Maine State House, was completed in 1832, Bulfinch spent most of the last fourteen years of his life in an uneventful retirement. One of his granddaughters recalled, "In my childhood, my little sister and I were sometimes indulged with the privilege and delight of looking at our grandfather's English books on architecture . . . the 'house-books,' as we called them, which were piled upon the dining-table."

Certainly, he left his imprint in Boston in uncounted ways (one was by giving the newly founded Massachusetts Historical Society the room above the central archway at the Franklin Crescent, quarters the Society occupied for close to forty years). But he also lived long enough to see the beginning of the next transformation in his native city. Just a year before his death in 1844, he would write to a friend, "Mr. Coolidge's noble mansion, trees and all, are swept away, and 5 new brick houses are now building on the site." It was a house he had designed for Joseph Coolidge, whose son Joseph had married his sister, Elizabeth Bulfinch. That marriage, in turn, had produced a number of children. The second of them, also named Joseph Coolidge, had married Jefferson's granddaughter, Eleanor Wayles Randolph.

JOHN TRUMBULL, the "patriot-artist," died in 1843 at age eighty-eight, having served his nation as a soldier, diplomat, and—most importantly—as a painter. His *Autobiography: Reminiscences and Letters of John Trumbull from 1856 to 1841* described his life and times. But his hundreds of portraits record the faces of the players and his dozens of history paintings offer a reconstructed glimpse backward at some of the most dramatic scenes of the Revolutionary era. He executed four murals, including a twelve-by-eighteen-foot copy of the *Declaration of Independence*, that were hung in the Capitol rotunda during Bulfinch's era as its architect.

The varied legacy of CHARLES WILLSON PEALE (he died in 1827) includes a thousand portraits of his contemporaries, America's first natural history and art museum, and an immense body of correspondence and manuscripts. In 1945, it was Kimball who acquired Peale's *trompe l'oeil* portrait of his sons, "The Staircase Group," the first great work by Peale to enter the Philadelphia Museum.

ROBERT MILLS had outlived the demand for his fireproof vaulting, but he didn't live long enough to witness the results of a fire that threatened to consume the Patent Office in 1877. The conflagration utterly destroyed the newer sections that had been built using the newfangled "fireproof " iron technology that had made his work obsolete. Meanwhile Mills's masonry wing remained standing, its contents largely intact.

The survival of his Patent Office was a surprising vindication, but it is the Washington Monument that remains his best-known legacy. The obelisk was completed in 1884, more than half a century after Mills's design had been chosen. It's the one national monument that everyone seems instinctively to admire. In a strange irony, the stark simplicity of the 555-foot-high obelisk is not what Mills had in mind at all. He thought the monument shorn of its temple base and other elaborations would resemble a "stalk of asparagus."

Robert Mills's generation spread sophisticated architectural notions across the nation. In Philadelphia, both architect WILLIAM STRICKLAND (1788–1854), and engineer FREDERICK GRAFF (1775–1847) were Latrobe-trained professionals who carried on well after leaving Latrobe's employ. In New England, Connecticut-born ASHER BENJAMIN (1773–1845) wrote his *Country Builder's Assistant* (1797), the first American builder's guide, which contained a meetinghouse modeled on one of Bulfinch's churches. In 1802, he moved to Boston, where more books followed, among them the *American Builder's Companion* (first edition, 1806), which was packed with designs in the Bulfinch mode. His *Practical House Carpenter* (1830), with its emphasis on the newer Grecian style, was reprinted twenty-one times, making it the most popular American architectural handbook of the century.

Another Connecticut Yankee, ITHIEL TOWN (1784–1844), moved to Boston where he became Asher Benjamin's assistant. He would build bridges in Connecticut before moving to New York where he formed the first architectural firm in the nation with the gifted ALEXANDER J. DAVIS. Town and Davis only lasted a few years (1829–1835), but other young architects trained there, notably a carpenter from New York's Hudson Valley, JAMES H. DAKIN (1806–1852), and JAMES GALLIER, SR. (1798–1866). Dakin and Gallier would, along with Charles Bingley Dakin, establish an architectural practice in the South, based in New Orleans. A one-time partner of James Gallier was MINARD LAFEVER (1798–1854) who would write widely influential builder's books, including the *Modern Builder's Guide* (1833) and *The Beauties of Modern Architecture* (1835). Other notable architects of the time, including ALEXANDER PARRIS of Massachusetts, New Yorker JAMES RENWICK, and Philadelphia-born THOMAS USTICK WALTER, were linked by their mentors to the core of the new profession. The network of professionals continued to grow and Town, Davis, Dakin, Lafever, and Walter would found the American Institution of Architects, a short-lived professional association that anticipated the American Institute of Architects.

Birthed by Jefferson, Latrobe, and Bulfinch, a new American profession had been established.

Glossary

Arcade   Series of arches supported on columns or piers.

Architrave   In classical architecture, the lowest portion of the *entablature* set immediately upon the columns or *pilasters* (originally, the architrave was the structural beam spanning the distance from column to column). See also *Cornice* and *Frieze*.

Balustrade   Series of balusters capped by a handrail.

Barrel vault   Arched roof or ceiling that is semicircular in section.

Baseboard   Interior, horizontal molding fastened at the base of the wall. Also called a skirting board in Great Britain.

Bay   Unit of space between the principal vertical framing members.

Bead   Round, convex molding, often found on paneling and the trim around doorways and windows.

Beam   Main horizontal structural member in the construction of a frame house.

Chair rail   Interior, horizontal molding fastened at waist height to protect wall surfaces. Also called a chair board and, in Great Britain, a dado.

Chamber   In the eighteenth century, a room generally given over to sleeping.

Cicerone   Tour guide who conducts sightseers.

Colonnade   Row of columns supporting an *entablature*.

Corinthian   *Order* of architecture characterized by capitals decorated with carved acanthus leaves.

Corner board   Vertical exterior trim board at the corner of a house.

Cornice   Band at the top of the classical *entablature* that projects at the crown of a wall. See also *Architrave* and *Frieze*.

Course   Horizontal row of bricks, shingles, stones, or other building material.

Dentils   Row of small blocks projecting from a cornice. See also *Modillion*.

Detail   Architectural drawing that portrays an element of a structure in detail.

Doric   *Order* of architecture characterized by its simple capitals without the carved acanthus leaves of the *Corinthian* or the scrolls of the *Ionic*.

Double-hung   Window in which the two sash slide up and down within the plane of the wall.

Double-pile   House plan in which the building is two rooms deep.

Elevation   Architectural drawing indicating how a completed interior or exterior wall will look; the point of view is that of an observer looking from a horizontal vantage. Also the wall surface represented in such a drawing.

Ell   Rear extension to a building at right angles to the main section.

Entablature   In the *Orders* of classical architecture, the assemblage of the horizontal bands of the *cornice*, *frieze*, and *architrave*, the elements immediately above (and supported by) the columns and capitals.

Entasis   Slight swell of the shaft of a column.

Fabric   Physical material of a building; the implication is of the interweaving between the various component materials.

Fanlight   Semicircular or half-elliptical window sash, often located over a doorway.

Fenestration   Arrangement and proportioning of the openings (windows and doors) in a building.

Festoon	Chain of flowers suspended in a curve between two points. See also *Swag*.
Fillet	Narrow, flat band of molding.
Floor plan	Top-view drawing in *section* that indicates outside walls, interior room configurations, and wall openings (windows and doors).
Frame house	House in which the structural parts are wooden or depend upon a wood frame for support.
Frieze	Horizontal band between the *cornice* and the *architrave* in the *entablature* in classical architecture.
Gable	End wall of a building formed by the eave line of a double-sloped roof in the shape of an inverted V.
Gouache	Painting made with watercolor pigments mixed with gum to produce opaque colors.
Grotto	Artificial cave.
Header	Brick laid with its end outward.
Hip roof	Gable roof with the ends shortened to form sloping triangular surfaces.
Historiography	Study of historical scholarship.
Indenture	Contract by which a person, often an apprentice, is bound to service.
Ionic	*Order* of architecture identifiable by the carved volutes (scrolls) of its capitals.
Jamb	Side or head lining of a window, door, or other opening.
Joiner	Craftsman skilled in making objects by joining pieces of wood.
Joist	Horizontal beam in a frame house that supports floorboards and/or ceiling surfaces.
Lath	Strips of wood nailed to the frame of the building to support plaster or shingles.
Mantelpiece	The decorative frame around the fireplace made of wood or stone.

Masonry	Brick, concrete, stone, or other materials bonded together with mortar to form walls, piers, buttresses, or other masses.
Mass	The collective external form of a structure. See also *Volume*.
Modillion	Ornamental blocks or brackets applied in series to the *soffit*, underside of a *cornice*.
Moldings	Strips of wood used for finish or decorative purposes with regular channels or projections which provide transitions from one surface or material to another (e.g. *baseboard*, *chair rail*, or *cornice* moldings).
Mortise	Cavity cut into the side or end of one framing member that forms a joint with a tenon cut into the end of a second member.
Muntin	Small wooden pieces that provide the divisions between the individual panes of glass in a window sash.
Newel	Large post at the top, bottom, turns, or landing of a stairway.
Ogee	Molding consisting of a double curve.
Orangery	A gallery or building with large windows in which plants are cultivated.
Orders	The various combinations of vertical (columns or *pilasters*) and horizontal elements (*entablature*) that distinguish the structure of a classical building. See also *Corinthian*, *Doric*, and *Ionic*.
Palladian window	Three-part window consisting of a taller center window, usually with an arched top, flanked by two shorter windows. Named after the sixteenth-century architect Andrea Palladio, it is also known as a Venetian window.
Paneling	Wall surface consisting of panels set within a framework of vertical stiles and horizontal rails.
Parlor	A multipurpose first-floor room that in early houses was used as a sleeping space; in two-room plans, the name was often interchangeable with *chamber*. Over the decades, *parlor* replaces the word *hall* in designating a formal sitting room used for entertaining.

Passage   In eighteenth-century America the space, usually extending front to back, that provided access to the rooms. See also *Chamber* and *Parlor*.

Pediment   Shallow, triangular area formed at the gable end of a roof by the two rooflines, echoing the temple end of a classical structure. A pedimented headpiece is sometimes found over doors and windows.

Perspective   Drawing in which the spatial relations of objects are represented on the two-dimensional sheet so as to appear in three dimensions.

Pilaster   Flattened column affixed to a wall and projecting only slightly from it.

Planter   Person who owned a plantation and who was of a certain elevated social class; or, one who derived his principal income from growing crops.

Plate   Horizontal structural member that caps a wall structure and supports the rafters in a *frame house*.

Portico   In classical architecture, a covered entry porch supported by columns.

Post   Principal vertical structural member in a *frame house*.

Quoins   Decorative projecting stones (or wooden elements carved to resemble stone) at the corner of a building.

Rafter   One of a series of inclined structural members that support the roof, running from the exterior wall to the *ridge*.

Rotunda   In classical architecture, a domed building or space in which the form is circular in plan.

Rustication   Masonry walling in which individual cut blocks of stone are emphasized by deeply recessed joints.

Sash   Single, light frame that holds the glass in a window unit and is designed to slide vertically in a track.

Section   A drawing or model of a part of a building that has been cut vertically or horizontally to reveal the interior or profile; a floor plan is an example of a section, where the cut is made through all the doors and windows so as to best show the construction.

Sidelight   One of a pair of windows flanking a door.

Siding   Finished surface of exterior walls.

Single-pile   House plan in which the building is one room deep.

Soffit   The underside of an overhanging *cornice*; also called a corona when used in context of a classical cornice.

Specifications   Series of sheets attendant to the architect's drawings that specify schedules of the materials to be used.

Stretcher   Brick laid lengthwise.

Stud   Secondary vertical wooden structural member used as a supporting element in walls or partitions.

Survey   The document prepared by a surveyor that delineates the extent and position of a tract of land.

Swag   A length of fabric suspended in a curve between two points. See also *Festoon*.

Tenon   Tongue-shaped projection at the end of a framing member that fits into a mortise.

Topography   Rendering on a map of the natural and man-made features of a place or region.

Undertaker   In eighteenth-century parlance, a builder or contractor; namely, one who *undertakes* the construction of a building.

Vernacular   Guileless, unpretentious buildings erected with local materials and labor guided by local tradition rather than national or international trends.

Volume   The internal space of a structure. See also *Mass*.

Watermark   Marking on paper stock usually produced by pressure exerted on a projected design in a mold and visible when the paper is held up to light.

Notes on Sources

THE RESEARCH FOR THIS BOOK PROVED A CONSIDERABLE ENTERPRISE. In a very real sense, I found myself doing the basic work required to write a half-dozen biographies in order to select the events in these pages. At the outset, then, it must be said that in addition to the sources cited below, there are as many more not listed that added in some general way to my overall understanding of the post-revolutionary period and its people.

In learning of Kimball, I turned first to George and Mary Roberts's *Triumph on Fairmount* (Philadelphia: J. B. Lippincott & Company, 1959). Their book is subjective and hagiographic in a way that has gone out of fashion, but remains valuable, largely for its account of Kimball's days at the Philadelphia Museum of Art. Not a little of it, I discovered, was a rewrite of memoirs that the Robertses found in Kimball's files. His original manuscripts have never been published; they are in no sense complete, surviving in longhand drafts in Kimball's own script. The tone is not Kimball-as-scholar but Fiske-as-raconteur, a mode his friends and acquaintances knew well. Those writings are rich in anecdote, packed with important names and, upon reading them, whence the Roberts's book came is instantly obvious.

Other students have examined Kimball, among them Lauren Weiss Bricker in her dissertation, *The Contribution of Fiske Kimball and Talbot Faulkner Hamlin to the Study of American Architectural History* (Santa Barbara: University of California, Santa Barbara, 1990). Another essential source is Joseph Dye Lahendro's thesis *Fiske Kimball: American Renaissance Historian* (Charlottesville: School of Architecture, University of Virginia, 1982). Mary Givens Kane—who herself appears in these pages, dowsing a fire—was for many years Kimball's secretary. Even after his death, she would show a devotion to duty, preparing the small but invaluable volume *A Bibliography of the Works of Fiske Kimball* (Charlottesville: University of Virginia Press, 1959).

Of Kimball's own books, I regularly consulted *Thomas Jefferson, Architect* (privately published in Boston in 1916, reprinted in New York by Da Capo Press in 1968), as well as his other still-standard works, *Domestic Architecture of the American Colonies and of the Early Republic* (Charles Scribner's Sons, 1922) and *Mr. Samuel McIntire, Carver, The Architect of Salem* (Portland, ME: Southworth Anthoensen Press, published for the Essex Institute of Salem, Massachusetts, 1940). His other books, though now dated and superseded by the works of others, include *A History of Architecture* (New York: Harper & Brothers, 1918); *American Architecture* (Indianapolis: Bobbs-Merrill Co., 1928); *The Creation of the Rococo* (Philadelphia: Philadelphia Museum of Art, 1943); and *Great Painting in America*, coauthored with Lionello Venturi (New York: Coward-McCann, 1948). Though incomplete (she wrote just three of the planned five books), Marie Kimball's multivolume life of Jefferson remains valuable. The three published volumes are *Jefferson: The Road to Glory, 1743 to 1776; Jefferson: War and Peace, 1776–1784;* and *Jefferson: The Scene of Europe, 1784–1789* (New York: Coward-McCann, 1943, 1947, and 1950).

The archival collections of Kimball's own papers proved my most essential sources, especially those at the Philadelphia Museum of Art and at the Harvard University Fine Arts Library. Those archives also contain manuscripts and printed versions of his voluminous writings on Jefferson, Latrobe, L'Enfant, and the many other architects whose lives and works he examined.

Before citing the sources that enabled me to write individual chapters, I must acknowledge a number of more general books that came regularly to hand as I tried to shape many stories into one. *The Eye of Thomas Jefferson*, William Howard Adams, ed., remains the single best introduction to Jefferson's life in architecture and the arts (Charlottesville: Thomas Jefferson Memorial Foundation, and Columbia: University of Missouri Press, 1976). A companion volume, *Jefferson and the Arts: an Extended View*, William Howard Adams, ed. (Washington: National Gallery of Art, 1976) contains a range of valuable essays.

For a more general understanding of the architecture of the period, I owe particular debts to *The Colonial and Neoclassical Styles* by William H. Pierson Jr. (New York: Oxford University Press, 1970); and *The Making of Virginia Architecture* by Charles F. Brownell, Calder Loth, William M. S. Rasmussen, and Richard Guy Wilson (Richmond: Virginia Museum of Fine Arts, 1992). *American Architects and Their Books to 1848*, Kenneth Hafertepe and James F. O'Gorman, eds., is a collection of most useful essays (Amherst: University of Massachusetts Press, 2001).

One of the many pleasures of this project has been the opportunity to read large portions of James Thomas Flexner's four-volume biography, *George Washington* (Boston: Little, Brown & Co., 1965, 1968, 1970, and 1972) and Dumas Malone's six-volume biography, *Jefferson and His Time* (Boston: Little, Brown & Co., 1948 through 1981). Both are masterworks that, while being compendious and authoritative, offer their readers an immersion experience in the past. Many books that have followed on Jefferson and Washington have distinct merits of their own, but none is likely to eclipse Malone's or Flexner's not only for richness of detail but for sheer reading pleasure.

I relied where possible on primary sources so I became well acquainted with the papers of Jefferson, Washington, William Thornton, Benjamin Henry Latrobe, Charles Bulfinch, and Robert Mills, as cited. Other early sources included *The Autobiography of Colonel John Trumbull* (originally published 1841, but republished as edited by Theodore Sizer, New Haven, CT: Yale University Press, 1953) and William Dunlop's groundbreaking *History of the Rise and Progress of the Arts of Design in the United States*, 2 vols., (New York: George P. Scott & Co., 1834).

CHAPTER I

William Buckland appears in these pages because of his undisputed importance in American architectural history and, in part, since his personal history is the best documented of any master builder of his time. But, again, I must acknowledge that he was not one of Kimball's finds, at least to the same extent that Jefferson was. Or even Latrobe. Thus, Dr. Kimball and I are both indebted to various Randall descendants, one of whom, Rosamond Randall Beirne, cowrote (with John Henry Scarff) the basic biography on Buckland, *William Buckland, 1734–1774: Architect of Virginia and Maryland* (Baltimore: Maryland Historical Society, 1958). But Kimball did go public somewhat earlier, telling of Gunston Hall and Buckland in his article, "Gunston Hall" in the *Society of Architectural Historians Journal* (vol. 13, May 1954).

Two unpublished master's theses provided numerous biographical details: *William Buckland in England and America* by Georgina Louise Joyner (Notre Dame, IN: University of Notre Dame, 1985); and *The Work of William Buckland in Maryland, 1771–1774* by Barbara Allston Brand (Washington: George Washington University, 1978). Essential sources for Buckland's craftsmanship include two articles by the sharp-eyed Luke Beckerdite: "William Buckland and William Bernard Sears: The Design and the Carver" (in *MESDA*, vol. 8, November

1982) and "Architect-Design Furniture in Eighteenth-Century Virginia: The Work of William Buckland and William Bernard Sears" (in *American Furniture: 1994*; Hanover, NH: University Press of New England with the Chipstone Foundation, 1994).

We are all indebted to Paul Buchanan for finding Buckland's sketches within the walls of Gunston Hall and to Carl Lounsbury for explicating the significance of the discovery in "'An Elegant and Commodious Building': William Buckland and the Design of the Prince William County Courthouse" (*Journal of the Society of Architectural Historians*, vol. 46, September 1987). The notes of Bennie Brown Jr. regarding Buckland's library are essential, too. They were published in the catalog *Buckland: Master Builder of the 18th Century* (Mason Neck, VA: Board of Regents of Gunston Hall, 1977).

CHAPTER 2

Thomas Jefferson's Paris by Howard C. Rice Jr. is a rich journey into the fabric of that antique city (Princeton, NJ: Princeton University Press, 1976). Other valuable sources for Jefferson's Parisian days were Marie Kimball's *Scene of Europe: 1784–1789* (New York: Coward-McCann, 1950) and *Thomas Jefferson: American Tourist* by Edward Dumbauld (Norman: University of Oklahoma Press, 1946).

The authoritative book on Clérisseau is Thomas J. McCormick's *Charles-Louis Clérisseau and the Genesis of Neo-Classicism* (Cambridge, MA: MIT Press, 1990). Another source for this chapter was Fiske Kimball's dissertation, *Thomas Jefferson and the First Monument of the Classical Revival in America* (Ann Arbor: University of Michigan, 1915). It has been published and republished over the years, most recently in an edited and annotated edition released as *The Capitol of Virginia: A Landmark of American Architecture*, Jon Kukla, ed. (Richmond: Library of Virginia, 2002).

There is a vast literature on Palladio, Jones, Adam and the rest. To study Palladio, one starts with the master's own *The Four Books on Architecture* and the edition of choice is the new translation from Robert Tavernor and Richard Schofield (Cambridge, MA: MIT Press, 1997). Professor Tavernor's *Palladio and Palladianism* (London: Thames and Hudson, 1991) is arguably the best brief introduction to Palladian studies. In following the Palladian thread through time, among the most useful of books I consulted was *The Palladian Revival: Lord Burlington, His Villa and Garden at Chiswick* by John Harris (New Haven, CT: Yale University Press, 1994). In collaboration with Gordon Higgott, Harris also gets credit for *Inigo Jones: Complete Architectural Drawings* (New York: The Drawing

Center, 1989). *Robert Adam and His Circle* by John Fleming (Cambridge, MA: Harvard University Press, 1962) remains the best first approach to Adam and his times.

CHAPTER 3

For the opening vignette at Federal Hall and Washington material elsewhere, key sources included *George Washington: A Biography*, vol. 6, by Douglas Southall Freeman (New York: Charles Scribner's Sons, 1954); Joseph J. Ellis's *His Excellency George Washington* (New York: Alfred A. Knopf, 2004); and Louis Torres's invaluable essay, "Federal Hall Revisited" (*Journal of the Society of Architectural Historians*, vol. 29, December 1970). Other Washington references included James Thomas Flexner's *George Washington and the New Nation, 1783–1793* (Boston: Little Brown & Co., 1970). When looking into the life of the president at home here and in other chapters, I drew upon the thorough and accessible *George Washington's Mount Vernon* by Robert F. Dalzell Jr. and Lee Baldwin Dalzell (New York: Oxford University Press, 1998).

The Papers of George Washington were perhaps the most essential resource for this chapter, in particular volumes 7, 8, and 9 (Charlottesville: University Press of Virginia, 1983). In seeking other original documents, I found very useful the *Papers of William Thornton*, C.M. Harris, ed. (Charlottesville: University Press of Virginia, 1995) and *Thomas Jefferson and the National Capital*, Saul K. Padover, ed. (Washington: U.S. Government Printing Office, 1946).

Regarding L'Enfant's capital plan, Allan Greenberg's "L'Enfant, Washington, and the Plan of the Capital" is cogent and authoritative (*Antiques*, July 1991). Other sources included Kimball's entry in the *Dictionary of American Biography*, Dumas Malone, ed. (New York: Charles Scribner's Sons, 1928 and after), as well as the basic biography of the man, *The Life of Pierre Charles L'Enfant* by H. Paul Caemmerer (Washington: National Republic Publishing Company, 1950).

Other sources for this chapter include a number of articles by Kimball, including "The Genesis of the White House" (*Century Magazine*, vol. 95, February 1918); "The Origin of the Plan of Washington" (*Architectural Review*, vol. 7, September 1918); "The Competition for the Federal Buildings, 1792–1793," in collaboration with Wells Bennett (*American Institute of Architects Journal*, vol. 7, January, March, May, August, and December 1919, and vol. 8, March 1920).

Two books of Glenn Brown's were of use. In the case of *The Octagon: Dr. William Thornton, Architect* (Washington: American Institute of Architects, 1917), I found his biographical essay illuminating, while it was the plates that were essential references in his *History of the United States Capitol*, 2 vols. (Washington: U.S. Government Printing Office, 1900, 1903).

CHAPTER 4

To look at Latrobe, one must begin with the monumental project conducted by the Maryland Historical Society, in cooperation with Yale University Press, to publish *The Papers of Benjamin Henry Latrobe*. The result is the three-volume *Correspondence and Miscellaneous Papers* (1984, 1986, 1988); the two-volume *Architectural Drawings* (1994); *The Engineering Drawings* (1980); *Latrobe's View of America, 1795–1820* (1985); and the three volumes of *Journals* (1977, 1980). Also useful was an earlier edited attempt at the same venture, *The Journal of Latrobe* (New York: D. Appleton and Company, 1905; introduction by J. H. B. Latrobe), not least because it first announced to the world the existence of Latrobe's trove of journals.

Despite the voluminous papers (or, perhaps, because of their sheer bulk) Talbot Hamlin's definitive biography, *Benjamin Henry Latrobe* (New York: Oxford University Press, 1955), remains the best entrée to Latrobe's world (a most excellent book, sadly out of print). Kimball's seminal essays, too, were essential here, including "Benjamin Henry Latrobe and the Beginnings of Engineering and Architectural Practice in America" (*The Michigan Technic*, vol. 30, December 1917); "Latrobe's Designs for the Cathedral of Baltimore" (*Architectural Record*, vol. 42, December 1917, and vol. 43, January 1918); and "The Bank of Pennsylvania, 1799" (*Architectural Record*, vol. 44, August 1918).

CHAPTER 5

For the opening vignette, the key source was the *Papers of Anna Maria Brodeau Thornton*, and in particular her entries from September 1802 concerning her visit to Monticello (Washington: Manuscript division, Library of Congress, n.p.). I referred regularly to Jack McLaughlin's *Jefferson and Monticello: The Biography of a Builder* (New York: Henry Holt & Co., 1988) in writing this chapter. The book is a thorough and enjoyable introduction to Monticello's complex history.

Other memoirs helped fill in many details. Among them were Margaret Bayard Smith's *The First Forty Years of Washington Society* (New York: Charles Scribner's Sons, 1906) and the several recollections in *Jefferson Reader: A Treasure of Writing about Thomas Jefferson* (New York: E. P. Dutton & Co., 1953). The *Reader* contains memoirs of Jefferson and Monticello by the Marquis de Chastellux

(1782), the Duc de la Rochefoucauld-Liancourt (1796), British Lieutenant Francis Hall (1817), Daniel Webster (1824), Monticello overseer Edmund Bacon (1862), slave Isaac Jefferson (circa 1840), and a brief recollection by grandson Thomas Jefferson Randolph (1858). I also drew upon *The Family Letters of Thomas Jefferson*, Edwin Morris Betts and James Adam Bear Jr., eds. (Columbia: University of Missouri Press, 1966).

In getting to know George Ticknor, the essential sources are *Life, Letters, and Journals of George Ticknor* (2 vols., Boston: Houghton Mifflin Co., 1909); David B. Tyack's *George Ticknor and the Boston Brahmins* (Cambridge, MA: Harvard University Press, 1967); and the essay about Ticknor and Jefferson in *Literary Pioneers: Early American Explorers of European Culture* (Cambridge, MA: Harvard University Press, 1935). *The Levy Family and Monticello: 1834–1923* by Melvin I. Urofsky (Charlottesville, VA: Thomas Jefferson Foundation, 2001) was a source for the days of Levy ownership. The best short history of the University is *Thomas Jefferson's Academical Village: The Creation of an Architectural Masterpiece*, Richard Guy Wilson, ed. (Charlottesville: Bayly Art Museum University Press of Virginia, 1993).

In thinking about Monticello's place in preservation history, the basic reference remains *Presence of the Past* by Charles B. Hosmer Jr. (New York: G.P. Putnam's Sons, 1965). When one comes to the artifact itself, Susan Stein's scholarly catalogue of Monticello's contents, *The Worlds of Thomas Jefferson at Monticello*, is accessible and rich with Jefferson surprises (New York: Harry N. Abrams, 1993). One means of understanding the bookish Jefferson is to consider his library and thus I found indispensable William Bainter O'Neal's *Jefferson's Fine Arts Library* (Charlottesville: University Press of Virginia, 1976).

The recollections of Thomas Jefferson Coolidge appeared, along with the Francis Calley Gray's account of his Monticello visit, in *Thomas Jefferson in 1814* (Boston: Club of Odd Volumes/Riverside Press, 1924). Other valuable recollections of the period are to be found in Harold Jefferson Coolidge's compilation of family letters found in "An American Wedding Journey in 1825" (*Atlantic Monthly*, vol. 143, March 1929).

The key sources to the architectural state of the house in its early days are, first, the article that launched serious consideration of Jefferson's favored hobby, Kimball's "Thomas Jefferson as Architect: Monticello and Shadwell" (*Architectural Quarterly of Harvard University*, vol. 2, June 1914) and second Gene Waddell's "The First Monticello" (*Journals of the Society of Architectural Historians*, vol. 45, March 1987). *Thomas Jefferson's Architectural Drawings*, compiled and with commentary and checklist by Frederick Doveton Nichols (Charlottesville,

VA: Thomas Jefferson Memorial Foundation, 1961, 1995) is another basic reference for any student of Jefferson's architecture.

Travis C. McDonald Jr. is the authority on Poplar Forest, and I drew upon various of his writings, among them *Notes on the State of Poplar Forest*, vols. 1–2 (Forest, VA: Corporation for Jefferson's Poplar Forest, 1991, 1994); "Poplar Forest: A Masterpiece Rediscovered" (*Virginia Cavalcade*, Winter 1993); "Constructing Optimism: Thomas Jefferson's Poplar Forest" in *People, Power, Places*, Sally McMurry and Annmarie Adams, eds. (Knoxville: University of Tennessee Press, 2000); and "Thomas Jefferson's Poplar Forest: Privacy Restored" (*Virginia Cavalcade*, Winter 2002). Also of use was S. Allen Chambers Jr., *Poplar Forest and Thomas Jefferson* (Forest, VA: Corporation for Jefferson's Poplar Forest, 1993).

Last but hardly least were others of the Kimballs' writings, in particular, *Thomas Jefferson, Architect*, but also Marie's *The Furnishings of Monticello* (Charlottesville, VA: Thomas Jefferson Memorial Foundation, 1954).

CHAPTER 6

The Bulfinch bibliography begins with *The Life and Letters of Charles Bulfinch Architect*, edited by granddaughter Ellen Susan Bulfinch (Boston: Houghton Mifflin Co., 1896). The book includes not only many of Bulfinch's letters but his own autobiographical notes. Harold Kirker's two books are also basic to any Bulfinch investigation. *Bulfinch's Boston, 1787–1817* (New York: Oxford University Press, 1964), written with his brother James Kirker, explicates Bulfinch's profound affect on Boston's streetscapes and topography. *The Architecture of Charles Bulfinch* (Cambridge, MA: Harvard University Press, 1969) is a building-by-building survey of the works. Another source was *Charles Bulfinch: Architect and Citizen* by Charles A. Place (Boston, MA: Houghton Mifflin Co., 1925).

Walter Muir Whitehill's classic *Boston: A Topographic History* (Cambridge, MA: Harvard University Press, 1959) takes the reader back in time. Other Boston sources include *The Memorial History of Boston*, Justin Winsor, 4 vols. (Boston: James R. Osgood and Co., 1885); and *Gaining Ground: A History of Landmaking in Boston* by Nancy S. Seasholes (Cambridge, MA: MIT Press, 2003). A number of period details came from various memoirs, in particular *Memoir of the Life of Eliza S.M. Quincy* written by her daughter, Mrs. Susan Quincy Morton (Boston: John Wilson and Son, 1821); Eliza Susan Quincy's journal reprinted in *The Articulate Sisters*, M. A. DeWolfe Howe, ed. (Cambridge, MA: Harvard University Press, 1946); and Samuel Eliot Morison's works on his great-grandfather, *Harrison Gray Otis, 1765–1848: The Urbane Federalist* (Boston: Houghton Mifflin

Co., 1969) and *The Letters of Harrison Gray Otis, Federalist*, 2 vols. (Boston: Houghton Mifflin Co., 1913). My thanks, too, to Jinny Nathans at the American Meteorological Society for giving me the tour of the Society's headquarters, Otis's former home at 45 Beacon Street.

Despite its age, the bible on McIntire remains Kimball's book, *Mr. Samuel McIntire, Carver: The Architect of Salem* (Portland, ME: Southworth Anthoensen Press, published for the Essex Institute of Salem, Massachusetts, 1940). I also drew upon numbers of the *Historical Collections of the Essex Institute*, chief among them "Samuel McIntire—A Sketch" (vol. 48, April 1932). For period testimony, the remarkable diary of Dr. William Bentley is unsurpassed (every town ought to have had its Bentley to chronicle its greatest days). His jottings were published as *The Diary of William Bentley, D.D.* (4 vols., Salem, MA: Essex Institute, 1905–1914). A number of essays (the contributors included Abbott Lowell Cummings, Kimball, and Nina Fletcher Little) appeared in *Samuel McIntire: A Bicentennial Symposium, 1757–1957*, Benjamin W. Labaree, ed. (Salem, MA: Essex Institute, 1957). I drew, as well, upon Joseph Downs's summary, "Derby and McIntire," in *The Bulletin of the Metropolitan Museum of Art* (vol. 6, Summer 1947). For his insights into Bulfinch's perspective drawings, I am indebted to James F. O'Gorman and his provocative essay published in conjunction with a symposium and exhibition, each of which bore the title *The Perspective of Anglo-American Architecture* (Philadelphia: Athenaeum of Philadelphia, 1995). In examining the Derby Room and the Philadelphia Museum of Art, I drew upon Fiske Kimball's "The Derby Room and Its Furnishings" (*Philadelphia Museum of Art Bulletin*, vol. 23, April 1930). For the early days of the museum, I found very useful both the text and archival photos in *Making a Modern Classic: The Architecture of the Philadelphia Museum of Art*, text by David B. Brownlee (Philadelphia: Philadelphia Museum of Art, 1997).

For the history of the Massachusetts State House, valuable references included an old capitol handbook, *The State House* by Ellen Mudge Burrill (Boston: Wright and Potter Printing Co., 1917) and Buford Pickens's "Wyatt's Pantheon and the State House in Boston and a New View of Bulfinch" (*Journal of the Society of Architectural Historians*, vol. 45, May 1970). Many numbers in the Bulletin of the Society for the Preservation of New England Antiquities, *Old-Time New England*, contain useful notes about Bulfinch, in particular "Charles Bulfinch and Boston's Vanishing West End" by Abbott Lowell Cummings (vol. 52, October–December 1961); "Early Buildings of the Asylum at Charlestown, 1795–1846" by Nina Fletcher Little (vol. 59, October–December 1968); and "The Tontine Crescent and Its Architect" by Emma Forbes Waite (vol. 42, January–March 1953). In considering the Barrell house, I drew upon "Joseph Barrell's Pleasant Hill" by Dean A. Fales Jr., which appeared in *Publications of the Colonial Society of Massachusetts* (Boston: Colonial Society of Massachusetts, 1966).

CHAPTER 7

The foundation work on Robert Mills, which contains a number of useful appendices transcribed from Mills's own papers, is *Robert Mills: Architect of the Washington Monument* by H. M. Pierce Gallagher (introduction by Fiske Kimball; New York: Columbia University Press, 1935). Building upon and updating Mrs. Gallagher's book are the very thorough *Altogether American: Robert Mills, Architect and Engineer* by Rhodri Windsor Liscombe (New York: Oxford University Press, 1994) and John M. Bryan's *Robert Mills: America's First Architect* (New York: Princeton Architectural Press, 2001). Also of use was the museum catalog published in connection with an exhibit at the Columbia Museum of Art, *Robert Mills: Architect, 1781–1855* by John Morrill Bryan (Columbia, SC: Columbia Museum of Art, 1976). For pointing me to the tale of Jefferson's gravestone, I am indebted to Andrew Burstein and his *Jefferson's Secrets: Death and Desire at Monticello* (New York: Basic Books, 2005).

The tale of the Washington Monument has been oft-told, but among the most valuable sources for its recounting here were F.L. Harvey's *History of the Washington National Monument and of the Washington National Monument Society* (Washington: N.T. Elliott Printing Co., 1902); the National Park Service's handbook *Washington Monument* (Washington: U.S. Department of the Interior/ National Park Service, 1942); and Ada Louise Huxtable's essay "Progressive Architecture in America: The Washington Monument—1836–1884" (*Progressive Architecture*, vol. 38, August 1957). Pamela Scott's valuable essay, "Robert Mills and American Monuments" appeared in the collection *Robert Mills, Architect*, John M. Bryan, ed. (Washington: American Institute of Architects Press, 1989).

The story of the battle over the Jefferson Monument in the late 1930s has yet to be told in full (though it is a skirmish that anticipates more recent culture wars). One contemporary perspective on the story appears in Steven McLeod Bedford's *John Russell Pope: Architect of Empire* (New York: Rizzoli, 1998), but the polemical writings of the time are most revealing. Many articles appeared in the arts and architectural press of 1937 and 1938, some of them in *Architectural Record*, *Architectural Forum*, *Art Digest*, *The Architect's World*, *Pencil Points*, and, in particular, *Magazine of Art*, which took a partisan role in the debate. Kimball's ingenious appreciation, "John Russell Pope, 1874–1937," appeared in *American*

Architect (vol. 151, October 1937). Transcripts of the Commission meetings and congressional testimony also make engrossing reading.

"Fiske Kimball and Colonial Williamsburg," was a paper delivered at *Fiske Kimball: Creator of an American Architecture: A Symposium* (Charlottesville: University of Virginia, 1995) by Edward A. Chappell and Mark R. Wenger. An appreciation of Kimball by art critic (and former Philadelphia Museum colleague) John Canaday, originally published in the *New York Times* in 1961, was republished in *Culture Gulch: Notes on Art and Its Public in the 1960's* (New York: Farrar, Straus & Giroux, 1969).

In the historiographical vein, I am indebted to W. Stull Holt's *Historical Scholarship in the United States* (Seattle: University of Washington Press, 1967); Robert Allen Skotheim's *American Intellectual Histories and Historians* (Princeton: Princeton University Press, 1966); C. Vann Woodward's *The Future of the Past* (New York: Oxford University Press, 1989); John Higham's *History: Professional Scholarship in America* (Baltimore: Johns Hopkins University Press, 1975); *The Rise of Architectural History* by David Watkin (London: The Architectural Press, 1980); *The Past is a Foreign Country* by David Lowenthal (Cambridge, England: Cambridge University Press, 1985); and Richard J. Evans's *In Defense of History* (New York: W. W. Norton & Co., 1999). *The Architectural Historian in America: A Symposium in Celebration of the Fiftieth Anniversary of the Founding of the Society of Architectural Historians* (Washington: National Gallery of Art, 1990) contains a number of important contributions, including essays by Lauren Weiss Bricker and Dell Upton that address Kimball's role in shaping the discipline of architectural history.

INDEX

Page references in **boldface** indicate the page number of an illustration and its caption.

A NOTE ON THE AUTHOR

Hugh Howard's books include *Thomas Jefferson, Architect;*
his memoir *House-Dreams;* the essay collection *The Preservationist's
Progress;* and an introduction to the architecture of Williamsburg,
Colonial Houses. He resides in upstate New York with his wife, writer
Elizabeth Lawrence, and their two teenage daughters.